Personal Discipline and Material Culture

Personal Discipline

and

Material Culture

*An Archaeology
of Annapolis, Maryland,
1695–1870*

PAUL A. SHACKEL

The University of Tennessee Press / Knoxville

The paper in this book meets the minimum requirements of the
American National Standard for Permanence of Paper for Printed
Library Materials. ⊚ The binding materials have been chosen for strength
and durability.

Library of Congress Cataloging-in-Publication Data

Shackel, Paul A.
    Personal discipline and material culture : an archaeology of
Annapolis, Maryland, 1695–1870 / Paul A. Shackel.
       p.   cm.
    Includes bibliographical references and index.
    ISBN 0-87049-784-7 (cloth: alk. paper)
    1. Material culture—Maryland—Annapolis.   2. Annapolis (Md.)—
Antiquities.   3. Annapolis (Md.)—Social life and customs.
4. Annapolis Region (Md.)—Social life and customs.   I. Title.
F189.A647S48   1993
975.2'56—dc20   92-30559
                                                      CIP

For Barbara J. Little

Contents

Figures

Tables

Preface

In organizing this book, I used Fernand Braudel's scales of history—which he used initially in his 1949 classic *La Méditerranée et al Monde Méditerranéen à l'époque de Phillipp II*—individual, social, and long-term. Braudel popularized his organizational scheme in 1979 by writing a three-volume set on geographical scales (*Civilization and Capitalism; 15th–18th Century*). These scales of history can be examined in any order. The global (long-term) context can be defined first and the data placed in relationship to this context. I chose instead to explain local and regional (individual and social) scales first by analyzing archaeological and probate data and demonstrating how these shorter and more intimate time scales are important to understanding global histories. Archaeological data contribute to the history of the individual, probate inventory data help establish social history, and etiquette books provide data for an analysis of long-term history. Each scale builds on and is dependent on the other scales, revealing social and material change as historical developments rather than as evolutionary and predetermined patterns.

I am indebted to many people for their help and advice while writing this book. First, I am grateful to Mark P. Leone for his continual support and encouragement during my participation in the Archaeology in Annapolis Project (a cooperative agreement between the University of Maryland and the Historic Annapolis Foundation), from 1985 to 1989.

His generosity and willingness to share data and ideas helped shape some major concepts in this book. It was Ezra Zubrow who originally encouraged me to pursue many of the questions this book addresses— without his support this research would never have taken place. Ben A. Nelson and William B. Stein also were supportive in the early stages of writing. Their friendship, advice, and concern will always be appreciated.

I am also grateful to Charles Orser and Robert Paynter for their extensive comments on the later drafts of the manuscript as they helped direct the intellectual course of this book. Their time, energy, and enthusiasm is appreciated. The comments and suggestions from many others along the way, including Parker Potter, Paul Mullins, Liz Kryder Reid, Julie Ernstein, and Sue Winter, were helpful. A special thanks to two unique professionals associated with the Historic Annapolis Foundation: St. Claire Wright and Pringle Symonds. Their spirit and wisdom aided my research.

Lois Carr of the Saint Mary's City Commission shared ideas and information that helped assure the accuracy and efficient analysis of the probate data. Although we disagreed with some of the interpretations, she offered her assistance and undivided attention. There were many archivists at the Maryland Hall of Records who aided my research. To name them all would be impossible, but a special thanks goes to Susan Cummings for her assistance.

I can never be grateful enough for the support and encouragement provided by my parents, Paul and Gloria Shackel. They always insisted that I enjoy life to the fullest. But most of all, I appreciate the help, understanding, encouragement, and support provided me by Barbara Little. She dedicated a great deal of time to reading through various drafts of this manuscript, often making insightful comments and suggestions as the book took shape. In gratitude to Barbara for her love, friendship, and enthusiasm, I dedicate this book to her.

Introduction: A Study of Meanings of the Material World

The fields of anthropology, archaeology as a whole, and even historical archaeology, are in the midst of a changing paradigm. Historical anthropology is becoming widely accepted, as Eric Wolf's influential analysis, *Europe and the People Without History,* [1] is now claimed by many anthropologists to be one of the most comprehensive analyses of the 1980s. Bruce Trigger, in his keynote address at the 1990 American Anthropological Association Archaeology Division meetings, called for the rediscovery of historical approaches in archaeology, claiming that historical archaeology has the greatest potential for exploiting historical methodologies. [2] Archaeologists are beginning to realize that culture change is less orderly than previously thought, and that it is not necessarily an evolutionary process, but a persistent change whose direction is often unknown. [3]

Wolf proposes reanalysis of anthropological data for the purpose of interpreting power relations and conflict between individuals and groups. [4] To ignore these aspects of culture is to deny important parts of everyday relations among people. Wolf recommends using Michel Foucault's analysis of power: discipline, as found in institutions such as factories, schools, hospitals, prisons, and military organizations, creates subjects of people through observance of hierarchical practices. [5] New surveillance techniques, mechanized production, and division of labor help create an increasing number of goods and standardize the work process so that any number of individuals can perform a particular task. The modern work system and its material by-products create individuals that are predictable, regular, and interchangeable.[6]

The excitement created by the rediscovery of historical anthropology, which replaces the static approach of functionalism, and by the greater acceptance of group-conflict analysis, which replaces the study of cross-cultural patterning, comes during the quincentennial celebration of the European discovery of the New World. Historical archaeology was recognized as a viable discipline about the time of the American bicentennial, and now, I believe, historical archaeology can make substantial contributions to historical anthropology and provide a perspective enriched by its many data sources. Historical evaluation of material culture from the Chesapeake Bay region is a way to illuminate the roots of modern ideologies—to identify the historical relations between groups and understand how these modern ideologies are maintained.[7]

Since the eighteenth century, a growing number of people have spent their lives in factory systems guided by capitalist wage relations. Society's domestic realm became saturated with factory by-products and influenced more and more by the new behavioral disciplines.[8] Modern behavior associated with work life and home life, eating, health, and hygiene appears natural, inevitable, and timeless, when in fact it is not. Meanings and uses of goods today are much different than those found in preindustrial society. Although today many people in Western society would feel uncomfortable rejecting time discipline, eating foods with only a knife, wiping their mouth on a table cloth, and not brushing their teeth, all of these behaviors dominated Western preindustrial society. In this book I use historical and archaeological data to discuss the development of modern behavior and to explain why material culture and behavior related to domestic and work life became increasingly standardized, precise, and exacting in the eighteenth and nineteenth centuries. My study focuses on the Chesapeake Bay region of the New World, but I suspect that the observations are applicable to most of colonial Anglo-America.

The Chesapeake has a long history of occupation and a relatively long history of archaeological and historical studies. Although early Chesapeake residents did not work under a capitalist wage system, residents purchased the system's by-products, thereby affecting the domestic sphere. This book explores the circumstances under which residents adopted mass-produced goods and standardized behavior and how people used new material goods to establish and reinforce intergroup and intragroup relations.[9] Specifically, I emphasize the role of artifacts in the struggle for social position and how goods played an integral part in creating identity in eighteenth-century Annapolis, Maryland, and surrounding Anne Arundel County.

General and particular data and theory demonstrate why material culture changed when it did and show how this change may have shaped and created the social order in the colonial Chesapeake. I borrow and expand the theme of eighteenth-century culture change presented by James Deetz, Henry Glassie, and Mark Leone.[10] Both Deetz and Glassie describe material change in the late eighteenth century as being related to a switch of mental templates and the loss of community; neither incorporates class structure into his assessment. Leone analyzes culture change in the eighteenth century as a product of the penetration of Enlightenment ideas of merchant capitalism, acknowledging that these ideas affected people differently, depending on their class. I pay specific attention to culture and consumption, the symbolic qualities of material goods, and how goods actively shaped and structured the social order. I use Fernand Braudel's three scales of history—individual time, social time, and geographical time (long-term history)—to provide an organizational framework for considering relationships.[11] Archaeological and historical data contribute unequal amounts of data to each scale and could provide separate and different histories if considered individually, that is, out of a broad historical context.

In tracing the development of medieval and Renaissance etiquette, I use Michel Foucault's concepts of power and discipline and Pierre Bourdieu's analysis of the meanings and uses of everyday material cultural. Together these sources and ideas inform an assessment of how personal discipline developed and became intricately related to changing material culture and fashion in Western culture as it became industrialized. Scholars have often ignored the social, political, and material implications of changing etiquette.[12] But etiquette is not empty formality. It is tied to human relations and the creation of hierarchies in society, it is dynamic, it supports interest groups, and it has material consequences. I argue that the elite used goods and the rules associated with their use to maintain social distance and stratification. As the lower wealth and status groups acquired goods and learned their meanings and how they operated in the upper classes, the elite either changed the rules or began to use a new type of material culture to create boundaries and maintain their distance. In colonial Annapolis the goods and their meanings did not change gradually, but sporadically, when social or political crises threatened the social hierarchy.

Understanding societal differences, what created these differences, and what conditions promoted and legitimized social changes are key to understanding eighteenth-century culture change. The explicit connection between social circumstance and changing uses of material culture, a subject often ignored by social scientists, is emphasized in this research.

THE HISTORY OF THINGS AND THE MEANINGS OF HISTORY

This analysis is organized according to the scales of history introduced by Braudel and the Annales school. The histories of individuals, of social time, and of long-term history may each stand alone, but each reveals only a partial history. Individual time, or the history of the event, is sensitive to particular events and individual actions. Social time is concerned with social groups over decades or a few generations and is less sensitive to the nervous vibrations of particular actions. Geographical time, the long dureé of the Annales school of history, unfolds slowly, being measured in centuries or millennia.[13]

The approach taken here differs from most historical archaeological studies in that it considers all three scales of history. Although each chapter is placed in the context of the appropriate scale of history, each examines broader contexts. An understanding of social time is built upon an analysis of the individual, and an analysis of geographical time is understood when individual and social trends are examined. Archaeological materials from several sites in Annapolis provide information about the history of the individual, probate data from Annapolis and Anne Arundel County furnish the basis for an understanding of social time, and medieval to Renaissance etiquette books from Western Europe yield details concerning geographic time. Each data set provides different interpretations and meanings and allows for an understanding of the creation of a new discipline at the level of a different scale of history.

Individual Time

In the analysis of the individual, I examine the separations created during transformation from a preindustrial to a modern ideology. Investigation of the material culture shows the development of new etiquettes that reinforced standardizing and segmenting behavior. Personal discipline became exacting and precise behavior that permeated many aspects of everyday life. Although many individuals adopted this modern ideology, others resisted.

In particular, I examine archaeological data derived from ceramics and toothbrushes to measure the dissemination of the ideas of personal discipline through society. Greater diversity in plate sizes and growing functional diversity of ceramics in an assemblage are interpreted as an indication of the increasing segmentation found at the dinner table, which helped reinforce a new standardized way of eating. Behavior that standardizes and segments requires one dish per person and a variety of dish sizes for different courses in the meal (e.g., butter dishes, dessert dishes, meat dishes, etc.). An assemblage containing such an assortment would be an indication of a new etiquette that reinforced a segmenting trend and, in turn, disciplined people's behavior at and away from the table. I expect this segmenting behavior to have begun first within the wealthier groups. Whether this behavior then spread through society to other wealth groups or was resisted by other groups may have been dictated by ideological and functional reasons. After segmenting behavior takes hold in a society, a disciplined behavior— whose presence may be detected through the use of matched sets— should also appear among the elite. Through time this process, which tends to foster individuality, may extend to other wealth groups as they become involved in the creation of group boundaries. The analysis of toothbrushes indicates the increasing participation of individuals in grooming and hygiene. The use of the toothbrush eventually became disciplined and its production became standardized, a segmenting process, which helped reinforce and create individuality. The study of the toothbrush is used to measure this segmenting process in the workplace. I measure both the toothbrush's use by different wealth groups and its manufacture as production became standardized.

Both of these artifact categories, ceramics and toothbrushes, provide data for an analysis of the range of the penetration of new personal discipline into different wealth groups. Archaeology can measure to what extent individuality and segmentation existed. Was having a variety of plates and a variety of teawares—which led to the segmentation of meals and, eventually, to a training ground for behavior in everyday life—important? Or was it more important to have matched sets of dishes, bowls, and teawares with people eating from similar plates and behaving in a similar standard fashion at meals? Archaeology can retrieve information regarding the behavior of groups as well as how and to what extent their behavior spread.

There is no doubt that few toothbrushes existed prior to the last quarter of the eighteenth century. Toothbrushes are absent from most probate inventories; however, they were an item with no market value and therefore may have been overlooked in the inventory process. Archaeologically recovered toothbrushes reveal data regarding the creation of the individual through both hygiene and the manufacturing process. The measure of plate sizes and the production and use of toothbrushes are examples of the recursive quality of material culture in developing a materially and behaviorally segmented and modern disciplined society.

Social Time

In evaluating social time, I examine probate inventory data from Annapolis and Anne Arundel County, Maryland, which revealed the development of a new discipline and an increasingly stratified society. The mid- to late eighteenth century was a period of social transformation throughout the Anglo-Atlantic world. The bourgeoisie became prominently defined by incorporating new standardizing and exacting forms of behavior and material culture in their daily lives. Enlightenment ideas reached members of the wealthiest groups first, and eventually other groups emulated their actions and material possessions.[14]

Increasing discipline in a society is a reaction to a series of stresses, such as population increase, economic instability, inflation, and wealth redistribution. In Annapolis and Anne Arundel County, these socioeconomic instabilities produced an increasingly competitive society that encouraged modern discipline and segmented everyday life. People began to use material culture in a new way—to create and reinforce boundaries as well as to support the ideology of the new social hierarchy. Mary Douglas and Baron Isherwood note that people create boundaries when they are in continuous contact with others, a phenomenon that occurs most dramatically in urban areas. [15] Therefore, an urban (Annapolis) to rural (Anne Arundel County) comparison provides a test case to see if this new discipline developed in the more competitive setting of a flourishing social and economic center or in a less densely populated and less socially competitive area. This is not to suggest that group boundaries would have been more prominent in urban areas, but that the existence of these boundaries may have been expressed differently, and material goods may have played a different role.

The development of a new etiquette and material culture associated with formal and segmented dining and increasing concern for personal appearance and hygiene are some of the tools people used to create explicitly different groups. Of particular interest to this study is Daniel Miller's interpretation of an emulation model that focuses on Enlightenment England. [16] Borrowing from Neil McKendrick's work, he explains that groups used symbolic manifestations of material goods to reestablish their threatened position in the social hierarchy. In a society where the hierarchy is well established and unquestioned, or where the distance between classes is too great to bridge, new patterns of consumerism are extremely difficult, if not impossible, to create. As the ancien régime lost power in Enlightenment England, there was a radical transformation of the amount and type of goods people used. Goods that had little or no symbolic meaning during the time of unquestioned hierarchy became, as the old order was challenged, more active in creating meaning and reinforcing social asymmetry. With the increased production of goods, emulation of the elite groups by those lower in the order became popular. Demand for goods increased with the ambiguity of the social hierarchy. [17] Because emulation threatened the hierarchy, the elite needed to reestablish differences and keep their social distance by creating new goods, new behaviors, and new social actions. They maintained this distance by controlling the access to knowledge about goods and their proper use.

I believe that the development of these concepts are heightened in a competitive society and, consequently, help to discipline and segment everyday life, create and reinforce group boundaries, and establish a hierarchical society. My specific expectations and conjectures follow.

First, items that segmented time and land, such as clocks, scientific instruments, weights and scales, and compasses, should be noticeable in inventories prior to any socioeconomic crises. These goods appear in Annapolis more often than in the surrounding rural area. In the hands of a select few, these instruments were used to facilitate the task of the division and measurement of land, time, and environment—reinforcing, creating, controlling, and ordering society.[18] It is the use of these objects that helped to legitimate control and power and the advent of individualism among the elite, because they understood the natural law through direct observation. These goods created and maintained wealth and behavioral differences between the wealthiest groups and the rest of society and naturalized the former's dominance. The use and observation of this new behavior laid the framework for the introduction of a vast quantity of segmenting and standardizing materials, stimulated by competition and economic crisis in society. This idea is opposed to the standard interpretation of wealth and material culture as examples of sumptuary items.

Second, during a time of social and economic instability, when distinct naturalized boundaries were in place, a new type of behavioral discipline, or etiquette, developed. This new etiquette, which had its foundations in the naturalization of time consciousness, acted to discipline behavior and segment people within and between wealth groups. Items associated with this new behavior that can be found in the probate inventory records include: forks, sanitary equipment (e.g., chamber pots and close stools), looking glasses, bed and table linens, handkerchiefs, napkins, items associated with grooming (e.g., dresser boxes, dressing glasses, dressing tables, shaving/wash basins, and combs), and objects associated with formal and segmented dining (e.g., functionally specific tables, dish covers, castors, butter boats, fruit dishes, buffet and custard cups, sets of dishes, cups and saucers, spoons, knives, and forks).

My third expectation is that the penetration of these ideas associated with the segmentation and standardization of material and behavior should occur at a faster rate in the urban areas or in the competitive centers suffering under socioeconomic strains. Even though some pre-twentieth-century urban areas were often considered to consist of urban farmsteads, as inhabitants carried on many of the daily routines of rural farmsteads,[19] the city dweller began to subscribe to a new order of disciplined behavior.

Fourth, the goods noted above initially should increase dramatically among members of the upper wealth group during times of social and economic strain in the Chesapeake, in general, and Annapolis, in particular, resulting in heightened competition among the elite. These objects aided in the creation and definition of a distinct upper wealth group that was adopting a new etiquette emphasizing individuality and social separation. As lower groups emulated the new disciplining behavior and acquired material that the upper wealth group already possessed, the latter changed the behavior and meaning associated with these goods in order to maintain social boundaries.

Quantification and analysis of these objects would be incomplete if there were no meaning associated with them. For example, knowing that a specific wealth group tended more often to have sets of forks is nothing more that a statistic describing the consumption patterns of a particular group. Absent is a knowledge of the social context. By discovering the meaning, an understanding of how material goods are symbolically used to create and reinforce boundaries may be found.

Long-Term History

For the analysis of long-term history I examine etiquette books from Western society and build upon local and regional contexts from the Chesapeake. Historical data furnish information for the transformation from premodern to modern behavior from the late medieval era through the Enlightenment. Long-term history provides a look at broader geographical areas and allows for an understanding of the interconnected relationships between diverse groups and wide-ranging time periods.[20]

Discipline is most closely associated with increasing consciousness of time. In order to provide an understanding of changing etiquette in Western civilization it is necessary to place this analysis in the context of time discipline. The analysis of geographical time demonstrates the changing rules of behavior, from premodern rules, which are foreign to us today, to rules of modern times, which feel natural and familiar. Etiquette books provide not only a basis for understanding this behavioral change but also a description of the material goods that reinforced the change. The history of individuals and social time needs to be understood in the context of long-term history, and broad-scale analyses can only be built upon the smaller scales of history.

Etiquette books, which recommended behavior for different social groups, survive from as early as the twelfth century. Their rules were restricted to those who were literate, but they were eventually emulated by the lower groups. The long-term history of manners in Western civilization, as well as in the local context of colonial Maryland, helps to explain the diachronic variability of material goods.

AN APPROACH TO UNDERSTANDING CONTEXT AND MEANING

The advantage of this interdisciplinary study is not in using one set of data, archeological or historical, to prove or disprove the other. Rather, I integrate the two sources of data, for each can provide information that the other cannot.[21] Robert Schuyler's distinction between *emic* and *etic* as historical and archaeological categories is relevant for understanding how materials from these two sources complement each other. Using only one of these data sources produces a partial interpretation of the subject; combining both emic and etic analyses creates a fuller understanding of the materials.[22] Mark Leone and Parker Potter argue against the lack of integration between the archaeological and historical records. They claim that sites are often excavated first and documentary records are then searched for comparative practices. Other archaeologists search the documentary records and fill in the historical gaps with archaeological data. Leone and Potter's approach, called Middle Range Theory, argues that both historical and archaeological data be used to identify anomalies. As ambiguities are identified, additional questions arise and the sources need to be reexamined, thus creating a dialectical relationship between the two sources. Together archaeological data and historical data can provide a richer interpretation of the meaning of material culture and account for the variability of goods through time and space.

Examining individual, social, and long-term history reveals that society cannot be seen in terms of a simple hierarchy but, rather, that society is involved in a continual struggle regarding hierarchy. An archaeology of discipline is only possible if there is an understanding of the context of uses and meanings of material goods. In any population alternative ideologies exist and are essential for understanding resistance to the dominant ideology. Archeology has the potential of revealing these tensions if an understanding of the uses and meanings of material culture can be achieved. Material culture can claim various meanings depending on the motives of subgroups. For example, a group can retain an appearance of conformity while maintaining alternative values for objects.[23] Breaks in the standard uses of items, or the substitution of items for less conventional or more traditional objects, also may indicate a form of social resistance. It has been archaeologically demonstrated that resistance may appear in some forms of material culture and not in others.[24] Most important, archaeology can serve alongside history to provide additional interpretations of the past. This is essential, because historical records are often a product of dominant groups, leaving subordinate groups underrepresented.

Meanings of Material Culture Change

Addressing the interactive qualities of material goods is relatively new in archaeology. Archaeologists need to go beyond descriptive and functional analyses of material goods and seek to understand how the goods structured everyday existence. The analysis of stylistic attributes and assemblage variability are important in discovering emic meaning.

Wobst's work regards style as a form of information exchange that often relays messages about group boundaries, rank, and ownership.[25] Style messages are usually aimed at groups beyond the household but may not be understood by socially distant groups. Other archaeologists argue that material culture plays an important role in daily social relations. Groups manipulate and negotiate meanings for material culture according to their strategies of survival.[26]

Evaluating the meaning of goods provides a basis for understanding their context. It is the emphasis on the interactive quality of material culture that sets this approach apart from the functional analysis dominating the new archeology:

> Rather than supporting that culture, including the rules, behavior, and things produced, is borne by people in a fairly passive and unaware fashion, the assumption is that people create, use, modify, and manipulate their symbolic capabilities, making and remaking the world they live in. . . . Like language, its use shapes our lives, and our lives would be shapeless without it. . . . Material culture [is] an instrument in creating meaning and order in the world . . . and not solely as the reflection of economics, social organization, or ideology.[27]

Michael Shanks and Christopher Tilley claim that style creates boundaries where interaction is intense. Functional studies assume that "style is a passive reflection of group or social identity and the cross-cultural generalizing perspective, in terms of which this research has often been framed, denies the specificity of cultural context, that in some situations style may relate to learning networks while in others it clearly does not."[28]

Uniformity or variability of material goods between or within groups is not caused only by patterns of interaction. Variability of goods in the Chesapeake region also can be understood as an expression of intragroup cohesion, competition over resources, and stress. All of these may affect the internal structures of society or the rules according to which observed systems of interrelations are produced.[29] According to Ian Hodder, "The exact form of any dichotomies overtly stressed between groups within complex societies will depend on the way in which social strains develop in relation to competition over resources or privileges and access to power in a particular instance."[30]

Goods are more than items of desire, they are a medium that reinforces social relations. They are "visible statements about the hierarchy of values to which their chooser subscribes." Material culture nonverbally communicates meaning and maintains social relationships, either inside or outside of a group. Consumption goods create the system of meaning. Taken out of the society in which they participate, these objects are meaningless. Whether and how they are used or refused constitutes whether they maintain, create, or undermine social relations. Their meanings are neither fixed nor randomly arranged, rather, they are structured around social purposes and "arranged in vistas and hierarchies."[31] The consumption of goods allows for the classifications of persons and events. It is a dynamic process that allows social categories to be continually defined and redefined.[32]

In the historic Chesapeake, the elite groups acquired new goods for the sole purpose of differentiation. The lowest groups were not threatened by assimilation and therefore either imitated higher ranking groups or created boundaries, separated themselves, and resisted the dominant ideology. The intermediate groups faced more complex situations, because they were superordinate to one group and subordinate to another. They either tried to distinguish themselves from lower groups by using goods and meanings different from both upper and lower groups, or they imitated the upper groups, which also separated them from the lower groups. Complex situations influenced material culture change, and both downward and upward movement caused variability. Grant McCracken questions, "Are there some social groups that drive upward by their own efforts, while other social groups are driven upward only by the pressure of those below (and never by the driving pressure of their own)?"[33]

In the seventeenth and eighteenth centuries in Western Europe, France and England in particular, competition for status and prestige led to an overt expression of behavior and material culture dominated by the upper class. Once a hierarchy was established, it was maintained by the competition of people within that group, "each being understandably anxious to preserve any privilege however trivial, and the power it conferred."[34] In court society, individuality was created as each person distinguished himself or herself from others in the group as well as from those outside of the group. Hegemonic tendencies appeared as groups expressed their identity through material goods and the behaviors associated with them, thus distancing themselves from others while transforming and creating their own identity.[35] The stronger the group, the greater its ability to control the envy that might ruin the cohesive bond, imposing, for example, values preventing deviant spending and excessive consumption.[36]

One way of enforcing and establishing group values is through ritual, which serves as a way of clearly and distinctly defining a meaning. Rituals help to reinforce and maintain a meaning and prevent that meaning from changing. "More effective rituals use material things," Douglas and Isherwood assert, and "the more costly the ritual trappings, the stronger we can assume the intention to fix the meaning to be."[37] Ceremonies among isolated gentry, particularly in rural areas, such as Anne Arundel County, did not play as big a role as they did in the more competitive, more densely populated urban areas. If gentry members of an urban area refused to participate in ceremonial activities, it meant their removal from the group, forfeiting of privileges, and a concomitant loss of power.[38]

SOCIAL RELATIONS AND MATERIAL CULTURE

To understand the context of the uses and meanings of material goods, it is necessary to understand power relations, hierarchies, and the strategies by which social behavior is reproduced. The social order of colonial Chesapeake may be examined in terms of Foucault's institutional structures and the roles they play in creating society, as well as through Pierre Bourdieu's analysis of the power and meanings behind everyday material culture. As Shanks and Tilley note, "Material culture can be considered an articulated and structured silent material discourse forming a channel of reified expression and being linked and bound up with social practices and social strategies involving power, interests, and ideology."[39]

Foucault argues, along with Althusser, that institutional structures, such as schools, families, and insane asylums, maintain class hegemony.[40] Foucault's ideas are essential in understanding power relations, the mechanisms of the dominant state apparatuses, and the success and longevity of dominant ideologies. For Foucault, however, the individual is elusive; the social actor is engulfed by the dominate ideology.[41] Both Foucault and Althusser have neglected the role of the active individual. Identifying the role of the human agency and its influence in understanding the role of domination is essential, however, to understanding the mechanisms of subordinate culture. Archaeology is able to uncover forms of dominant ideology on institutional levels as well as show how individuals conformed to or rejected the dominant ideology.

Foucault asserts that power is productive as well as repressive.[42] His ideas on power differ from traditional Marxist interpretation, which claims that power tends to come from economy and is "concrete possession analogous to commodity which can be wielded, transferred, seized, or alienated."[43] That is, traditional Marxism believes that power arises from class interest, flows from superordinate structures, such as class and state apparatuses, and is exercised on subordinate populations. According to Foucault, however, power is linked to social relations. Because social relations are based on power, they shape and create forms of social interaction, and because power, which has many meanings, is important for social interaction, it not only should be linked to social oppression or economics but also should be regarded as part of all encounters of which the social world exists.[44] Thus Miller and Tilley distinguish *power to,* which has positive social affects, and *power over,* which is negative and repressive.[45] Power creates the individual and produces the social context in which individuals and groups operate.[46]

Power to is a complex set of relations practiced and reinforced socially, through relations existing in all forms of daily activities, including institutions and family life. Power is not held by, and does not radiate from, one person, but is part of complex and interlinking social interactions. A monarch, for instance, is only one part of a power structure: he or she does not hold or wield power alone.[47] Support for dominant relationships comes from subordinate groups and is "sustained by power in families, local groups, offices, etc."[48]

"If [power] were anything but repressive," Foucault asks, "do you really think one would be brought to obey it?"[49] Subordinates must see power as productive in order for it to operate as a repressive force. Therefore, power can both produce and repress social action. Power is not centralized, repressing resistance in discrete locations; rather, power dilutes resistance along power networks embedded in the social order.

In Foucault's view the Enlightenment was not simply a humanitarian movement but was the creation of a new system of domination expressed in new surveillance technology.[50] Discipline and social control of people became a major concern. Institutional buildings—prisons, factories, and schools, for example—began to look alike as they created space for surveillance.[51] Controlling and structuring space allowed for enforcement of discipline. Tilley asserts that "enclosure and measured subdivisions or partitioning, fixed positions, [and] paths for circulation" are "complex spaces at one and the same time architectural, hierarchical and functional."[52] Such discipline standardizes behavior and determines the use of private space. The large open rooms found in medieval houses, where guests could be received and view the various household activities, were replaced in the Renaissance by many rooms with fixed living spaces, where only specific activities took place, such as kitchens, living rooms, dining rooms, and bedrooms.[53] Functionally specific rooms necessitated a specific and standardized behavior in each room. It will be apparent later that in Annapolis a new material culture and new rules helped to reinforce this new behavior. Material goods related to dining and hygiene practices became increasingly important in creating this new individuality and standardized behavior.

"Discipline creates subjects of everyone," Foucault argues. It also provides procedures for training. The workplace, which became separated from the home, became increasingly monitored, and "the factory-based labor process [rendered] bodily behavior routine, repetitive, subject to codifiable rules and accessible to surveillance and calculation." According to Foucault, the body is directly involved in a political field: "Power relations have an immediate hold over it; they invest it, mark it, train it, torture it, force it to carry out tasks, to perform ceremonies, to emit signs."[54] The power of discipline is not that it crushes or alienates people, but rather that it produces willful subjects who willingly work within the capitalist system. Discipline creates a standardized subject.

Bourdieu's work is also concerned with power, particularly that involved in the reproduction of class relations.[55] Bourdieu believes that the dominant ideology penetrates daily social encounters, and that the "very language and forms through which people express themselves provide instruments for their own oppression."[56] It is necessary to document the culture of any community in order to understand why people docilely obey and accept their subordinate position or are oblivious to their condition.

One of Bourdieu's analyses involves a nonstate, small-scale society in which social domination is created and maintained through repeated social practices.[57] Those who are the dominant agents in the asymmetrical relationship must work daily to maintain their power. The interpersonal bond is necessary in order to appropriate labor, services, goods, and honor. The dominant exercise their control and create differences through speech, gesture, task, and appearance, and claim that these cultural differences justify their right to rule. This is what Bourdieu calls symbolic violence, which is "more economical in terms of power than pure violence."[58] A study of meaning and context from Annapolis, Maryland, and the surrounding countryside reveals how the elite used symbolic violence by creating new formal behaviors to justify their position in society.

Hierarchy is continually being contested and boundaries are always being redrawn, providing an arena for resistance.[59] Material culture and ritual become important in power relations as they reinforce the order through intimate experiences of cultural form. Bourdieu examines the power and meanings of what superficially may be seen as trivial material and social classifications, such as the body, foods, play, and opinion: "These are constructed within a systematic opposition between a range of 'higher' cultural practices and distinctions, disdainful and disinterested in representations and context, in response to which the culture of the dominated class presents an aesthetic valuing immediate sensual gratification based in a culture of necessity."[60]

Bourdieu recognizes strategy as an important means of reproducing social behavior. Domination often negotiates between its "coercive-legitimatory, collectivist-individualist, structural-calculative, [and] practical-representational natures,"[61] and may break down unless agents actively maintain the balance. Daniel Miller explains that domination is the condition in which the practice and ideas of a minority control all of society and are successful in reproducing these conditions.[62] Groups may dominate through coercive actions or through ideology, so that their claims to power are seen as legitimate.

Because Bourdieu finds traditional anthropological structuralism mechanical and inflexible, he modifies this structuralism to find "the nature of dispositions and power strategies."[63] He notes that Mauss used ethnographic examples to understand the social contracts involved when exchanging gifts.[64] Bourdieu adds that gift reciprocity is more than a set of rules, it is a set of complex negotiations for strategies of power.[65] He examines culture through the concept of *habitus*, a "set of dispositions which provides a basis for the enactment of strategy according to interest, perspective and power."[66] *Habitus* is a structured set of classification schemes that is learned and provides a sense of cultural priority. By exploring the hierarchies of classification, which are reinforced by material objects or physical settings, we may be able understand ideology and power.

How one reads an object's meaning, which may be influenced by an underlying experience, determines how one reacts in differing social circumstances. Bourdieu claims that it is the order embodied in manners and the trivial objects that often express meaning in the everyday world. Everyday objects "assert their presence as simultaneously material force and symbols."[67] Our image of objects are continually modified by their presence. Objects can and do play a major role in social reproduction.

When threatened by resistance, the dominant group may either appeal to mass participation or turn inward for personal salvation. Miller explains that turning toward mass participation involves the dominant group referring to an original text that supports a particular ideology.[68]

Bourdieu and Foucault have observed power and discipline on the individual, group, and institutional levels. To make this analysis applicable to historical archaeology in the Chesapeake, it is necessary to realize that power is not instantaneously generated at the institutional level. Rather, power is generated by individuals and supported and reinforced by other individuals and groups. It is this power that creates industrial capitalism, a meta-institution that is supported by schools, factories, and so forth. This study is about the development of modern discipline from its most basic level, the individual, and how the individual operated within a regional and international context. As modern discipline became accepted, people were trained through surveillance either by institutions or by peer groups. Surveillance is only successful on the level of everyday intercourse if material goods and codes of meaning are understood by the appropriate players.[69]

Studies that explore the symbolic and the active nature in material culture are rare, and those studies that integrate archeology, history, and theory are even rarer. Many social scientists neglect to analyze goods in the cultural context in which they operate.[70] Only a few anthropologists and archaeologists have focused on the importance of the object in social reproduction.[71] Even with the overwhelming amount of material goods in modern life, there has been little academic discussion on the meaning of artifacts.[72] Using the three scales of history, this analysis of the eighteenth- and nineteenth-century Chesapeake explores how individuals and groups actively used material goods to define power relations and create social hierarchies. This archaeological and historical analysis provides a basis and context for an understanding of the meaning and uses of goods in a long-term history of material goods and behavior.

1. Individual Time: Archaeology of the House Lot

Archaeological analyses of four house lots within the city of Annapolis provide a perspective on a history of the individual. The archaeological preservation within the city is impressive compared to many urban areas, because most of Annapolis's eighteenth-century deposits are undisturbed by subsequent urban development. To date archaeologists have tested or excavated more than twenty sites, some dating to as early as the late seventeenth century (the majority date from the mid- to late eighteenth century). Annapolis was a small port town until the provincial capital was moved there from Saint Mary's City in 1695. Governor Francis Nicholson (1693–98) established a baroque city plan that emphasized the dominance of the church and the state. These institutions were placed on the two highest points of land, were surrounded by circles, and had streets radiating from them (fig. 1). The provincial government attracted support services, and many of the elite who participated in the social and bureaucratic affairs of the colony maintained residences in town. During Annapolis's "golden age" (1763–86), the town's elite constructed large Georgian mansions that either destroyed the previous archaeological record or protected it under newly constructed house wings, sheds, barns, and stables.

Although still the capital, Annapolis lost most of its prominence as a social center by 1790, as development and industry moved to Bal-

BIRD'S EYE VIEW OF THE CITY OF ANNAPOLIS.
CAPITAL OF THE STATE OF MARYLAND.

Figure 1. A nineteenth-century bird's-eye view of the city of Annapolis. Maryland State Archives Special Collection MSA SC 1556-150.

timore. Annapolis remained a relatively underdeveloped port town through the nineteenth and early twentieth centuries. Because of this, well-defined stratigraphic deposits exist and allow for exact chronological control. This control helps to provide a changing history of individual time. Although generalities will be drawn from the data, these short chronological components are sensitive to the idiosyncracies of short-term and particular events.

This archaeological study examines two types of material culture to test how the ideas of a new discipline penetrated society. The first items examined are functional, related to dining. They include a variety of ceramic types and sizes and the functional categories of plates, bowls, and teawares. It is traditionally assumed that with the advent of the Industrial Revolution in the second half of the eighteenth century, consumption became democratized and ceramics became more readily available.[1] To what extent, and how rapidly, did this new idea—one plate for one person—spread to the New World? Were people concerned with reproducing disciplined and standard behavior around the table, thus creating individuals with similar behavior? Which social groups were concerned with this new behavior and how did this discipline enter society?

The second item studied is toothbrushes. The examination of toothbrushes found in the archaeological record adds two dimensions to the aspect of behavioral and material segmentation. From the late medieval era, cleanliness became a growing concern in Western society. In late eighteenth-century Anglo-America, regular toothbrush use and dental care became important as cleanliness, including clean teeth and inoffensive smelling breath, became a requirement of polite society. The toothbrush is related to grooming and hygiene and, therefore, to personal discipline, which required its regular and systematic use to create the individual. The toothbrush is indicative of new behavior not only through its use but also through the attributes of its manufacture. By studying the toothbrush's manufacture, it is clear that it is an object whose mass production required an increasingly disciplined and segmented workplace.

THE SITES

This analysis includes four major sites within the historic district of Annapolis, containing undisturbed eighteenth- and nineteenth-century

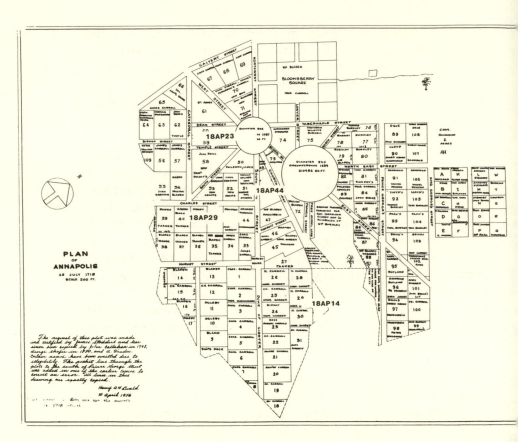

Figure 2. Map of Annapolis, locating the Victualling Warehouse, Thomas Hyde House, Reynolds Tavern, and Jonas Green Print Shop. Maryland State Archives Special Collection MSA SC 1477-4.

components (fig. 2). These sites are the Thomas Hyde House at 193 Main Street (18AP44), a residence of wealthy merchants; the Victualling Warehouse (18AP14), a residence of a middling merchant; the Jonas Green Print Shop (18AP29), a residence and work site of a crafts-man with high social status within the community; and the Reynolds Tavern (18AP23), the residence of a wealthy merchant.

The materials for these analyses come from sheet refuse found in the yards of these sites. Two sites, the Thomas Hyde House and the Reyn-olds Tavern, contain materials from privies that date to the early and mid-nineteenth century, respectively. Because stratigraphic analyses are available for the Thomas Hyde House, Victualling Warehouse, and Jonas Green Print Shop, an analysis of dining ceramics will use data from these sites only. A ceramic minimum vessel count for each of these three sites was performed, and data were grouped chronologically. An analysis demonstrating the various uses of disciplining and segmenting items provides information on how different wealth and social groups used these items every day to reinforce a modern discipline, and on how attitudes changed from the eighteenth through the nineteenth century.

Because major features have been catalogued and analyzed from the Reynolds Tavern, toothbrush data from this site as well as from the Jonas Green Print Shop will be analyzed. Toothbrushes were not found at the other sites. Specifically, manufacturing techniques, such as the standardization of drill hole placements, will be compared to the acceptance of a new personal discipline in the workplace. A relationship between manufacturing techniques and greater concern for hygiene will be examined. The following is a history of the lots encompassing each of the sites.

The Victualling Warehouse (18AP14)

The earliest ownership of the Victualling Warehouse,[2] a waterfront lot, can be traced to Amos Garrett, a wealthy merchant who owned a substantial amount of property in Annapolis, by at least the 1720s. By 1747 the Dulany family owned the property, and deeds indicate that they possessed two brick warehouses on this land.[3] Because Daniel Dulany, a loyalist, owned the property at the time of the American Revolution, it was confiscated by the state in 1781. The warehouse was used as a victualling office, handling supplies for the Continental army. After the war the property was leased by William Wilkins, who operated a dry goods store.[4] One year later he purchased the warehouse, a dwelling, and other property through a public auction.

Wilkins's career as merchant began in the 1760s, during Annapolis's golden age. It seems that Wilkins most often sold coffee, tea, chocolate, sugar, molasses, soap, medicines, and window glass.[5] Occasionally he added other goods to his inventory, such as Irish linens, osenabrigs, and writing paper. Wilkins also advertised for sale "a Lusty Country-born

Negroe Wench that was bought for a House Wench, but does not an-
swer the Purpose, having been chiefly used for Plantation Business."[6]

Wilkins, a successful and influential middling merchant, remained in
Annapolis throughout the revolutionary war. He was one of only two
merchants who had goods to advertise in the *Maryland Gazette* during
the British blockade of the Chesapeake in 1777–78.[7] In the postwar
optimism, Wilkins purchased the waterfront warehouse and eventually
converted the building into a store/residence. He continued to sell
goods, although dinnerware such as ceramics remained noticeably absent from his advertisements.[8]

On 21 January 1790, a fire destroyed Wilkins's business and home as
well as other structures on the block. He relocated his business to
Church Street, and the lot remained unoccupied into the nineteenth
century. In 1807 Wilkins advertised in the *Maryland Gazette* to sell his
business in Annapolis so that he could move to Baltimore. He also advertised to sell his "lot of ground near the dock where his house was
burned."[9] One can infer from this advertisement that the structure had
not yet been rebuilt. Wilkins finally sold his lot to John Barber of Annapolis for one hundred dollars.[10] There was no mention in the deed of
any building on the premise.[11]

The warehouse was rebuilt soon after the property was sold, for in
1816, and again in 1819, Barber sold dry goods from his business at "the
new store on the wharf." The historical documents are unclear as to
when Barber rebuilt the warehouse (probably between 1810 and 1816),
but restoration of the building in the 1970s indicated that the present
building incorporated a portion of the earlier foundation.[12] Barber successfully operated his store and residence on this site until his death in
1822. Adam and John Miller leased the property and sold goods from
the store, perhaps until the 1850s.[13]

The fire and demolitions at the site created four distinct chronological layers, thus allowing relatively straightforward correlations to time
periods. The strata include the layers before the fire (c. 1747–90), at
the time of the fire (1790), after the fire until the demolition (1790–c.
1810), and during the early occupation of the rebuilt store (c. 1820–
40). All of these layers were overlaid by a concrete floor covering the
whole site. Some grading had occurred, which removed any strata post-
dating the early nineteenth century.[14]

The Thomas Hyde House (18AP44)

The Thomas Hyde House at 193 Main Street (formerly known as Church Street) lies within lot forty-eight of the 1718 Stoddart survey.[15] At that time the lot was owned by Philemon Lloyd. The property was inherited by Henrietta Maria Lloyd Chew, wife of Daniel Dulany, who later sold this lot along with lots forty-nine and fifty to Edward and Henrietta Marie Dorsey. The deed included the sale of several houses on the lots, although it was not specified which lots contained houses (Anne Arundel County Court Land Records 1748: 6). In 1757 the Dorseys subdivided the lot and leased a portion each to Charles Wallace and Thomas Hyde for ninety-nine years at £3.5.0 per year (Baker 1973). Hyde's portion is currently known as 193 Main Street. It was not until 1773 that Hyde purchased the property for £54.5.0 sterling. There is no documentary evidence that a dwelling existed on this land prior to 1767; at that time the *Maryland Gazette* contained several references to Thomas Hyde's store and residence on Church Street.[16]

Most of the excavated material at 193 Main Street belonged to Thomas Hyde and his family. Thomas Hyde was fifteen years old in 1734 when his father, Isaac, died and left him a penniless orphan. He was apprenticed to read, write, and make shoes. By 1745 he owned his own shoemaking and tanning business near the waterfront. In 1760, still listed as a tanner in a *Maryland Gazette* advertisement, he announced the sale of dry goods. He also held the public office— "commissioner and endorser of bills of credit." His shoemaking and dry goods business prospered such that in 1767 he was able to build his store and residence at 193 Main Street. The structure was a five-bay, two-story brick building with several outbuildings. Even though Thomas Hyde increasingly became known as a merchant, he leased a tanyard from 1775 until the revolution, when he re-leased it to the state. By 1783 he was ranked as the fourth wealthiest person in Annapolis with a taxable estate valued at £1,726. He died in 1795 at the age of seventy-four.[17]

The 1798 Federal Direct Tax List provided a description of the house and outbuildings on the property. Francis T. Clements, whose wife inherited the property, was charged with one two-story brick dwelling, thirty by twenty feet. Also on the property was a one-story brick kitchen measuring sixteen by sixteen feet.[18] George Maccubin, a successful Annapolitan merchant, purchased the lot in 1833 and in turn sold it to Sarah E. and Dr. Francis Thompson, a general practitioner, in 1864. Dr. Thompson successfully practiced medicine and lived in the structure until the turn of the century. The property remained in the family until 1929, when it was purchased by the Novelty Amusement Company. In the 1930s all of the structures on this lot were destroyed to create a parking lot for the theater adjacent to and east of 193 Main Street.

Stratum I of the site consisted of twentieth-century fill. The next stratum (II) included materials from the early to mid-nineteenth century. Stratum III contained deposits from the mid- to the late eighteenth century, and stratum IV contained diagnostic artifacts dating to the mid-eighteenth century.

The Jonas Green Print Shop (18AP29)

The history of lot forty-two, 18AP29, the Jonas Green Print Shop site,[19] can be traced back to 1718 when the property was resurveyed for William Bladen. In 1724 Thomas Bladen, who inherited this land from his father, sold it to Daniel Dulany. The following year the property, with a house, was sold to Dr. Charles Carroll for £16 sterling. Evidence suggests that Carroll leased the house to Jonas Green, official printer for the Maryland province, when Green first arrived in the city in 1738. The lot, including all the houses and edifices, was sold to Samuel Ogle, governor of Maryland, for £160 sterling.[20]

Most of the archaeological residue form the Jonas Green Print Shop site is a product of the Green family occupation. Three generations of Greens lived and practiced the craft of printing at the site. Jonas Green was born in 1712 and moved to the province with his wife, Anne Catherine, in 1738. Starting in 1745 he published the weekly *Maryland Gazette*. In the 1760s he sat on the Annapolis Common Council and was elected city alderman. Jonas served as a vestryman for Saint Anne's Church, as secretary of the local Masonic lodge, and on the jury of the mayor's court. He belonged to the prestigious Tuesday Club, which satirized eighteenth-century social and political life. When Jonas died in 1767, he left a probated estate worth £376.10.6., which placed him in the upper-middle wealth category.[21] (See chapter 3 for a discussion of wealth groups.)

Anne Catherine Green succeeded Jonas in the printing business and became the official printer of the province. In 1770 she purchased the lot where she lived and printed, and two years later she took her son, Frederick, into partnership. Little is known about Anne Catherine's social obligations. When she died in 1775, her probated inventory and accounts of administration placed her in the middle wealth group.[22]

Frederick Green became head of the household and took charge of the printing business. He served as a vestryman for Saint Anne's parish, a councilman for ten years, a city alderman, and a clerk of the House of Delegates. According to the 1783 tax assessment, Frederick Green's property holdings placed him in the top 20 percent of the estate in Annapolis. Green printed the *Maryland Gazette* on Charles Street until about 1786, after which the business moved several times and the house may have been rented. Frederick died in 1811 with an estate valued at $2,730.49, placing him in the uppermost wealth group.[23]

Frederick's son, Jonas, succeeded him in the printing business. The state did not award Jonas the title of official printer to the state, he lost most of the family's public printing business, and competition from other papers soon drove Jonas and his brother into insolvency. Their personal property was sold, and the *Maryland Gazette* ceased to publish in 1839, almost one hundred years after their grandfather had founded the paper.[24]

The stratigraphy found at the Jonas Green Print Shop site can be grouped into four distinct chronological layers: stratum I dated from the late nineteenth through the early twentieth century; stratum II contained artifacts dating mostly to the mid-nineteenth century; stratum III dated to about 1800; and the earliest layer at the site, stratum IV, dated to about 1780. Throughout most of the site, sterile soil underlaid stratum IV, although some areas had scatters of early deposits related to the occupation during the mid-eighteenth century.[25] These deposits are not large enough to include in this analysis.

The Reynolds Tavern (18AP23)

Lot sixty-one of the 1718 Stoddart survey is where Reynolds Tavern (18AP23) is located.[26] The lot originally was owned by Saint Anne's parish, probably as early as the beginning of eighteenth century. In 1747 Saint Anne's parish leased to William Reynolds, hatter, all of lot sixty and part of lot sixty-one with two hundred feet on Cathedral Street. The term was for sixty-three years at £4 sterling per year. In 1761 he leased about forty-seven feet of this property on West Street to William Faris for forty-one years at £4 sterling per year. Two years later the lease was extended to forty-seven years at the same rate. [27] Reynolds, an aspiring craftsman, merchant, and tavern keeper, continued to sublease portions of this land. In 1770 he leased additional land to William Faris for forty years at £1.6.8 sterling per year, and in 1772 he subleased to David Douglas sixty-one feet on West Street for thirty-eight years at £6.6.0 sterling per year. [28]

In 1777 William Reynolds died, and his wife Mary and daughter Margaret inherited the remainder of the lease. Two years later, Mary Reynolds married Alexander Trueman. [29] The structure on this lot soon became a boardinghouse, and in 1785 Alexander Trueman advertised his boardinghouse opposite Church Circle. [30] The following year, Trueman advertised the dwelling for rent, as it was a "very large, elegant, and convenient house, fit for public or private business." Later that year, Cornelius Mills advertised that he had opened a boardinghouse in "that commodious house opposite the Church . . . formerly occupied by Maj. Alex. Trueman." [31]

Trueman sold the remainder of his lease, including the lot formerly owned by William Reynolds, to Gabrial Duvall in 1789. Part of this land was put in trust for Duvall to sell in order to pay Trueman's debts. Later that year, Duvall advertised the sale of this property as the land, formerly owned by Trueman and William Reynolds, now being rented to Thomas Price. [32] One year later the land formerly belonging to Alexander Trueman was still advertised for sale in the *Maryland Gazette*. [33]

In 1794 the Corporation of Annapolis brought Gabrial Duvall to court for nonpayment of debts to the city. The corporation noted that "Reynolds Tavern" was decaying and ordered that the lot be sold. In the proceedings Duvall testified that Mrs. Reynolds and her two daughters had lived in the house until 1791, after which he had rented it. That same year the house and lot were sold to John Davidson for £1,020. Davidson died in 1794, and his wife Eleanor inherited the property. In 1798, the Federal Direct Tax List assessed her estate as having a house near Church Circle measuring thirty by twenty-four feet, a frame stable sixteen by twelve feet, and a frame smokehouse ten by eight feet, all of which was assessed for twelve hundred dollars. [34]

In 1811 Saint Anne's Church renewed Reynolds's lease, which was now in the hands of Eleanor Davidson. The next year Davidson leased Reynolds Tavern to Farmer's National Bank, and it became the residence of the bank's cashier. Six years later the lands and house were sold to the bank for $350. The bank held the title until 1936, when they sold it to the Public Library Association of Annapolis and Anne Arundel County for $17,500. In 1974 the property was sold to the National Trust for Historic Preservation for one dollar.[35]

A partial stratigraphic analysis of Reynolds Tavern exists, allowing the dating of artifacts, such as the toothbrushes located beneath the flooring of the house as well as those found in the privy. The archaeological contexts under the flooring provided a late eighteenth-century date, whereas the privy had a mean date of 1828. For this analysis these two contexts are the only areas that can be confidently examined.

Site Summary and Prospects for an Archaeology of Capitalism

The wealth and status of the Hydes, Maccubins, and Thompsons at the Thomas Hyde House (193 Main Street) site; the Greens at the Jonas Green Print Shop site; and the Wilkinses and Barbers at the Victualling Warehouse site varied from the mid-eighteenth into the nineteenth century. Thomas Hyde began his career as a penniless apprentice shoemaker, became a merchant, and succeeded in becoming the fourth wealthiest Annapolitan in 1783. His Main Street estate was purchased by another financially fortunate merchant, George Maccubin, and by the 1860s Dr. Francis Thompson and his family lived there. At the Victualling Warehouse site, William Wilkins, a middling merchant, ranked in the top 20 percent in the 1783 tax list and appears to have remained comfortable during his occupation of the site.[36] John Barber's occupation of the Victualling Warehouse site also appears to have been successful. Although the Greens, who occupied the Jonas Green Print Shop site, were craftsmen, they were well respected among the Annapolis elite. Soon after Frederick's death in 1811, the family's fortunes dissolved. William Reynolds, a merchant and craftsman, made hats as well as operated his tavern. The site was located in a prestigious part of town, across the street from the Anglican Church, and the house remained the Reynolds family residence until the turn of the century.

Studying Standardization, Precision, and Exacting Behavior

In order for the culture of capitalism to be successful, it must penetrate the everyday routines of all segments of society.[37] As behavior became standardized and regimented, it encouraged the development of a modern discipline that allowed for a successful manufacturing process and promoted the consumption of goods, such as ceramics, that reinforced this behavior every day and at special, ritualized meals.

New ceramic technology from the second half of the eighteenth century was made possible only by new labor organization. Alienated labor and time discipline helped create standardized products, which, when used by the consumer, subconsciously taught the concepts of individuality. One plate for one person helped to reinforce standardizing, precise, and modern behavior in one aspect of domestic life. Emulation models suggest that the wealthy acquired high status items, and these goods eventually trickled down to the less wealthy. Middle- and lower-class people thought they were becoming more like their wealthy counterparts by using the same tableware that the wealthy used. What also happened was that the middle and lower classes learned to think and operate according to a new social pattern that encouraged individuality and time discipline. This new behavior reinforced the lower classes' ties to their inferior social position, and they eventually became the laborers of the new industrial era.

A functional analysis of ceramic dining items from these sites provides an understanding of how mass-produced goods entered the everyday life of various social and economic groups in eighteenth- and nineteenth-century Annapolis. Although conventional archaeological wisdom tells us that a variety of ceramic forms can be found by the beginning of the nineteenth century, more precise descriptions are needed, and I provide a measure of the acceptance of mass-produced goods in various wealth groups.

To measure the penetration of the new segmenting behavior in the archaeological record, a diachronic analysis was performed, identifying functional variety of wares and types of ceramics related to dining activity. For this analysis the Victualling Warehouse, Thomas Hyde House, and Jonas Green Print Shop sites were examined. A presence/absence table demonstrates ceramic types and their functional variability with

Table 1.   Ceramic Types and Functional Variability

Ceramic Type					
Creamware				×	
Pearlware			×	×	×
Whiteware		×		×	×
Sizes	7.0	7.5	8.0	8.5	9.0

the assumption that this data indicates the typical assortment of table-ware in a household.[38] In table 1 "Ceramic Type" indicates the standard ceramic wares present and "Sizes" is the number of different plate sizes present, rounded to the nearest one-half inch. In table 1 there is at least one 7.5-, 8.5-, and 9-inch whiteware plate, at least one 8- and 9-inch pearlware plate, and at least one 8.5-inch creamware plate present in the assemblage. There are three types (creamware, pearlware, and whiteware), six type-sizes (the total number of sizes present within the x-y coordinates of the table), and four plate sizes represented in the assemblage.

Table 2.   Two Models of Low Variability

Type				
W	×			
X	×			
Y	×			
Z	×			
Size	A	B	C	D

Type   = 4
Type-Size = 4
size   = 1

Type				
Z			×	
Size	A	B	C	D

Type   = 1
Type-Size = 1
size   = 1

Table 3. A Model of Middle-Range Variability

Type				
W				×
X			×	
Y		×		
Z	×			
Size	A	B	C	D

Type   = 4
Type-Size = 4
size   = 4

An assemblage with few types and sizes signifies a lack of variation and segmentation at the table, thus denoting nonparticipation in the new order of modern discipline (see table 2). A variety of types and sizes signifies that there is some segmentation at the dinner table and a partial participation in the new order (see table 3). An assemblage containing few types and many sizes signifies a high degree of segmentation and discipline at the table and the acceptance and use of the new order (see table 4). There are variations on all of these general groupings.

The tables' values are not gauges of wealth and should not be used the way many archaeologists use Miller's ceramic indexes to create an absolute scale of wealth. Rather, the tables gauge the penetration of modern discipline and are meaningful only with comparisons in similar contexts. Comparisons within a town are feasible, but comparisons between towns must take into account additional variables linked to commerce, information systems, and changes in social and economic situations.

Table 4. A Model of High Variability

Type				
Z	×	×	×	×
Size	A	B	C	D

Type   = 1
Type-Size = 4
size   = 4

Table 5.   A Model of Assemblage Variability

Ceramic Type							
Creamware, queensware	×	×	×				
Creamware, undecorated				×	×		
Pearlware, hand painted						×	×
Pearlware, transfer print								×

Function categories	10"d	12"d	9"p	7"m	5"t	3"tc	5"s	7"pit

Key: d = dish; p = plate; m = muffin; t = tureen; tc = tea cup; s = saucer; pit = pitcher
Type Function   = 8
Type   = 4
Function categories = 8

For a more complete analysis of the archaeological assemblage, other artifact categories also need to be considered. The measure of variability among plate sizes can easily be expanded to include different functional vessels. In all cases decorative patterns and function categories need to be considered. Function categories include serving vessels such as tea cups, saucers, bowls, pitchers, soup plates, and so forth. Type-function represents the various sizes and functions in an assemblage within the x-y coordinates of the table. Table 5 is a model of an analysis of a more complete assemblage.

Such analyses can easily be applied to sites dating from the beginning of mass-produced ceramics, the mid-eighteenth century, as long as there is a sizable sample and an adequate recovery strategy. Research goals should include the excavation of domestic refuse, because limiting excavations to architectural features may skew the data. Other materials, such as glass, may also be incorporated into an analysis. Due to new manufacturing techniques, glass tableware was mass produced and mass consumed from the late nineteenth century. As the time frame for this study ends before the late nineteenth century, however, glass will not be included in it.

In presence/absence tables 6, 7, and 8, function categories from the three sites are grouped according to layers and time periods. The function categories of plates, bowls, and tewares offer intra- and intersite comparison. An examination of the function category variations in the tables indicates that assemblages from the mid-eighteenth century are not very differentiated.

Table 6.   Diversity of Functional Categories at the Hyde House

Stratum I (1870–1880)

Ceramic Type	Ceramic Functions																		
	Plates											Bowls				Teaware			
Por,E	×	×	×	×	×	×	×		×										
Por,C	×			×												×	×		
PW	×																×		
PW,Se					×	×													
WW	×	×	×		×	×							×						×
IS	×	×											×	×		×			
Size (inches)	7	7.5	8	8.5	9	9.5	10	10.5	11	11.5	12	5	7	9	11	2	3	4	5

	Type	Size	Type-Size
Plate	= 6	9	21
Bowl	= 2	2	3
Teaware	= 3	3	5
	Type	Size	Type-Function
Totals for Stratum I =	6	14	29

Stratum II (1820–40)

Ceramic Type	Ceramic Functions																		
	Plates											Bowls				Teaware			
WSsw			×															×	
Por,E																×			
Por,C			×									×	×						
CW			×																
PW	×				×	×		×					×						
WW		×	×		×	×	×		×					×	×		×		
Size (inches)	7	7.5	8	8.5	9	9.5	10	10.5	11	11.5	12	5	7	9	11	2	3	4	5

	Type	Size	Type-Size
Plate	= 6	8	14
Bowl	= 3	4	4
Teaware	= 3	3	3
	Type	Size	Type-Function
Totals for Stratum II =	6	15	21

Table 6. (*Continued*)

Stratum III (1790–1810)

Ceramic Type	Ceramic Functions — Plates											Bowls				Teaware			
Size (inches)	7	7.5	8	8.5	9	9.5	10	10.5	11	11.5	12	5	7	9	11	2	3	4	5
WSsw					×							×		×		×			
Por,C							×												×
CW			×	×															
PW		×		×		×						×							

		Type	Size	Type-Size
Plate	=	4	7	7
Bowl	=	2	2	3
Teaware	=	2	2	2
		Type	Size	Type-Function
Totals for Stratum III	=	4	11	12

Stratum IV (c. 1750)

Ceramic Type	Ceramic Functions — Plates											Bowls				Teaware			
Size (inches)	7	7.5	8	8.5	9	9.5	10	10.5	11	11.5	12	5	7	9	11	2	3	4	5
Por, E	×																		
Por,C																	×		
CW				×															
PW							×												

		Type	Size	Type-Size
Plate	=	3	3	3
Bowl	=	0	0	0
Teaware	=	1	1	1
		Type	Size	Type-Function
Totals for Stratum IV	=	4	4	4

Key: CW = Creamware; IS = Ironstone; PW = Pearlware; PW,A = Pearlware, annular; PW,Tr = Pearlware, transfer print; PW,Hp = Pearlware, hand-painted; PW,Se = Pearlware, shell-edged; Por = Porcelain; Por,E = English porcelain; Por,C = Chinese porcelain; Por,S = Semi-porcelain; TG = Tin-glazed earthenware; ST,Ew = Slip-trailed earthenware; YW = Yellow ware; WSsw = White salt-glazed stoneware; WW = Whiteware

Table 7. Diversity of Functional Categories at the Victualling Warehouse

Stratum I (c. 1820s–1840s)

	Ceramic Functions																		
Ceramic Type	Plates											Bowls				Teaware			
CW			×		×		×												
PW,Tp	×	×	×		×	×										×			
PW,Hp																×			
WW													×	×				×	
Size (inches)	7	7.5	8	8.5	9	9.5	10	10.5	11	11.5	12	5	7	9	11	2	3	4	5

		Type	Size	Type-Size
Plate	=	2	6	8
Bowl	=	1	2	2
Teaware	=	3	1	3

	Type	Size	Type-Function
Totals for Stratum I =	4	9	13

Stratum II (1790–1810)

	Ceramic Functions																		
Ceramic Type	Plates											Bowls				Teaware			
Por,C	×		×				×												
CW		×														×	×	×	
PW,Se					×	×							×						
PW,Tr	×																×		
WW													×	×			×		
Size (inches)	7	7.5	8	8.5	9	9.5	10	10.5	11	11.5	12	5	7	9	11	2	3	4	5

		Type	Size	Type-Size
Plate	=	3	6	7
Bowl	=	2	2	2
Teaware	=	2	3	4

	Type	Size	Type-Function
Totals for Stratum II =	5	11	13

Table 7. (*Continued*)

Stratum III (1790)

Ceramic Type	Ceramic Functions																		
	Plates												Bowls			Teaware		
Por,C																×	×	×
CW	×												×					
PW,Se		×					×											
Size (inches)	7	7.5	8	8.5	9	9.5	10	10.5	11	11.5	12	5	7	9	11	2	3	4	5

		Type	Size	Type-Size
Plate	=	2	3	3
Bowl	=	1	1	1
Teaware	=	1	3	3
		Type	Size	Type-Function
Totals for Stratum III =		3	7	7

Stratum IV (1747–90)

Ceramic Type	Ceramic Functions																		
	Plates												Bowls			Teaware		
CW	×																	
Size (inches)	7	7.5	8	8.5	9	9.5	10	10.5	11	11.5	12	5	7	9	11	2	3	4	5

		Type	Size	Type-Size
Plate	=	1	1	1
Bowl	=	0	0	0
Teaware	=	0	0	0
		Type	Size	Type-Function
Totals for Stratum IV =		1	1	1

Key: CW = Creamware; IS = Ironstone; PW = Pearlware; PW,A = Pearlware, annular; PW,Tr = Pearlware, transfer print; PW,Hp = Pearlware, hand-painted; PW,Se = Pearlware, shell-edged; Por = Porcelain; Por,E = English porcelain; Por,C = Chinese porcelain; Por,S = Semi-porcelain; TG = Tin-glazed earthenware; ST,Ew = Slip-trailed earthenware; YW = Yellow ware; WSsw = White salt-glazed stoneware; WW = Whiteware

Table 8.   Diversity of Functional Categories at the Jonas Green Print Shop

Stratum II (c. 1860)

Ceramic Type	Plates											Bowls				Teaware			
WSsw	×								×										
Por,C			×						×			×							
CW	×		×				×					×							
PW			×						×			×	×					×	
WW												×	×						×
Size (inches)	7	7.5	8	8.5	9	9.5	10	10.5	11	11.5	12	5	7	9	11	2	3	4	5

		Type	Size	Type-Size
Plate	=	5	5	13
Bowl	=	2	2	2
Teaware	=	2	2	2
		Type	Size	Type-Function
Totals for Stratum II =		5	9	17

Stratum III (c. 1780–1800)

Ceramic Type	Plates											Bowls				Teaware			
Por,E	×								×										
CW	×						×					×	×					×	
PW							×					×	×				×		
Size (inches)	7	7.5	8	8.5	9	9.5	10	10.5	11	11.5	12	5	7	9	11	2	3	4	5

		Type	Size	Type-Size
Plate	=	3	4	7
Bowl	=	2	2	2
Teaware	=	2	2	2
		Type	Size	Type-Function
Totals for Stratum III =		7	8	9

Table 8.   (*Continued*)

Stratum III (c. 1780s)

Ceramic Type	Ceramic Functions		
	Plates	Bowls	Teaware
CW	×		
PW	×	×	×

Size (inches)	7	7.5	8	8.5	9	9.5	10	10.5	11	11.5	12	5	7	9	11	2	3	4	5

		Type	Size	Type-Size
Plate	=	2	2	3
Bowl	=	0	0	0
Teaware	=	1	1	1
		Type	Size	Type-Function
Totals for Stratum III	=	2	3	4

Key: CW = Creamware; IS = Ironstone; PW = Pearlware; PW,A = Pearlware, annular; PW,Tr = Pearlware, transfer print; PW,Hp = Pearlware, hand-painted; PW,Se = Pearlware, shell-edged; Por = Porcelain; Por,E = English porcelain; Por,C = Chinese porcelain; Por,S = Semi-porcelain; TG = Tin-glazed earthenware; ST,Ew = Slip-trailed earthenware; YW = Yellow ware; WSsw = White salt-glazed stoneware; WW = Whiteware

By the turn of the nineteenth century, the occupants of the Thomas Hyde House had increased dramatically the variety of their ceramic tableware, as indicated in table 6 by a type-function value slightly higher than the assemblages of the middling merchant (table 7) and the craftsman (table 8). Ceramic plates were probably beginning to be used to rigidly segment behavior at the dinner table by Thomas Hyde, a wealthy merchant who substantially elevated his status in the mid-eighteenth century. Most of the increased variation was a result of the growing use of dinner plates. The occupants of Hyde's lot acquired a white set made of mostly medium-cost pearlware and creamware, with a serving assemblage of high quality porcelain. This trend toward greater variety continued through the post-Civil War era, as the assemblage belonging to Dr. Francis Thompson nearly twice the ceramic variety as those of occupants at the other sites. Another white set of dinner plates was introduced, predominantly whiteware, with a serving set of high quality porcelain. This wealthiest site generally contained the greatest ceramic variety.

No plate sets exist in the assemblages of the middling merchant and craftsmen/printer families in the mid-eighteenth century. The early occupation of the middling merchant family, the Wilkinses, at the Victualling Warehouse (table 7) shows very little variation or use of ceramics as segmenting dining items, but by the 1790s Wilkins's ceramic variability had increased a great deal. Although there was less plate variation than during the same period at the Hyde site (table 6) and the Green site (table 8), teaware increased noticeably. From the beginning of the nineteenth century, ceramic variability rose. Plate size variation increased, whereas the teawares decreased. At the Jonas Green Print Shop site (table 8), some form of segmenting dining was found in the archaeological record by the 1780s. Both households began to assemble a white tableware set consisting of pearlwares and creamwares (the porcelains tended to be the serving vessels, although neither household developed a full porcelain set). By the turn of the nineteenth century, the Green family had increased significantly their plate size variation, and slightly increased their use of bowls and teawares. By the 1860s, however, the Greens had increased their ceramic variability only slightly. The site's type-function variability was about one-half the value of the wealthy merchant occupants at the Main Street site (see table 9). Both the middling merchant and craft/printer households appear to lag behind the wealthy merchant's household in adopting new material culture associated with the consumer revolution.

The archaeological data gathered—plate diameters, function category variation, and the consumption of ceramic sets—indicate a trend. In Annapolis segmentation and discipline at the table appeared earliest among the elite by at least the mid-eighteenth century, but by the turn of the nineteenth century, all socioeconomic groups measured—the wealthy merchant, the middle-class merchant, and the craftsman—had similar assemblages and variability index values. Whether all groups applied the same rules of disciplined dining is not known. But from the data one can infer that segmenting and disciplined dining practices had penetrated at least the upper and middle groups by the early 1800s. Most of the variation resulted from consumers using a variety of wares rather than matched sets. Large-scale consumption of matched sets (table 9) is not noticeable until the mid- to late nine-

Table 9.   A Diachronic Comparison of Type-Functions of Three Annapolis Sites

Year	Thomas Hyde (18AP44)	Victualling Warehouse (18AP14)	Jonas Green (18AP29)
1870–1890	29		
1860			17
1820–1840	21	13	
1790–1810	12	13	11
1790		7	4
1747–1790		1	
c. 1750	4		

teenth century. The middle groups imitated the consumption patterns of the elite, and although they might have believed that they thereby reached some kind of parity with their wealthy counterparts, in fact they learned a new social discipline that trained them for industrial society. Thus parity was never really achieved; rather, social distance was reinforced. By the second half of the nineteenth century, consumption differences between the groups had once again increased. Matched sets had become customary, creating and reinforcing a new discipline that allowed for the growing commoditization of time and goods.

Many of these consumer goods were produced under a labor system that used new surveillance technologies and new definitions of space use. This discipline enforced social controls and created standardized and repetitive behavior. Although the working classes were subjected to this new order in the factories, the elite began using the material by-products of disciplined factory methods, such as matched tableware sets, earlier than the poor. Matched sets and greater functional variety reinforced a disciplining behavior at the table and provided the elite with a new behavior and new material goods to socially separate themselves from the lower groups. Even though this new discipline was imposed on the lower classes, they were initially prohibited from acquiring the new goods by their still-alien behavior and the cost of the goods themselves.[39] As mass-produced goods became cheaper and discipline became an integral part of Western culture, goods entered the lower stratum of society, reinforcing the new culture of capitalism. It is traditional wisdom to believe that matched sets were developed because of increased standardized manufacturing techniques. However, a demand for these goods also had to exist. This demand apparently created group differentiation and further trained people for industrial society.

PERSONAL DISCIPLINE AND THE TOOTHBRUSH

A Brief History of the Toothbrush

References to teeth cleaning occur occasionally in early Renaissance literature. As early as the fifteenth century, dental health was a topic found in the scientific literature. Motley notes that in the fifteenth century Giovanni of Arcoli suggested that a person "should avoid indigestion; that excessive movement after eating was harmful, as was vomiting; that sweet or viscous food should not be eaten."[40] He also prescribed that teeth be cleaned with slivers of wood. Often a rag wrapped around a finger served as an early toothbrush. Renaissance studies of the human body included research in dental anatomy. Leonardo da Vinci, Andreas Vesalius, and Fallopius studied the masticatory musculature, the nerve supply to the teeth, dental anatomy, and their relationships. By 1530 the first book devoted solely to dentistry was published.[41] In the sixteenth century, Erasmus was offended by people who used napkins or tablecloths to clean their teeth and therefore prescribed that the mouth should be cleaned daily with fresh water.[42] In the seventeenth century, Cardinal Richelieu was offended by people picking their teeth with the sharp point of the knife and therefore ordered that knives should be rounded.[43]

Although the Chinese developed a type of toothbrush well before the sixteenth century, it was not until 1498 that a British citizen was credited with inventing the first documented toothbrush in the West.[44] It was not until the nineteenth century, however, that brushing became an accepted daily practice in the West and that studies of dental anatomy and tooth care increased dramatically.

Whether John Baker or Robert Woofandale was the first qualified dentist in the United States is not known. What is known is that Baker taught people such as Paul Revere, Isaac Greenwood, and H. Josiah Flagg the trade of dentistry. Revere took over Baker's practice in Boston, whereas Greenwood, "an ivory turner as well as a dentist, was a pioneer in America advising toothbrushes and dentifrices to remove tartar in its first state."[45] This new concern for the teeth is one measure of Enlightenment ideas about hygiene used in the New World.

Toothbrush Making

Toothbrush making was developed as early as the sixteenth century in England, as trade records from the Russia Company (founded in 1553) indicate that they were importing bristles from the Siberia region.[46] In 1734 as many as nine brushmakers were working in Bristol. The founding of the brushmaking industry is attributed to a man named Pitchard, a comb manufacturer, in the early eighteenth century. Throughout the mid-eighteenth century, the number of brushmakers in England grew as demand for their products rose.[47] In 1747 brushmakers unionized in Manchester, making the National Society of Brushmakers the oldest trade union in the world.[48]

Brushes in general and toothbrushes in particular became increasingly popular in the late eighteenth and early nineteenth centuries. The toothbrush became an accepted personal disciplining device, requiring systematic use to be effective, and it was used regularly by the upper classes by the beginning of the nineteenth century. It aided hygiene practices and helped create individuality. It also was useful as a social stratifier: the British crown effectively sanctioned its use. William Bracey Kent, a respectable brushmaker, was assigned to make toothbrushes for King George IV (1820–30) and held the royal appointment for the next two monarchs, King William IV and Queen Victoria.[49]

With the popularity of toothbrushes came a large number of manufacturers, especially in London. By 1835 there were 353 brushmakers in the city, employing an average of 4.55 journeymen and 1.30 apprentices. The large number of shops with an average of only four to five workers indicates that mass production in the form of large factories had not reached the craft at this point, yet the discipline and standardization process was underway.

The toothbrush consists of two different parts, the stock and the bristle. The stock was usually cut from the thigh or pelvis bone of the cow or the leg bone of an ox.[50] With a saw, five or six blanks could be cut from a single bone. The highest quality bristles, stiff and long, came from boars, hogs, and pigs raised in cold climates. Trade for bristles for use in toothbrushes began as early as the sixteenth century through the Russia Company. Early trade routes in the northern climates of the eastern hemisphere were extensive. Boar hairs were collected from the following species: *sus scrota* (Germany, Poland, Russia, and China), *sus cristatus* (India), *sus leucomystax* (Japan), and *sus scrota moupinensis* (Tibet). Chinese boar hairs were black and therefore not desirable until the 1890s.[51]

A discussion of the three major stages related to the development of the brush follows shortly, but to provide an understanding of the growing standardization of the toothbrush, I will first describe the different drilling methods, from basic hand drilling to multiple-template drilling.

The earliest toothbrushes were manufactured with a hand-held drill; the holes were bored freehand without benefit of a pattern. Their depth and spacing were judged by the craftsman, which usually resulted in brushes having unevenly spaced holes drilled to uneven depths. Eighteenth-century toothbrushes generally had two or three columns of drill holes, and their bristles were packed more loosely than the bristles in nineteenth- and twentieth-century toothbrushes. In the next stage of manufacturing technology, craftsmen pulled the stock toward fixed revolving drills. Here again holes were usually spaced by the eye of the craftsman, creating unevenly spaced rows. Eventually marking devices and/or templates were used for finer work, and finally up to six stocks were drilled at a time while the operator followed a metal template.[52] This increased mechanization created a more standardized product.

With the change in the drilling technology also came changing methods of constructing brushes, including toothbrushes. The earliest brushes were created through a process called pitch panning. When a craftsman had finished boring a number of stocks, he would proceed to the pitch pan. The exact number of bristles to fill the hole was chosen, and the bristles were dipped into the pitch pan to the required depth. Any excess pitch was wiped away and a "thrum [a short piece of thread] was tied around the bristle, and was again dipped into the pitch. Finally, it was placed into the bore hole, and this process was repeated for the next hole."[53]

Wire drawing, another construction process, required smaller holes placed on the reverse side of the bored stock. A wire was inserted through these holes, then the bristles were inserted, doubled, and a complete knot was made, pulled back, and drawn tight. When the process was

Figure 3. An example of wire drawing with cut grooves. (Drawn by Alan Ernstein).

completed for all of the holes in the column, the wire was broken off and looped under a wire several knots back, "pulled tight, looped under once more and pulled tight another time, finally to be broken off."[54]

Another type of wire drawing process involved cut grooves or channels on the reverse side of the brush (fig. 3). There were as many channels as columns of bore holes. The wire was drawn as described above and the grooves were filled with a molten wax or a hard cement. This technique was usually exclusively used on bone and ivory brushes (including toothbrushes).[55]

There is a third wire drawing process called trepanning wire drawing (fig. 4). In this case, holes are drilled in columns as with other brushes, but they are connected by holes bored horizontally through the length of the stock. These horizontal holes connect all of the vertically drilled holes in a column. The wires placed in these channels are not visible and are pulled through the holes with a crochet-like hook. The bristles

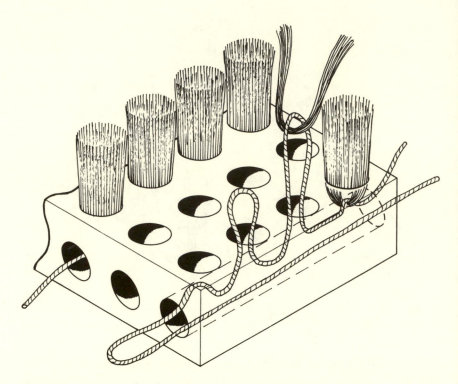

Figure 4. An example of trepanning wire drawing. (Drawn by Alan Ernstein).

are placed under the wire and the wire pulled back. When the column is finished, the hole at the end of the brush is plugged.

Generally, early toothbrush manufacturing was unmechanized and depended on the skills of individual craftsmen, resulting in a nonstandardized product. By the beginning of the nineteenth century, the toothbrush making process became increasingly standardized with the development of new technological developments. The English crown sanctioned its regular use, and eventually the toothbrush became part of the everyday life of consumers.

A Personal Discipline

There are at least two important ideas to explore regarding the discipline related to the production and use of toothbrushes through time.

First, wealth groups should be compared to see which first used mass-produced artifacts. Second, the relationship between factory discipline and the acceptance of a new personal discipline should be examined.

To date, only two of the four Annapolis sites have produced toothbrushes, and then only in small quantities. To make any conclusions about the relationship of toothbrushes to social and economic status based on this small data set would be unsound. But if all of the toothbrushes are examined as a complete set, some inferences regarding the discipline process in general and the workplace in particular may be drawn.

Rule making, or disciplining procedures, eventually became involved in the manufacture of toothbrushes. One way to gauge the discipline in toothbrush manufacturing is to measure the distance between drill holes in the brush. I used vernier calipers and measured drill holes to the nearest one-thousandth of an inch. A standard deviation, which calculated the average deviation between the average distance of the drill holes within a row, was assessed for each toothbrush. A higher standard deviation meant that the manufacturing process, with regard to the placement of the drill holes, was less standard.

The toothbrushes were grouped in four chronological categories, regardless of the site from which they came (table 10). Eighteen brushes were used for this study, all from the Jonas Green site, which was occupied by several generations of craftsmen, and the Reynolds Tavern site, occupied by a merchant/craftsman. Other brushes were found at other sites, but because their proveniences are not precise, they cannot be used here.

The first group of toothbrushes consists of four brushes that came from Stratum II of the Jonas Green site and had a mean date of 1860. The standard deviation between bristle holes ranged from 2.55 to 7.42, with an average standard deviation of 4.48.

The chronological category of the next group was 1818 to 1828, with the majority of the toothbrushes found belonging to the later date and coming from the privy at Reynolds Tavern. Only one toothbrush from this era was from the Jonas Green site. These eleven toothbrushes had standard deviations ranging from 3.04 to 10.82, with an average standard deviation of 6.29.

Two toothbrushes belonged to the next earliest group, from 1800 to 1804. These were from the Jonas Green site and had standard deviations of 7.07 and 5.32, with an average standard deviation of 6.20.

Table 10.   Toothbrushes from Two Annapolis Sites according to Chronology

Toothbrush	Date*	Total Holes	Mean Distance between Holes	Standard (S.D.)	
18AP29172.B1	1860	11	93	7.42	
18AP29172.B2	1860	4	79	3.11	
18AP2985B	1860	9	66	2.55	
18AP29120C	1860	59	23	4.83	
	1860		Average S.D.	4.48	
18AP23333B1317	1828	86	27	5.82	
18AP23333B1312	1828	88	22	4.59	
18AP23333B1311	1828	133	27	5.29	
18AP23333B1316	1828	56	74	10.77	
18AP23 3331314	1828	94	26	4.66	
18AP23 131	1828	89	89	5.31	
18AP23 131.5	1828	44	25	6.46	
18AP23 131.8	1828	82	82	6.61	
18AP23 344.131	1828	36	66	10.82	
18AP23333B1313	1828	134	23	3.04	
18AP29 F96a	1818	18	71	5.81	
	1818–28		Average S.D.	6.29	
18AP29 180c	1800	23	32	7.07	
18AP29251.39	1804	76	36	5.32	
	1800–1804		Average S.D.	6.20	
18AP23 5B2	1785	5	651	347.51	— —
18AP23 5B1	1785	26	79	14.38	14.38
18AP23 1B	1766	37	47	8.48	8.48
			Average S.D.	123.47	11.43

*Calculated by mean ceramic dating

Toothbrushes in the earliest grouping ranged from 1766 to 1785 and came from the Reynolds Tavern. The standard deviation between bristle holes were 8.48, 14.38, and 347.51, with an average of 123.47. If the outlier brush were removed from the population, an average standard deviation of 11.43 could be calculated. Errors in the drilling process, which were not found in later brushes, were found in these three earliest brushes. In all three the makers drilled some of the holes through the bottom of the brush, an unnecessary process because these were all wire-drawn brushes with cut grooves on the reverse side for the placement of fastening wires.

The earliest toothbrushes appear to have been manufactured with a nonstandardized process. Holes were often drilled deeper than needed, and spacing between holes was not standardized. Through the middle of the nineteenth century, the manufacturing process became increasingly standardized, and errors in manufacturing decreased significantly.

This diachronic study of toothbrushes indicates several trends. First, toothbrushes did not appear in Annapolis until the late eighteenth century, then dramatically increased in number in the nineteenth century. In the nineteenth century they became more standardized because they were being mass produced and affected by greater factory discipline. Through mass manufacturing and standardized manufacturing techniques, the production of toothbrushes increased and their cost decreased. As consumption became democratized during the eighteenth century and health and hygiene practices became social requirements, toothbrushes were accepted by a larger proportion of society. With their adoption came personal regularity, predictability, and personal discipline: "Such rule observance is the production of the self as the individual who in turn produces . . . a product."[56]

SUMMARY: THE ARCHAEOLOGY OF SOCIAL DISCIPLINE

As Robert Paynter points out, one of the goals of historical archaeology is to understand why material culture since the eighteenth century changed, as well as to make sense of the expanding amount of standardized materials found in the archaeology record.[57] Since the eighteenth century, more and more people have spent their lives in a factory system guided by capitalist wage relations. The domestic realm became saturated with the factories' by-products and was increasingly influenced by its new discipline. New mechanized production and division of labor helped create more objects, but they also standardized much of the work process so that anyone could perform the task of the laborer. The new work system created both products and individuals that were to some degree predictable, regular, and interchangeable.[58]

An examination of archaeological materials from eighteenth- and nineteenth-century contexts provides some information regarding the uses of goods and their relationship to a behavior growing ever more precise and exacting—modern discipline. The occupants of the sites discussed came from varying social and economic standings within the community. Only the poorest segment of the population is not represented here, as they have not been the focus of the Annapolis archaeology program until recently. Questions regarding the penetration of Enlightenment ideas can be answered from an archaeological analysis of functional categories of ceramic dinnerwares and toothbrushes. Foucault notes that the Enlightenment created a new system of domination through surveillance technology. New social relations were based on discipline and surveillance. The adoption of these Enlightenment ideas can be measured from the domestic assemblages of eighteenth- and nineteenth-century Annapolis.

The distribution of mass-produced goods to a growing number of people can be explained in part by economics. As goods became mass produced, they also became cheaper, thus available to a larger proportion of society. In Annapolis the wealthiest group examined appears to have owned more of these goods than the lower groups. Two immediate questions arise from this. First, why did the elite buy these mass-produced goods in the first place? And second, why weren't the poorer groups, who were more commonly subjected to factory discipline, the first to use these goods?

I suspect that the elite first incorporated modern discipline and behavior related to new material into their everyday behavior as a shield to prevent outsiders from encroaching. Modern discipline was a new behavior, and if an intruder did not know the rules, he or she could not join the group. It was the group in power, the manufacturers, who knew discipline and imposed it upon the lower groups in the form of factory discipline. Even though work processes, such as ceramic making or toothbrush making, incorporated discipline, the elite were the first to explicitly display discipline in the form of manners, eating behaviors, and health and hygiene practices. By the mid-nineteenth century, disciplined behavior associated with eating appears to have reached all wealth groups. No longer did segmenting dining practices separate the upper groups from the rest of society, though the wealthy tended to have a more rigid and exacting discipline. The culture of capitalism had spread to all socioeconomic groups.

2. Social Time:
The Middle Scale of History

In providing a study of social time, or the middle scale of history, this chapter focuses on the social history of the Chesapeake, including Annapolis, Maryland, and the surrounding countryside, Anne Arundel County. This information provides a context for the analyses of data and material culture on the local and regional level. Primary sources, including letters, a traveler's accounts, newspapers, the administrative journals of Saint John's College, and the minutes of the Tuesday Club are reviewed, along with many secondary sources.

In this investigation, material goods associated with dining etiquette and health and hygiene are linked to the structuring of eighteenth-century colonial society. Many material culture studies tend to have description as their final goal, but this study analyzes the material holdings of various wealth groups with regard to the symbolic meaning of goods and the influence these meanings had over a particular group's relationship to power. The history of social time for the Chesapeake and Annapolis allows for the material culture patterns revealed in historical sources to be placed in a social context and demonstrates how the elite responded to threats on the hierarchical order. Following is a social history that demonstrates how the gentry codified their position through legal means and by adhering to a new, rigid behavior associated with a modern etiquette.

A REGIONAL HISTORY OF THE CHESAPEAKE

Because Maryland and Virginia were economically dependent upon the tobacco trade, any interpretation of the Chesapeake economy must include an understanding of the tobacco industry. In the early Chesapeake, there were two long periods of growth with some major fluctuations. The first period of growth occurred from 1616 to 1680, followed by a leveling off period to about 1715; then there was steady growth to the time of the American Revolution.[1]

New communities in the early seventeenth-century Chesapeake area were "characterized by low levels of wealth and by the crude egalitarianism of frontier life."[2] The frontier areas usually included a mix of recently freed indentured servants, the newly married, and young men and women in search of opportunity. Landowners who settled early capitalized on the tobacco industry.[3]

A rare commodity in the English markets, tobacco commanded a high price in the 1620s. Many factors in the Chesapeake, including overproduction, cheap credit, falling prices of manufactured goods and foodstuffs, greater output per worker, savings in distribution costs, and lower customs charges, helped reduce the costs of raising tobacco and made early expansion into the European market possible. After about 1660 planters and merchants were unable to achieve any major cost reductions and faced increased land and labor costs.[4] Distribution costs did drop slightly, but increased land and labor costs nullified these gains, and by 1680 expansion in the tobacco industry had ceased.[5] Wars of the League of Augsbury and the Spanish Secession raised shipping costs, thereby decreasing European consumption, and French privateers targeted English shipping, further intensifying the depression in tobacco-producing colonies.[6] The market did not recover until the 1710s.[7] During this thirty-year depression, plantations became more flexible in their production of goods, and plantation industries such as carding, spinning yarn, and candle and spoon making became important.[8]

Indentured white servants provided much of the labor on tobacco plantations until about the fourth quarter of the seventeenth century. Planters preferred English-speaking white servants, but as the population increased, white labor could not fill their needs, and they resorted to alien workers. In 1660 about seventeen hundred blacks resided in the Chesapeake, and by 1680 this population had increased to four thousand.[9] By the turn of the eighteenth century, white planters relied heavily on black slaves. By 1710 the Chesapeake black population had increased to about 31,500.[10] This increase coincided with an expansion in the number of laws in Maryland restricting the rights of blacks. The earliest legislation in the seventeenth century generally prohibited the congregation of blacks in public places. By the 1710s and 1720s, there was a tremendous increase in the number of laws restricting the rights of black slaves.

The empowered used legislation to legitimize racial bigotry and inequality and justified restrictions as natural, thereby employing a naturalizing ideology. For instance, the law prohibited interracial marriage or copulation, because it was said to be "unnatural and inordinate." In 1728 legislators passed an act "for the punishment of free negro women, having bastard children by white men; and for as much as such copulation are as unnatural and inordinate as between white women and negro [men]. . . ."[11]

This sort of legislation was, in part, a product of the number of family dynasties elected to the Maryland assemblies in the early eighteenth century who wished to protect their place in the hierarchy. By the 1720s 60 percent of those elected to the Maryland assembly had Maryland-born fathers. After this date the number increased to 84 percent.[12] Discriminatory legislation created a clear position in the hierarchy for the growing slave and indentured servant population, which otherwise might have posed a threat to the established order.

From about 1715 to the early 1720s, European demand for tobacco increased and created an upswing in tobacco prices, "followed by over a decade of depressed prices [until] prices rose again in the mid 1730s, then fell [sharply] from 1743 to 1748."[13] Settlers responded to these depressions by migrating from the Chesapeake area in search of inexpensive land.[14] The rate of frontier settlement increased dramatically during the depression of the late 1720s and early 1730s and can be measured by the growth of taxed lands south of the Rappahannock River, a frontier of the Chesapeake. Between 1702 and 1733, the growth rate of taxed lands was 1.7 percent per year, but by 1735 it was 3.3 percent. (This rate was calculated by an increase from 2.2 to 2.9 million taxable acres between 1702 and 1733 and to 4.6 million acres in 1735).[15]

During the economic lows in the tobacco industry, planters turned to the provincial government for legislative aid. Maryland and Virginia responded by creating acts that they hoped would centralize trade, encourage diversification, and increase tobacco prices by improving the quality and decreasing the quantity of tobacco exportation each year.[16] During the depression of 1703–13, the Maryland and Virginia legislatures mandated several "town acts" calling for the creation of towns and the centralization of trade.[17] This legislation encouraged farmers to shift from tobacco cultivation to planting staples such as wheat for the displaced planters now living in towns. Town development was meant to encourage manufacturing. Centralized port towns would decrease the number of stops a ship had to make to acquire the necessary tobacco for export, thus lowering the cost of transportation. These acts ended in failure, producing only small towns with populations ranging from fifty to one hundred people.[18]

The depression of 1722 to the mid-1730s was more persistent and more severe than the previous one, due to overproduction, lagging demand, and the high costs of shipping.[19] During this era Maryland and Virginia legislation established twelve new towns. All met the same fate as those created by the earlier acts.[20] Planters continued to build wharves on navigable waters, and "even the tobacco inspection act (which forced planters to bring tobacco to designated warehouses) failed to centralize trade."[21]

Virginia passed the Inspection Act of 1730, which required tobacco to be brought to public warehouses for inspections by public officials. This act was designed to eliminate "trashy tobacco" and cut the quantity of exports, thereby raising the price. The smaller planters opposed this legislation, as they often produced only one or two hogsheads of poor quality tobacco on the inferior land they cultivated. They feared that "trashy tobacco" from their richer neighbors would pass inspection and their own would not. The protest led to the burning of four tobacco warehouses in northern Virginia in March 1732; by May the violence had spread to southern Maryland. These riots subsided shortly afterward.[22]

Maryland legislators did not impose inspection laws. Instead, in 1733, "the Maryland assembly decided that an issue of paper money, supported by a tax on each hogshead of tobacco exported from the province, would revive the economy by encouraging consumption of manufactured goods."[23] Each planter's household received thirty shillings of

Maryland currency per taxable person on their estate. Additionally, every planter was to burn 150 pounds of poor quality tobacco and receive six pennies of paper money in return. Most planters escaped the latter regulation as they would have lost more than five shillings if they had obeyed. It appears that the inspection act and distribution of paper money may have worked, for by the mid-1730s tobacco prices rose. The tobacco riots subsided in the Chesapeake, and many planters abided by the new act. [24]

A commodity price index, based on data pertaining to the lower western shore of Maryland, can be applied generally to the Chesapeake region. This index is a standard measure of price change demonstrating the proportional difference between prices for different years compared to a base period. The difference represents the percentage change required to adjust the values for that particular year to the constant value. [25] Prices were somewhat stable until about 1732, then rose dramatically until 1740. As noted above, there was a serious depression in the tobacco trade beginning in 1722, bottoming out in 1732, and ending in the mid-1730s. The rise in prices began in the 1720s but may have been neutralized by the depression. [26] According to Carr and Walsh, "The exchange rates between sterling and Maryland currency were beginning regularly to appear in inventories, an indication that Maryland currency was beginning to buy less physical wealth than formerly." [27]

Other inflation indicators are found in two components of the commodity price index: imported labor and imported manufactured goods. These two components rose substantially beginning in the 1720s, suggesting that inflation began to climb at this time. This trend continued until about the early 1740s. After 1733 the introduction of Maryland paper money contributed to the inflation. [28]

In 1743 the poorer quality tobacco in Maryland caused prices to plummet far below those found in Virginia. Whereas Virginia did not revise its inspection act, the Maryland assembly debated over whether to impose new tobacco regulations. During the summer of 1747, the assembly passed an inspection act, and by 1748 tobacco prices had climbed.

For the remainder of the colonial era, the tobacco industry prospered. "Although the boom-and-bust cycle characteristic of tobacco production continued," Allan Kulikoff asserts, "depressions were less severe and recoveries more forceful then they had been earlier in the century.

Prices rose in the 1750s . . . and peaked in 1759."[29] Although there were several minor depressions, one in the early 1760s and one in 1772, tobacco prices generally climbed as the "income from tobacco per laborer rose more that twice as rapidly after 1750 as before that year."[30] Continental demand increased despite rising prices caused by interrupted transatlantic shipments during the Seven Years' War (1755–63).[31]

The gentry manipulated tobacco production, wealth, property, and social relations to create power. They devised a complex "series of inheritance and marriage strategies designed to maintain the family's wealth. As a result, gentlemen and their sons increasingly controlled the assemblies of the Chesapeake."[32] As early as 1733 in Prince George's County, Maryland, 40 percent of the sons of wealthy gentlemen inherited sufficient property to rank among the wealthiest in the country. Only 5 percent of the immigrants' sons or sons of native freeholders ranked among the wealthiest.[33]

The men who built great fortunes in the eighteenth century were those who pursued mercantile activities and loaned money to small planters (who had to settle their debts after poor harvests). Merchants and gentlemen, a relatively small group when compared to the total population, held between two-thirds and seven-eighths of the mortgages in four Virginia counties from 1738 to 1779. Kulikoff notes that "the majority of debtors were the smaller planters who usually borrowed less than 100 pounds to settle debts, or purchase land or slaves." One example of a successful creditor was Charles Carroll of Annapolis. In 1764 his estate consisted of unoccupied land worth forty thousand pounds, twenty-four thousand pounds out in interest bearing loans, and ten thousand pounds' worth of shares in an iron works.[34]

By the mid-eighteenth century, a series of changes in the Chesapeake area had enabled the gentry class to visibly emerge, distancing themselves from the lower classes with a new material culture and set of precisely defined behaviors. Large five-part Georgian mansions and associated formal gardens became an expression of the elite's domination. Not only did the wealthy differentiate themselves from others by the amount of goods they owned, but they also distinguished themselves by the types of material they possessed.

A new dining etiquette became an expression of a new social segmenting behavior. Dining was highly formalized among the elite and served as the center of social ritual. It took place in a reserved space with matched sets of dishes and with each person sitting in a carefully defined social space. There were rules for utensil use, and etiquette books prescribed the "proper" courses to serve as well as how and when to serve them. Children ate in a separate room until they learned to conform to correct dining etiquette. The dining ceremony included the master saying grace and carving the meat, a drink to health, and conversation.[35]

This strictly defined behavior brought about a balanced and symmetrical architecture that designed space according to function. "The new style of building conveyed a whole set of social values and assumptions through attention to mathematical proportions and through the invariable usage of a three-part design," states Rhys Issac. "A strong sense of gradations of dominance and submissions was expressed in the elevation of a central unit by means of balanced subordinate lateral elements." In these Georgian structures, rooms served functionally specific purposes and reinforced the transition from communality to individuality. This newly refined behavior in dining and the new architecture was necessary to create and maintain the hierarchy and its distance from the lower classes.[36]

Before the American Revolution, the elite lacked the means to bargain effectively with the authorities of the British Empire. Their position was compromised and their social distance from the lower groups was narrowing. They therefore created a common front with the lower classes to defy the authority of the crown in the name of liberty.[37] This common front was symbolically formed by the widespread consumption of tea among all wealth groups. A probate inventory analysis of estates in Annapolis indicates that during this time most of the wealth groups possessed a relatively plentiful amount of tea-related goods. This popularity made tea an appropriate symbol of unity and resistance among most colonists, regardless of class.[38] Landowners created a bond with the lower classes and inspired the revolution, and they eventually became the new ruling class.[39]

THE LOCAL HISTORY OF ANNAPOLIS

Annapolis was established and developed within the regional context described above. Richard Acton received the earliest recorded patent for land on the Annapolis peninsula in 1651, in an area then called

Figure 5. Location of Arundelton on a 1680 map of Virginia and Maryland. Maryland State Archives Special Collection MSA SC 1427-47.

Providence. Later that year other patents were obtained by Thomas Todd, a shipwright; Robert Proctor, an innkeeper; and Richard Hill, a captain.[40] Between 1657 and 1683 there is a gap in Providence's recorded history as documents from that time were lost or damaged when legislators moved the capital from Saint Mary's City to Annapolis in 1694. A fire at the state house in 1704 also destroyed many records. Between these years Providence became known as "the town at Proctor's Landing." In 1683 the legislature declared this town a port of entry, named it Anne Arundel Town, and ordered Richard Beard to survey the settlement.[41] Although this was part of the attempt to encourage the growth of towns, Anne Arundel Town, also known as Arundelton, remained comparatively small throughout the seventeenth century (see fig. 5).

During this period of limited growth, political conflict mounted between Catholics and Protestants in the province. In the sixty years of the existence of Saint Mary's City as the capital, Protestants attempted several times to move the center of government from the Catholic stronghold. Short-lived relocation attempts occurred between 1654 and 1659, and again in 1683. William and Mary, who were Protestants, became sovereign rulers of England in 1689 as a result of the Glorious Revolution, and the Protestants of Maryland seized upon this opportunity to take control of the government, an act approved by the Crown. In 1694 Protestants gained enough power to move the provincial capital from Saint Mary's City. Anne Arundel Town, a Protestant stronghold, became Annapolis and the new capital of Maryland in 1695.[42] By 1698 Annapolis had about forty dwellings, only a handful of which served as inns, and a population of about 250. The state house and a free school were already built with brick, along with the foundation of the Anglican church.[43]

The design of the city of Annapolis (fig. 6), attributed to Governor Francis Nicholson, deviated from the traditional orthagonal plan and incorporated many elements of baroque urban planning, including formal symmetry, imposing open spaces, the closing of street vistas by important structures, and the location of major buildings on commanding sites.[44] The original drawings of the town plan were destroyed in the 1704 state house fire; the earliest plan of the city is a copy made in 1743 of a resurvey drawn in 1718 by James Stoddart (also see fig. 2).

Governor Nicholson chose a knoll, the highest point in the area, as the ideal location for the state house, which he surrounded with a 520-foot-diameter circle. He constructed a 125-foot-diameter circle, known as Church Circle, around the monumental Saint Anne's Church, just west of the state house on the second highest elevation. To the north of Church Circle was Bloomsbury Square, which Nicholson, in his vision of grandeur for Annapolis, named after the square in the fashionable

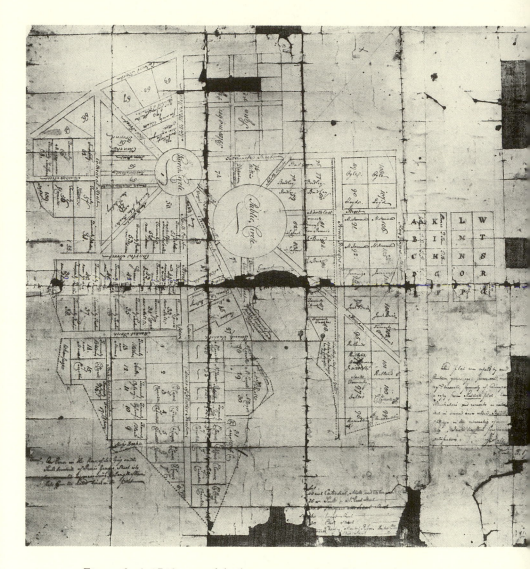

Figure 6. A 1743 map of the baroque city plan of Annapolis. Maryland State Archives Special Collection MSA SC 1477-501.

London neighborhood of Bloomsbury.[45] It measured 360 square feet and was divided by four streets, each entering a midpoint of the square's sides. Bloomsbury Square shares similar characteristics with Londonderry in Northern Ireland.

Though Nicholson designed Annapolis with many baroque concepts, he violated many of its principles. Most of the streets do not intersect at a common point within the circles. If West, South, and Doctor streets (southwest of Church Circle) are lengthened, they meet at a common point, but not at the center of Church Circle. The geometry at State Circle is even less exact. West, School, and East streets imprecisely divide both circles but do not share similar bearings. School Street, which connects Church and State circles, is not a wide boulevard with the monumental architecture (the church and state house) found at both ends, and the church and state house are not aligned with each other.[46] The geometric imbalance may have occurred because Nicholson did not fully appreciate the objectives of baroque street design. John Evelyn, who submitted a baroque plan for the city of London after it burned in 1666, influenced Nicholson's planning. Evelyn's concept lacked complete geometric symmetry, and if Nicholson had studied his plan, Evelyn's ideas would have carried over to the New World.[47]

The plan also may have been distorted by other factors. The new street plan conformed to a preexisting one, creating a somewhat asymmetrical design. If Beard's 1683–84 survey is imposed upon the current street plan, several streets are similar to both plans. These include Duke of Gloucester, Market, Shipwright, and perhaps even Francis and Prince George streets.[48] It appears that Nicholson imposed a baroque design over an orthagonal-like plan, incorporating many of the predetermined streets.

Edward Papenfuse outlines the social and economic development of Annapolis in three phases.[49] From 1684 to 1715, the "uncertain years," Annapolis had the characteristics of a small village, its existence and growth being uncertain except for a few services catering to the courts and assemblies. Few craftsmen resided in the town, and Annapolis remained small, even after becoming the provincial capital in 1695. Ebenezer Cook described the town's sparseness in a 1708 poem:

> Up to Annapolis I went
> A city situated on a plane
> Where scarce a house will keep out rain

The buildings-fram'd with Cyprus rare,
Resemble much our Southwork Fair,
But stranger here will scarcely meet
With Market-place, Exchange or street. . . .[50]

Annapolis never became a major tobacco trading center as originally intended by the 1683 act declaring it a port of entry. The tobacco economy discouraged the development of major port towns and a supporting hierarchy in the hinterlands. Throughout the eighteenth century, Annapolis lacked a dependent hinterland. This low degree of interaction between urban merchants and the countryside can be demonstrated by analyzing the relationship of the distribution of debtors to Annapolis businessmen. Data suggest that Annapolitans mainly traded with the adjacent parishes of Middlesex, Westminster, and All Hallows. These urban merchants did not expand their networks in the eighteenth century, although some peripheral mercantile expansion occurred in the farthest parishes, such as Queen Caroline, in the late eighteenth century.[51]

The surviving accounts and probate inventories from rural Anne Arundel County merchants suggest there was little differentiation between economic activity close to and distant from the capital. This observation suggests that few planters concentrated on the production of meat, firewood, and other goods for the urban market; rather, they occasionally shipped their surpluses to the city. It appears that most of the city merchants' interactions were with local Annapolitans. An examination of probate inventories produced no differences in the types of commodities that land holders possessed, regardless of their distance from Annapolis. "Even after Annapolis began to grow," notes Lorena Walsh, "rural communities continued to be served by their own local and rural craftsmen."[52]

Although Annapolis did not develop as a major tobacco center, the city was a principal political and social center. With the town's growth, particularly in the second quarter of the eighteenth century, services developed for the courts, assemblies, provincial bureaucracy, and cultural activities.[53]

Between 1715 and 1763 there was a time of "industrial expansion and bureaucratic growth"—Papenfuse's second phase. Government became a year-round activity, and bureaucrats became permanent residents of the town. This growth created a market for local goods and services and resulted in the development of an increasingly diversified economy. By this time Annapolis had taken on distinctively urban characteristics. As well as becoming a center for the tanning industry, many luxury craftsmen, such as goldsmiths, watchmakers, hatters, and musicians, were attracted to the city.[54] This growth came at a time marked by optimism and a sense that profit could be made in the city, especially through land speculation. This optimism is indicated in the 1718 resurvey of city lots. The survey was made three years after the Calvert family regained its proprietorship of the Maryland colony and people were confident that they would not move the capital back to Saint Mary's City. Entrepreneurs felt investment in Annapolis was more stable, and growth followed.

This second phase may be more finely divided by reference to regional events. As described earlier, the 1720s and 1730s were decades of extraordinary economic fluctuation in the Chesapeake region. A severe depression in the tobacco trade from 1722 to 1735 was followed by high inflation during the 1730s. Prices rose dramatically until 1740, after which they rose slowly.[55] It is also during this economic instability that wealth shifted among Annapolitans. Probate data indicate that the wealthiest group of people increased its share of wealth from 21 percent (held by 8 eight of the population) between 1700 and 1709 to 85 percent (held by 20 percent of the population) between 1768 and 1777, whereas the poorest group saw its wealth diminish from 8 percent (held by 46 percent of the population between 1700 and 1709) to 2 percent (held by 30 percent of the population) between 1768 and 1777[56] (table 11). These probate data are from a deceased population, and therefore these trends probably began sometime before the dates recorded.

During this time of major socioeconomic change, most of the original settlers no longer lived or owned property in the city. By the second decade of the eighteenth century, the original settlers of Annapolis and Anne Arundel County had fled to western Maryland.[57] This reorganization began as early as 1699, and by 1725 four Annapolitans—Charles Carroll, Amos Garret, Thomas Bladen, and Thomas Bordley—owned more than half the town's land. In fact, two decades earlier an observer had noted that "most of the Lotts in the Said Town and Porte are Ingrossed into three or four Peoples hands to the great Discouragement of the neighbors who would build and Inhabitt therein could they have the

Table 11. Wealth Held by Groups in Annapolis

Year	Group 1 Wealth (%)	Group 1 Population (%)	Group 2 Wealth (%)	Group 2 Population (%)	Group 3 Wealth (%)	Group 3 Population (%)	Group 4 Wealth (%)	Group 4 Population (%)	Total Wealth Inventoried	Total Population Inventoried
1689–99	28	75	0	0	72	25	0	0	£ 321	4
1700–09	8	46	14	23	51	23	21	8	£ 2175	13
1710–22	5	38	18	42	21	13	56	8	£ 8444	40
1723–32	2	30	7	30	13	21	78	18	£ 41769	33
1733–44	3	37	8	27	12	16	77	20	£ 19804	51
1745–54	3	48	4	13	7	13	86	26	£ 15292	31
1755–67	2	26	7	34	7	15	84	25	£ 32673	53
1768–77	2	30	8	43	5	13	85	20	£ 17697	30

Key: Group 1 = estates valued between £0–£50
  Group 2 = estates valued between £51–£225
  Group 3 = estates valued between £226–£1000
  Group 4 = estates valued more than £1000

Source: Russo 1983; Leone and Shackel 1987, 1990.

opportunity of taking up Lotts."[58] The landless were subjugated to a leasehold system, a tenure by lease that persisted throughout the colonial period.[59]

The population of Annapolis grew rapidly between 1720 and 1730, probably adding to the competitive base of the city and subjecting more people to the leasehold system. The earliest population figures indicate that Annapolis had 252 residents in 1699, an estimate based upon an average number of occupants per known structures. By the 1783 census, the population had increased to 1,280, still somewhat small compared to other port cities, such as New York.[60] Between 1720 and 1730, the city's population rose by 65 to 70 percent.[61] This rate was twice as fast as during any other ten-year period, including its glorious golden age, 1763 to 1786 (table 12). Whether the growth was a product of immigration or a matter of the birthrate increasing faster than the deathrate, or a combination of both, is not yet known. Nevertheless, the remarkable population growth during this decade was a key to the city's development.

During this era of growth, the elite of the city expressed their new social position through architecture. In the 1720s the most affluent citizens of Annapolis began to build stone foundations, brick exterior walls, and brick chimneys. It appears that interclass cooperation diminished among the upper class and the meaning of their goods, services, and wealth changed. The earliest brick dwellings known to have been built in Annapolis were erected by 1721. Soon thereafter other wealthy merchants followed this lead, and the building of permanent structures increased throughout the eighteenth century.[62]

The number and variety of goods and services drawn to Annapolis grew substantially with the influx of a mounting residential bureaucracy. During the early eighteenth century, wood- and leather-related occupations were predominant. By the 1740s and 1750s, however, luxury crafts increased substantially and catered to the wealthy.[63] This trend continued through the 1770s.

Papenfuse's third phase of socioeconomic development, the "age of affluence," lasted from 1763 to 1774 and is also commonly known as the golden age. Many small industries, such as tanning and shipbuilding, suffered during this time. "Prosperity was not based on industry," Papenfuse notes, "but on the concentration of political power in Annapolis, as growing numbers of socially or politically oriented wealthy planters

Table 12.   Annapolis and Anne
Arundel County Populations

	Annapolis	
Year	Estimate	Census
1704	272	
1705	272	
1706	311	
1707	331	
1708	333	
1709	330	
1710	326	
1711	324	
1712	319	
1714	329	
1715	340	
1716	383	
1717	389	
1720	400	
1723	520	
1726	588	
1728	642	
1730	678	
1740	746	
1755	875	
1760	951	
1764	989	
1768	1071	
1775	1299	
1782	1152	
1783		1280

	Anne Arundel County	
Year	Estimate	Census
1650	300	
1675	1297	
1700		4121
1704	4630	
1710	4778	
1712		5003
1755	13150	
1775	17906	
1782	19968	
1783		22598

Source: Walsh 1983b.

were drawn to town." Merchandizing rose significantly in the 1750s as the wealthy spent more on imported goods. Papenfuse supports this observation by documenting that the number of merchants advertising in the *Maryland Gazette* increased from three in 1745 to twelve in 1753.[64] Four of these merchants held other professions before merchandizing. Prior to this mercantile activity served as a seasonal activity and economic supplement.

After 1763 wealthy planters and merchants built enormous Georgian brick mansions throughout the city. By the beginning of the 1770s, although the town was considered prosperous and genteel, general conditions were far from perfect. William Eddis, a British resident who wrote letters to his homeland describing Annapolis at the beginning of its golden age, noted that the "roads [are] too much exposed to lade and unlade with safety and convenience."[65] Nevertheless, by 1774 residents erected at least fourteen major dwellings and four residence-businesses. These structures served as winter retreats for planters when responsibilities on plantations were at a minimum. Social and political activities increased during the winter, and entertainment and other forms of social interaction were emphasized by the elite. With this social interaction came the desire to obtain and display finely made imported goods—a desire that apparently became greater as social competition increased with the influx of the gentry in the 1770s.

With the development of a gentry class came the rise of social clubs. In the 1730s gentleman planters and merchants who lived near Annapolis established the South River Club. They met monthly for dinner and exchanged ideas and news, a pattern that continued into the nineteenth century. In 1745 Dr. Alexander Hamilton, along with other well-respected Annapolitans, established the Tuesday Club. Membership required intellectual achievement, wit, and oratorical skills. The club was discontinued when Hamilton died in 1756, but gentry members re-created the Tuesday Club's tradition with the establishment of the Homony Club, which existed from 1770 to 1773.[66]

As Annapolis became a social and political center of the New World, residents rebuilt the city. During the late 1760s, many believed that Annapolis would slowly transform into a metropolis, although it was still a rustic port town. William Eddis described the city in 1769:

The buildings in Annapolis were formerly of small dimensions and of an inelegant construction; but there are now several modern edifices which make a good appearance. There are few habitations with gardens, some of which are planted in decent style and are well stocked.

At present, the city has more the appearance of an agreeable village than the metropolis of an oppulant province as it contains within its limits a number of small fields, which are intended for future erections. But in a few years it will probably be one of the best built cities in America, as a spirit of improvement is predominant. [67]

Eddis continued his letter, acknowledging that Annapolis would never be a large commercial city, for its harbor was very small and could not handle large fleets of commercial traffic. He said, however, that the city was "the seat of government; the public offices are here established; and as many of the principal families have chosen this place for their residence, there are few towns of the same size in any part of the British dominion that can boast a more polished society."[68]

Annapolis prospered for several years after the revolution, and in 1783, because of its reputation as a major social and political center in America, it became the temporary capital of the United States for six months. By the 1780s few industries such as tanning and shipbuilding remained in the city as most of the commerce focused upon luxury crafts and international trade, which depended upon the patronage of the affluent.[69]

From 1785 to 1786, Annapolitans found themselves in the midst of an economic depression. The most influential international merchants, Wallace, Johnson, and Muir—who together were the major component of the Annapolitan business community—disbanded their operations due to an internal quarrel. This dissolution hurt the local economy severely, because no local firm could replace them. Papenfuse describes Annapolis in 1786 as being in a grim economic situation, with high taxes and money in short supply. [70] As a result, many wealthy people left Annapolis for other social centers.

At this time Baltimore was growing as a social center, and its independent merchants competed for the tobacco and grain trade.[71] Greater profit could be made cultivating grain than tobacco. Wheat was less labor intensive and proved more profitable as its value increased steadily throughout the eighteenth century. In the long run, wheat was more reliable than tobacco, as its prices did not fluctuate as drastically. Part of Baltimore's growth may be attributed to the extensive support system in the hinterlands that used the city as the marketplace for grain. [72]

In the late 1780s, Annapolis lost most of its gentry, for both economic and social reasons, as nearby Baltimore developed into a major
Chesapeake urban center. The economy of Annapolis, with its focus on
luxury crafts and merchandising, collapsed once there was no gentry to
serve. By the 1790s Baltimore with its diversified economy had replaced
Annapolis as the center of gracious living. A letter from Harriet Anderson of Annapolis to Mrs. Mary Grafton Ridout conveys what might
have been the general spirit of the city: "You must not expect any news
from this part of the world. We seem all to be trotting on in the same
dull pace as when you left us. Not the least deviation from the long
beaten path."[73] Annapolis steadily declined, exchanging its status as a
political and social center for that of a regional market town and way
station for travelers.[74]

This brief economic and social history of the Chesapeake and Annapolis provides insight into several events that led to a competitive society. Regionally these events included several long-term depressions in
the first half of the eighteenth century, the most severe occurring between 1722 and 1735.[75] The commodity price index sharply climbed in
the 1730s, partly as a result of the printing of Maryland paper money in
1734. Other inflation indicators, such as imported labor and manufactured goods, rose during the 1720s but were not noticeable due to the
cyclical lows of the depression.[76] Locally the population of Annapolis
grew slowly but steadily through the course of the eighteenth century.
An analysis of wealth redistribution through probate inventories provides some insight into the city's shifting wealth in the 1720s.[77] These
phenomena produced a competitive society that created distinct social
groups through overt material expressions.

Anne Arundel County faced many of the same stresses found in Annapolis. Inflation, population increase, and tobacco depression affected
the residents in the rural areas. The rural population used and rejected
the material correlates of social stress differently from the urban population and probably used different forms of material culture in the context
of social competition.

THE LOCAL CONTEXT OF MEANINGS
AND USES OF GOODS

To provide a contextual analysis of Annapolis and Anne Arundel
County, various primary sources were consulted. These include a trav-

eler's accounts, the Tuesday Club minutes, newspapers, administrative journal accounts of Saint John's College, and letters. These sources compose a complete survey of literature that may be used to interpret the symbolic nature of material culture in Annapolis and Anne Arundel County. The data derived are described according to specific genre. This format focuses on the themes of time discipline, formal and segmented dining, and appearance/hygiene as they became important aspects of behavior.

During the eighteenth century, the upper wealth groups increasingly used polite behavior to socially segment themselves from other groups. In 1733 Voltaire wrote, "Politeness is not in the least an arbitrary matter, but is a law of nature."[78] People considered manners to be part of the natural qualities of humans, and knowing the natural order legitimized their domination over lower groups. These ideas of "good behavior" were said to be embedded in nature and were prominent in the creation of groups, individuals, and in the development and maintenance of a stratified society. The following passages supply data on the growing naturalization of a modern discipline in Annapolitan society. More important, they demonstrate that what were once unnatural behaviors— the segmentation and regimentation of time, space, and behavior— came to be considered part of the natural order.

The *Maryland Gazette*

The *Maryland Gazette* was published by William Parks from 1727 until 1734, and resurrected by Jonas Green on 17 January 1745. It continued to be published weekly with few interruptions until 12 December 1839. Jonas Green fashioned his newspaper according to many leading British papers; the front page of every issue claimed it contained the "Freshest Advice Foreign and Domestic." Several articles can now be analyzed for their insight into culture and how contemporaries perceived the new order of behavior to be embedded in nature.

The following passage from a 1746 issue of the *Maryland Gazette* is a composition on the value and origins of taste. It is an important essay, for it is the earliest passage I've found that elucidates the ideas of the Enlightenment as used by Annapolitans, making such things as geometry and painting appear to be innate in human nature. The author Horatius (a pseudonym) describes how the world is ordered and claims that taste discerns what is decent in company, elegant in art, just in society, and beautiful in the world. Nature provides the basis of taste, but it is instruction and education that cultivate good taste. Good taste can be seen in the way a man lays out his garden, models his house, sets his table, and improves his leisure hours:

> A Taste is what Men very much differ about. . . . The true taste may be called, the Faculty of the mind, and elegant in Arts, what is just in Society, and beautiful in Nature, and the order of the world. We must not suppose we come into this World with such Taste; Nature may furnish a Genius fitted to graft it upon, but Art and Improvement are necessary to form it; and as this Art and Culture can never be innate, to a just Taste can neither be gotten, made, nor conceived with us, it is when a proper instruction and Education, which must form a true taste.
>
> A true Taste is intirely founded on Nature; to Nature for When and Fancey, is not the way to acquire it, as there is a certain Beauty and Deformity in natural Things, properly to called, so there is likewise in moral subjects; The true Taste, adopts the first, and rejects the last, and the judicious Choice finishes the Character of the polite Gentleman, and the true Philosephers [sic]. . . .
>
> A man who models his Taste a right, with relation to natural Objects, such as Painting, Music, Architecture, or Geometry, will never attempt to bring Truth to his own Humor, but leave these just where he found them, he will accommodate his Taste and Fancy to their Standard; and if he does the same in the moral System he will in reality become a great and a wise Man; as he is on the other Side, a refined and polite Gentleman; By the first Taste, he understands how to lay his Garden, Model his House, fancy his Esquipage, appoint his table, and improve a leisure Hour; by the other he learns the just value of these Amusements, and of what Importance they are to a Man's Happiness, Freedom, and self Enjoyment, A Taste so truly modelled would discover that the right Mind, and generous Affection, have more Beauty and Charm, than all the Symetries of Life besides.[79]

In Annapolitan society time discipline and the efficient use of time became an important concept as early as the 1740s, and probably much earlier. Time discipline demonstrates how the artificial divisions of time became internalized and part of everyday society. The following is a portion of an article from the 1746 *Maryland Gazette* emphasizing the profitability of using time wisely:

Gaming indicates a degeneracy of Taste: Cards and Dice matches waste
Time and Money to little purpose, the opulent may 'tis true, without a
Vice, be lavish or the last, but as the first is not to be bought or retarded
with Price, it cannot be too carefully husbanded; add to this, that these
amusements carry very little Improvement in them; and as a Philosophi-
cal Friend of mine used to say, "was one to sit a Thousand Years at them,
he would rise, not grain wiser, than when he first sat down.[80]

On 24 December 1745, the *Maryland Gazette* published the following
poem, which originally appeared in the *London Magazine*. Here the poet
reinforces the idea that such concepts as art and charm are embedded in
nature. It is the use of printing that helped establish close connections
with the mother country concerning the ideas of the Enlightenment:

> Attend ye Fair, Calliope the song
> Indites to you, the slugs of Arts
> That form the Mind, and every Charm improve;
> Which Nature gave, when from Hand profuse
> Your Beauties pour'd. . . .

Literature pertaining to the rules of behavior, creating a segmented
society, were probably accessible to many literate people in Annapolis
society. No doubt most of this literature came from England, but there is
evidence from an advertisement in the *Maryland Gazette* that as early as
1748 Jonas Green was printing behavioral guides: "Just publish'd. And
to be Sold by the Printer Hereaft, A Present for an Apprentice; or a Sure
Guide to Gain both Esteem and Estate. With Rules for his Conduct to
his Master and in the w————. By the Late Lord Mayor of London."[81]
Oral hygiene generally, and the care of teeth specifically, indicates
that people became interested in creating their personal identity. Good
teeth, free of disease and decay, became important in polite society.
The earliest documentation found on this subject in the city of Annapolis appeared 15 August 1776 in the *Maryland Gazette*. The advertisement was headed "Operator upon the Teeth, is just arrived in this
City, on His way to Baltimore, and intends returning about the middle
of September Next." The advertisement was one column long and discussed the various disorders that may occur if the teeth are not given
proper care. Also it stated the importance of clean teeth in specific social circumstances:

. . . the teeth serve for mastication, for the distinct articulation of sounds, and for ornament. The foulness of the teeth by some people is little regarded; but with the fair sex, with the polite and elegant part of the world, it is looked on as a certain mark of filthiness and sloth; not only because it disfigures one of the greatest ornaments of the countenance, but also because the smell imparted to the breath by dirty rotten teeth, is generally disagreeable to the patients themselves, and sometimes extremely offensive to the olfactory nerves in close conversation. . . . And above all the art of pleasing in conver[sati]on and social life, are matters of the highest co[ncer]n to individuals: but in this no one can excel, whose loss of teeth, or rotten livid stumps, and fallen lips and hollow cheeks, destroy articulation, and the happy expression of the countenance.

By the 1790s advertisements for toothbrushes, tooth powder, and toothpicks became prominent in the *Maryland Gazette*. It is worth noting that a 1793 advertisement regarding tooth-care products was in the middle of a one-column advertisement for a "Hair Dresser and Perfumer."[82] Included in this ad were hair powders, soaps, oils, razors, and so forth, signifying that tooth care was important to those who could afford these other luxury items. By selling and advertising these items, merchants helped to create and reinforce individuality and a socially segmented society.

Letters

Few letters survive from eighteenth-century Annapolis and Anne Arundel County. Most notable are those of William Eddis in the 1760s and early 1770s. The Ridout collection of letters also provides insight into Annapolis family life and perspectives of the world during the late eighteenth century.

Society among the upper wealth groups on the American continent considered it to be of great importance to have what they considered the natural abilities of good social graces. These characteristics helped define a person in his or her social class. In a letter to John Ridout in 1780, Horatio Sharpe described the training in the gentlemanly qualities received by Samuel Ridout, John's son, who was studying in England:

. . . in every respect he has been such to give one the highest Satisfaction, indeed there is such an equality and steadiness in all his Actions that I have a real pleasure in whatever I do for Him. . . . He has not by what I can find advanced in his Studies with all that rapidity which is peculiar to some Boys yet what he has gott he retains and will not be easily forgot; this is a valuable quality and as I am doth not was for Natural Abilities, has perseverance and is free from all Vice. I make no doubt but he will in time become a valuable acquisition to Society.

Sharpe continued, saying that Samuel was "serious" and ambitious, and that he could "also with trust say there are few Holidays he letts past in Idleness."[83]

Later, Anne Ogle of Annapolis added her comments regarding the social grace of Samuel, whom she felt had not yet developed. In 1782 she regarded him as clumsy and awkward but well disciplined with regard to time. She sent his sister Harriet to a convent to become refined. Ogle wrote that she was "anxious to have them appear well to the world. Harriet has been in a convent at Mountruill these five months. She is well made and genteel. [Samuel] misspends not his time but is always imployed in things to his advantage—he has begun to learn to play on the flute since he came here—the French he is obliged to translate into latin."[84]

The idea of group identity, the separation of groups by specific behavior or etiquette, was prominent in the 1760s in Annapolis. In a letter of recommendation for an unspecified person, Bladen wrote to Anne Ogle: "I have the pleasure of knowing him as by giving him a letter to Mr. Dulaney. I think I have given him an opportunity of being united with the most agreeable man at Annapolis, I should also be glad he should see and converse with the most amiable women."[85]

In a letter to John Ridout in 1783, Thomas Ridout discussed the need for cultivating good manners in children. Again, he noted that good sense was embedded in nature and a necessity of "polite society." Thomas Ridout claimed that Betsy Finch had been neglected in her upbringing but was "capable of doing credit to the education—She reads well and writes tolerably, but her manners are not yet such. I wish them to be a natural desire to please to be thought well of if properly attended to will I dare say her to show to advantage the good sense nature endowed her with."[86] He later suggests that a year's residence in a convent would help her develop her social graces.

Marylanders as a whole, and Annapolitans in particular, appear to have been equal to the high standards of civility in most regions in the

New World. Anne Ogle received a letter from her daughter, who was in Philadelphia, that stated, "I cannot find time to write by this Post. I am now dressing for the Drawing Room. You will easily suppose I have not much leisure when I tell you I have seen and wished 50 ladies, fatiguing work this—we Marylanders make a respectable figure here."[87] Elizabeth Ridout Ward wrote to her son Samuel about a formal dinner she had attended. Above all it was the etiquette and proper behavior that impressed Ward. She wrote: "Mr. Brooks . . . pay[ed] us a morning Visit and engaged us all to Dine with him, and a most Sumptuous Dinner and desert after we had; pineapples with every [?] the season could produce but their friendly and polite behavior exceeded everything else. . . ."[88]

Land asserts that the upper class used specific behaviors to close themselves to outsiders.[89] They protected themselves from intruders by adhering to specific codes of behavior. If these codes were violated by someone who had "frontier manners" it was often noticed, usually resulting in the expulsion of the intruder. Charles Carroll wrote his son of an occasion in which Robert DeButts, took to "rastling at the Govenor's . . . drunken frolic [and] so much alarmed [Mrs. Eden] . . . at the disturbance they made in the house that she miscarried." Eddis noted that "Annapolis society knows good manners and [insists] on decorum" and that Annapolitans quickly adopted English fashion and he found "very little difference . . . in the manners of the wealthy colonist and the wealthy Briton. Good and bad habits prevail on both sides of the Atlantic."[90]

Manners among the upper class Annapolitans in 1770 appear to have been as precise and standardized as those found in the great social centers in England. Eddis wrote, "I am persuaded there is not a town in England of the same size as Annapolis which can boast a greater number of fashionable and handsome women; and were I not satisfied to the contrary, I should suppose that the majority of our belles possessed every advantage of a long and familiar intercourse with the manners and habits of your great metropolis." Eddis believed that

> the American ladies possess a natural ease and elegance in the whole of their deportment; and that while they assiduously cultivate external accomplishments, they are still anxiously attentive to the more important embellishments of the mind. In conversation they are generally animated and entertaining, and deliver their Sentiments with affability and

propriety. . . . I am persuaded, [that they] might appear to great advantage in the most brilliant circles of gaity [sic] and fashion.[91]

Saint John's Board of Visitors and Governors

Saint John's College of Annapolis was officially chartered in 1785 with a curriculum that focused on the humanities, a program that exists there today. From the early days of this institution, a document titled *St. John's Board of Visitors and Governors* recorded many of its business and financial transactions. Within this journal can be found several cases concerning the regulation of daily activities and the enforcement of proper etiquette.

The concept of time discipline serves to demonstrate the internalization of order and regularity as an important factor in the early days of Saint John's College. By 1790 the Board of Governors found it necessary to enforce order by passing a set of regulations to guide and train students' daily habits. They resolved that professors, masters, tutors, and students must adhere to the following schedule: "From the fifteenth day of April until the first of September. From six o'clock in the morning until eight. From nine 'till twelve. From two 'till five. From December the first 'till February the first. From nine 'till twelve. From two 'till five. From February the first 'till the fifteenth of April. From eight 'till twelve. From two 'till five. On Saturdays the schools are to break up at 11 o'clock A.M."[92]

To enforce this schedule, the board of governors emphasized that attention should be "paid to good order and regularity." With this came the ringing of a bell to call students' attention to the beginning of class. The bell rang for ten minutes, after which a roll was "called over, in which the absentees [were] carefully marked . . . the absentees called on, and punished for each absence, unless they [satisfied] their respective professors, that there was a sufficient reason for their non-attendance." If a student was not punctual, or showed behavior contrary to the makeup of good conduct (such as gaming or rudeness) in school or elsewhere, he was often physically punished. This was performed "by a stroke of the terula on the hand, or by brick, [with] the consent of a majority of the teachers, who [had] the immediate care of the delinquents education."[93]

Saint John's College encouraged and reinforced polite behavior in school and in the community. On 22 June 1796, the Board of Governors passed several rules about the treatment and care of students and a list of orderly behaviors expected of students while they resided in the board-inghouses. The board also required that the students receive the best tea or coffee with fresh bread and butter during breakfast and supper. Good cream or milk, to mix with the tea or coffee, was also to be provided with every meal.[94]

Also emphasized was the increasing concern for cleanliness at the table: "A servant, or servants, shall wait at table. A clean table cloth shall be provided, at least four times every week. Knives, forks, and other utensils, shall be always clean and decent."[95] There were also instructions related to the cleaning of bedrooms and the bed, stating that the bed sheets should be changed regularly—once every two weeks from the first of May through the first of October. The rest of the year the schedule was once every three weeks. Each bedroom was to be swept clean every day and washed once a week. Chamber pots were to be placed under each bed, washed and aired, every morning. They were to be replaced in the room by nine o'clock in the evenings.[96]

In Annapolis education served to reinforce and regulate disciplined behaviors. Punctuality became a primary concern for educators, and deviation could be met with various forms of punishment. Regulation of everyday behaviors became an important aspect of a liberal arts education.

Traveler's Guide

The traveler's account consulted, a log written by Dr. Alexander Hamilton of Annapolis in 1744, details his journey from Annapolis to Boston and back. He was most famous locally for his role in founding and serving as secretary for the Tuesday Club. In a passage written after he met a rural family outside Annapolis in 1744, he conveys his distaste for what he perceived as a "rustic" way of life, because the planters lacked all the goods needed for a proper and formal dinner:

> [The house] was kept by a little old man whom I found at vittles with his wife and family upon a homely dish of fish without any kind of sauce. They desired me to eat, but I told them I had no stomack. They had no cloth upon the table, and their mess was in a dirty, deep wooden dish which they evacuated with their hands, cramming down skin and all.

Figure 7. "The Royalist Club," drawn by Alexander Hamilton. John Work Garrett Collection, Johns Hopkins University.

Figure 8. "Mr. Neilson's Battle with the Royalist Club," drawn by Alexander Hamilton. John Work Garrett Collection, Johns Hopkins University.

They used neither knife, fork, spoon, plate, or napkin because, I suppose, they had none to use. I look upon this as a picture of that primitive
simplicity practiced by our forefathers long before the mechanic arts had
supplyed them with instruments for the luxury and elegance of life.[97]

Hamilton was quick to satirize social clubs other than his own by noting their improper social and dining behavior. Two illustrations from
Hamilton's Tuesday Club minutes perhaps exaggerate the drunkenness
and communal drinking at the rival Royalist Club, portraying a man
passed out underneath a table and an unmannerly treatment toward
guests (figs. 7 and 8).

As noted, material culture is a communicator of varying messages
and may symbolize status, wealth, and/or group identity. Hamilton's log
recounts a dinner with two Philadelphians who wore improper clothing
for the time of day. He describes the unease he and his guests felt as they
considered the social implications:

> I dined with Mr. Fletcher in the company of two Philadelphians, who
> could not be easy because forsooth they were in their night-caps seeing
> everybody else in full dress with powdered wigs, it is not being customary
> in Boston to go dine or appear upon change in caps as they do in other
> parts of America. What strange creatures we are, and what triffles make
> us uneasy. It is no mean hest that such worthless thing as caps and wigs
> should disturb our tranquility and disorder our thoughts when we imag-
> ine they are wore out of season. I was myself much in the same state of
> uneasiness with these Philadelphians, for I had got a great hole in the
> lappet of my coat, to hide which employed so much of my thoughts in
> company, that for want of attention, I could not give pertinent answer
> when I was spoke to.[98]

According to Hamilton, appearance was a symbol of a person's position in society. His comment on two men's appearance—"I took them
for weavers, not only for their greasy appearance, but because I observed
a weaver's loom at each side of the room"—illustrates this. Rules for
speech and polite conversation in specific social circumstances also governed the way Hamilton interacted with people. He noted: "They sa-
luted me very civilly, and I as civilly as I could, returned their compli-
ments in neat short speeches such as, 'Your very humble servant, I am
glad to see you,' and the like common place phrases used upon such occasions."[99]

Records of the Tuesday Club

Alexander Hamilton established the Tuesday Club in 1745, and it became the most prestigious in Annapolis until its dissolution in 1756. The club was limited to fifteen of the most sociable and polite Annapolitans.[100] It changed the intellectual atmosphere of the mideighteenth-century Chesapeake as it encouraged gentility, social and political satire, and enlightenment. The Tuesday Club filled an intellectual void and "helped transform a seemingly backward community into a leading intellectual center; by 1750 Annapolis had become the most important locus for social and cultural life in the bay colonies."[101] The club also provided satirical commentary on politics and everyday life (fig. 9).

Several passages from the minutes of the Tuesday Club, recorded by Hamilton, its secretary, are of interest. Although there are few references specifically regarding polite behavior, it is important to note how people began to see all cultural phenomena as part of the natural order. These are the ideas of the Enlightenment that the elite knew and controlled. A letter recorded in the club minutes in December 1749 describes how society was founded upon the principles of right reason:

Gentlemen/

As without Society, man would be the most wretched creature upon earth, So, to this he owes, tho' not has rational powers and faculties, yet the use and Improvement of them. Arts, Sciences, all the advantages and pleasures of life flow from this fountain which alone renders it more Secure and Comfortable than the Condition of the Irrational tribes, for, without this, even reason itself, would avail us very little, our nobler powers would Languish and perhaps be employed in mutual destruction; but society founded upon principles of right reason, directed by Just laws, Impartially executed under the administration of wise and virtuous rulers, what a glorious Idea is it! What heart can conceive a greater blessing upon earth? It is the very prelude, or rather type of heaven, where nothing is to be found but order, peace, love, and all happy enjoyments, worthy of the rational nature.

Wherever Such well constituted Societies are to be met with upon earth, be they more public, or more private, formed for more General advantages, or the Comforts of a more private life, what wonder is it that men Should wish and endeavor to be members of Such Societies, who,

Figure 9. "The Tobacco-pipe Procession," drawn by Alexander Hamilton.
John Work Garrett Collection, Johns Hopkins University.

being prompted by a natural and reasonable Self love, wish themselves
happy. —

> . . . your most loving, Devoted
> and obedient Servant
> Alexr. Malcolm[103]

In May 1751 the orator of the club spoke of the natural order and how
the number three and all the forms of it are part of the grand system of
the world:

> There is also my Lord, a certain harmony in the number three in music,
> for all harmonic Compositions Can be Included in a Trio, or piece of
> three parts, and whatever greater number of parts musicians may add in
> their Compositions, they are only trios repeated. There are likewise in
> music but three principal chords, to wit, a third, a 5th and an 8th or an
> octave or Diapason. There is also, my Lord, that great rule in arithmetic,
> the rule of three, on which in a great measure depends the doctrine of
> proportions. There is Likewise my lord, That part of mathematics called
> Trigonometry, or the doctrine of Triangles or trilateral figures, of Such
> Singular use in mathematics on which is founded the whole of practical
> geometry, the mensuration of Surfaces, heights and distances, by which
> we discover the order, the regular disposition of the members of this
> grand System of the world, but what need I Say any more my Lord, about
> the number three, when I have once mentioned the great power of the
> number. . . .[104]

DISCUSSION

A description of the local context illuminates the changing codes of behavior and the use of material culture related to dining and personal
appearance. This social history reveals some deep structures in the creation of a modern discipline. The elite responded to crises in two different ways. First they codified the legal relations of the colony, and later
they created a rigid upper class that adhered strictly to the new rules of
etiquette.

Communality and premodern traditions characterize the earliest
Chesapeake settlements. White indentured servants and black slaves
provided the labor for the tobacco-based economy. Before the mid-
seventeenth century, the tobacco industry encouraged isolated settlements, which worked against the social cohesion necessary to forge

highly structured hierarchies. As the number of freed servants increased, they threatened the power structure, and the elite legislators legitimized racism. Interracial marriages became illegal and were often called unnatural. Blacks, who were once part of the daily social and economic workings of the tobacco industry, lost many of their rights to negotiate as free people and became a marginalized, although economically essential, group.

In two major instances in the eighteenth century the wealthy recodified behavior by introducing new etiquette after their position in the hierarchy was threatened. The first was during the 1720s, when Annapolis and the surrounding countryside felt the affects of tobacco depression, inflation, wealth restructuring, and demographic change. The second instance was prior to the American Revolution, when the Baptists and other poor groups challenged the authority of the elite. In both cases the elite responded by reasserting their dominance. During the 1720s Chesapeake lawmakers enacted more discriminatory legislation than in any previous decade. In the 1760s the elite built large Georgian, five-part mansions and reasserted their domination through ostentation. With this restructuring of the hierarchy came a new precise, standardized, and exacting behavior, which came to be perceived as part of the natural order. By the 1740s, if not earlier, the Enlightenment had become a way of life for the upper class of Annapolis.

3. Probate Data and Social Time

Probate data are used for this analysis of the social time of Annapolis and its surrounding countryside. The probate records are a rich source for studying the material culture of colonial and early America. This analysis examines the introduction and use of items found in probate inventories that may reflect a new standardizing and precise behavior implemented through modern etiquette. The introduction of disciplining items, such as clocks and sets of dishes, should correspond closely to many of the social and economic fluctuations in the Chesapeake region. The use of these new items reflect the changing social relations among the different wealth groups and may be a way that the elite used to differentiate themselves from other groups during times of social instability.

Traditionally probate inventories have been used to determine interior furnishings, ceramics, clothing, and fireplace equipment in early American households.[1] Other scholars examine changing life-styles, vernacular architecture, and the changing functional uses of rooms.[2] Historical archaeologists have realized the importance of incorporating probate inventories into their analyses.[3] Some observe changing colonial lifeways, and others examine subsistence patterns on a rural eighteenth-century farmstead.[4] Some scholars retrieve folk taxonomies, and, along with others, offers a typological system for ceramic identification.[5] Other archaeologists present ecological analyses and acculturation studies.[6]

Steven Pendery uses probate and archaeological data to study the changing social relations in early Charlestown, Massachusetts.[7] Barbara Little demonstrates the changes in daily life of a colonial printer's family and uses this data to suggest gender-based differences in organizing household goods.[8] I use probate inventory data in conjunction with etiquette books and archaeological data to analyze changing behaviors related to dining and hygiene.[9]

Anglo-American colonists performed probate inventories on Chesapeake Bay area estates beginning in the earliest decades of settlement. These documents provide an excellent opportunity to analyze material culture and early life-styles. Unless the estate was managed by prescription of a will, the court appointed an administrator, called an executor, to the estate. The executor's duties included caring for the estate, settling the debts, and dividing the remainder of the estate among the heirs. Appointing an executor was sometimes "avoided because the fees could be substantial, but it protected both heirs and creditors and was especially desirable if the heirs . . . were minor children."[10] A judge of a commission of probate appointed an executor and two or three appraisers familiar with the occupation of the deceased. The appraisers inventoried and assessed the value of the estate and determined the value of the belongings in the current market.[11] This inventory included "ready money, household furniture, clothing, negroes, stock of cattle, corn, [and] the crop on hand."[12]

A study of probate records provides insight into the changing consumption patterns in the Chesapeake. The typical colonist left little in the way of written records. The elite often produced the documents from which traditional histories have been written. Histories of the largest segments of the population—the middle classes and poor—have received less attention. Because inventories were recorded for large cross-sections of the population, these documents provide a broad accounting of both the nonelite and the elite.

Although inventories were meant to be a true and accurate record of the estate, appraisers often omitted items with no market value, such as small quantities of fruits and vegetables from kitchen gardens. The colonists probably considered these items perishable and therefore not worth listing. Clothing is usually missing from the inventories; close relatives usually took possession of these items soon after the death of the relative.[13] Before 1715 the court allowed a wife to keep a pot and bed

from her husband's creditors, but it is not known whether appraisers included these items in the inventories.[14] After 1715 English law passed a
"statute of distribution" that required one third of a man's estate to pass
to his wife and the remainder to be divided among his children.[15]

An executor's account greatly improves the data regarding an estate
as it is a final report on a decedent's assets. The document included
items such as the value of crops in the field at the time of death or debts
not accounted for at the time of appraisal.[16] The account also recorded
funeral expenses, an allowance of 10 percent of the estate for the execu-
tors or administrators, and 5 percent for extraordinary trouble in collecting debts.[17] The court usually subtracted these expenses from the
final estate value. The executor of the estate, usually a relative of the
deceased, would not avoid taking the inventory because of the high administration fee, because the money would stay in the family. Pauper's
families (usually with estate values of ten pounds or less) did not pay fees
on inventoried estates.[18]

Although the recording of inventories seems to have been consistent
throughout the population, there are several biases associated with probate inventories. First, males comprised the majority of the inventoried
population because women lost their right to own property when they
married. Therefore only single or widowed women appear in the probate records. Children did not legally own property, and therefore their
belongings were not inventoried. Inventories also are biased toward the
elderly: wealth in the form of goods tends to increase with age and naturally more older than younger men die and are subsequently probated.[19]
Slaves were also not probated, as they themselves were considered property.

The goods appraised in the Chesapeake differed from those in other
colonies. The colonists in Maryland and Virginia only inventoried
chattel property; other colonies often included real estate as well. Chattels are movable property, which could be removed from the estate and
hidden from heirs and creditors if not listed in a public document. Even
though the inventories from the Chesapeake included chattels and not
land, they furnish detailed information and market value on bound labor, trade goods, debts receivable, household goods, and personal belongings.[20]

Even with these biases and deficiencies, probate records are useful for
studies relating to economic growth, wealth distribution, social strati-

fication, regional economic variation, agricultural productivity and practices, labor systems, slave demography, credit networks, and lifestyles.[21] Probates can also reveal patterns in the changing relationships of goods to wealth patterns and social stratification.

There was a recording rate of nearly 70 percent for probate inventories in the Chesapeake before the American Revolution. There was a 40 to 60 percent recording rate for Anne Arundel County.[22] These high percentages contrast favorably to a rate of less than 40 percent in some New England areas.[23] Because of the high recording rates in the Chesapeake, probate inventories serve as a reliable sample of material culture among varying wealth groups. They are an important record of the changing goods found in colonial America and are an indicator of the changing behavior associated with these goods.

PROBATE DATA ANALYSIS—AN EXAMPLE OF HISTORICAL PARTICULARISM

Many scholars would not be able to analyze Chesapeake material culture without the excellent and rigorous scholarship of Lois Carr and Lorena Walsh. It is my goal to build new ideas and interpretations upon their pioneering work and contribute new dimensions to material culture studies in the Chesapeake.

According to Carr and Walsh, material culture is a reflection of economic prosperity.[24] They note that "economic prosperity meant that most family members sat on individual chairs instead of stools, beds, chests, or communal benches; ate from a table, made use of candles after dark; had more pewter dining and drinking vessels, more and better beds with linens, bedsteads, and hangings; a greater variety of cooking equipment; and now and then a picture or looking glass"[25] Throughout the eighteenth century, status symbols consisted of time pieces, pictures, and silver plate. Carr and Walsh consider forks and knives possessions of the upper wealth group. By the 1770s these items had become essential in the daily lives of those with lower status.

Large-scale probate inventory analyses were performed for Saint Mary's County, the area of the first permanent English settlement within the province of Maryland. The 2,612 inventories surviving from 1658 to 1777 provide the data. The reporting rate for these 119 years appears to be somewhat stable. The main goal of this initial work was to analyze "amenities," or those items believed to make life more comfortable or luxurious. Although the upper wealth group had "exclusive enjoyment of a few of these goods, a substantial majority of these items had a much wider circulation."[26]

Carr and Walsh created an amenities index to measure the penetration of these goods into all wealth groups. This index has five categories with varying amounts of items within them. The following goods are considered in the index:[27]

1. Earthenware and bed or table linen for convenience and sanitation.
2. Table knives, forks, and fine earthenware for refinements in convenience and sanitation and for increasing elegance at the table.
3. Spices for variety in diet.
4. Religious and secular books for education and perhaps some leisure time.
5. Wigs, watches or clocks, pictures, and silver plate for signs of luxury and display.

From these categories an amenities index can be formulated by adding the total number of categories recorded in all estates then dividing by the number of estates.

This analytical method reveals little change in the amenities between different wealth groups throughout the seventeenth century until 1716. During this time, the mean score was about two. Carr and Walsh state that "while the rich possessed a few luxuries—silver plate in particular—before 1715 their lifestyle was distinguished more by access to ordinary 'decencies' than by the ownership of many true luxury goods." By 1716 the mean score among the wealthy rose dramatically and continued to rise until it reached about five in the 1770s. People belonging to all wealth groups showed a noticeable increase in their scores, but the distance between the rich and poor remained large.[28]

According to Carr and Walsh, improvements made in transportation, marketing, and technology facilitated this increase in amenities.[29] These factors also decreased the cost of ceramics, nails, glassware, tin goods, cutlery, wool cards and stockings. The lower prices allowed for a surplus of capital that encouraged purchases and helped keep the inhabitants in the Chesapeake abreast of the life-styles in England. Also, during the late seventeenth century, the Chesapeake's economy shifted toward crop diversification, which helped the region endure the highs and lows of the tobacco industry. Other local phenomena—the growing number of home industries, for example— allowed for the production of goods such as wool, candles, spoons, and flax. These developments lowered the price of necessities, enabling people to purchase amenities.

Carr and Walsh also created a "modern index," using 7,590 probate inventories spanning the years 1634 to 1777 from four Chesapeake counties: Saint Mary's, Somerset, and Anne Arundel in Maryland; and York County in Virginia.[30] The modern index includes items that these historians consider basic household equipment for comfort and cleanliness: a mattress, a bedstead, some bed linen, a table, one or more chairs, pots for boiling, equipment to prepare food in at least one other way, some coarse ceramics, table forks, and some means of interior lighting. Analysis of Chesapeake inventories indicates that the acquisition of these "modern" goods did not follow the amenities index pattern; little change occurred over time in any wealth group. Although the population studied had

> increased their index scores, the mean was still less than three items, and the "modern" scores showed only modest progress. Such families still lived in small, poorly equipped houses with at most two rooms and a loft and a wooden chimney. Family members might enjoy a cup of tea but their living conditions were still primitive. The biggest changes were confined to the middle and upper groups.[31]

These concepts of comfort and modernism are based on our expectations. The needs and desires of a preindustrial community are different from those of an industrial society. The eighteenth-century Chesapeake was changing from a preindustrial society with its particular concepts of status to an incipient industrial society in which modern discipline and exacting behavior were developing. Some of the items found in the amenities index can also demonstrate an emerging modern discipline, whereas other items, such as coarse ceramics, may have been used solely for containing food. Goods such as sets of tableware reinforce the standard of one item for one person, thus rejecting the preindustrial, medieval concept of communalism. Although the Chesapeake did not industrialize until the nineteenth century, it did participate in the new culture of capitalism that became widespread in late eighteenth-century

England and its colonies. Therefore it is necessary to understand the social context of goods and how they created a modern society.

The Social Context of Goods

The social context and the meaning of goods are essential components in comprehending the dynamic nature of consumption patterns. Material culture does more than reflect behavior or serve as an index of wealth. Goods give meaning to social behavior as they enforce, reinforce, and create behavior. Because goods can have an ideological and symbolic element, they may be actively manipulated in social circumstances. They will have different meanings in different contexts.[32] As early as the eighteenth century, Saint Simon remarked that what matters "is not the thing itself but what it means in relations to certain people."[33] Objects can create and reaffirm social boundaries as long as the codes are understood by those in control of the meaning.

Goods may function as media that disguise social relations in the form of hegemony.[34] They are instruments that create meaning, order the world, and maintain social relationships through nonverbal communication. Whether and how they are used or refused constitutes whether they maintain, create, or undermine social relations.[35] The meaning and context of goods and their interactive quality help us understand how goods were used in the development of a modern discipline.

"Goods provide a communicative medium of symbolic significance . . . and provide a medium for social domination as an expression of power and ideology," according to Shanks and Tilley.[36] It is the control of material goods and their meaning that allows some to dominate others and produces asymmetrical allocations, thus creating power relations between groups.[37] Competition to acquire goods produces boundaries that exclude outsiders. Those within a group will attempt to synchronize their consumption patterns with their peers. In a developing complex or urban society, consumption goods are diversified and the upper wealth groups have a finely tuned understanding of the meaning of these goods in different social circumstances.[38]

Standardization of behavior usually develops at the center of a competitive system, such as the growing urban center of eighteenth-century Annapolis, "where close comparisons of value are required. At the fringe of a market system [such as Anne Arundel County], where turn-over is slower, where knowledge is incomplete, and bigger profits riskier, discrepancies in standards can pass. But where competition is hottest, standardization emerges."[39] This competition is characteristic in most urban society. Whenever standardization of precise rules and discipline occurs, one is probably near the center of a competitive system in which even the smallest deviation matters. On formal occasions behavior and goods are standardized, and if they are tampered with, there is the dan-ger of giving wrong signals.

Douglas and Isherwood note that there are three ways to maintain social boundaries.[40] The first is to demand a high fee for admission, making it impossible for less wealthy people to join. The high cost of membership may discourage people from joining a particular group. The second way is to "set the normal rate for settling of internal transactions so high that only the very rich can afford to join the game." If the cost of maintaining acceptance remains high, it may exclude many who can-not afford the ongoing costs of belonging to the group. The final way to maintain social boundaries is to refuse any transactions with members of other groups. This method legitimizes discriminatory practices.

I would like to add a fourth method of exclusion. I believe that cere-monies involving material culture change at an unspecified rate, de-pending on social pressures, thus keeping those who do not keep pace with these changes outcasts. Those in control of the group change the rules and ceremonies so that those who do not keep abreast with the changes are marginalized. With these changes in behavior, there may also be a change in material culture, reinforcing the association be-tween the new behavior and the new goods. Even if there is equal access to the "physical means of production," people tend to create groups and control specific types of material culture, thereby dominating access to information regarding the meaning and use of their goods. Those within a group will synchronize their consumption with other group members, who are guided by similar circumstances.[41]

Ian Hodder's work demonstrates that in areas of the greatest tension and competition, catalyzed by economic stress, groups sometimes em-phasize distinct material differences between ethnic groups: "The com-petitive relationship may be based on the overt distinctions." There may also be active use of material culture to express tensions within eth-nic units. Hodder explains that "material culture of many forms is used to justify between-group negative reciprocity and to support the social and economic dependencies within groups."[42] Some categories of goods may be used as media to implicitly relay information that is intelligible only to certain actors.

Some social scientists have successfully demonstrated that goods create and maintain social boundaries.[43] In particular, I find most useful the works of Hodder, Douglas and Isherwood, and Miller.[44] Their works are used as a basis for demonstrating that the use of material goods in colonial Annapolis played a role in structuring relations in society.

The Meaning of Consumer Goods

To understand the structure of social relations in the Chesapeake and the penetration of a modern, segmenting, and exacting discipline for the history of social time, I quantified and analyzed probate inventory data from Annapolis and Anne Arundel County. I recorded some items from inventories in the form of a presence/absence of sets, which is a finer indicator than a gross presence/absence count. These items include sets of chairs, sets of cups and saucers, sets of knives, sets of forks, and sets of plates. With the presence of sets, we can assume that one object was used by one person, thus rejecting the premodern communal tradition. To distinguish sets, I used Miller's criterion of six or more of one object.[45] I did not count "lots" and "parcels" of objects as sets, because of the improbability that a true estimate of the quantities these terms represented could be determined. Therefore all data related to the presence of sets are a conservative or minimum estimate.

These items were coded from 1688 to 1777 for all 255 inventories for Annapolis and for a systematic sample of the rural data, which included three-year groupings at approximately fifteen-year intervals (n = 351). The three-year grouping at fifteen-year intervals for the rural data was the preferred sampling method as it helped generate a representative sample.[46] Although not completely equivalent to the urban data this systematic analysis of rural data provides a general trend of material culture change.

For the analysis of urban and rural Chesapeake data, I divided the inventories into four wealth groups. Group 1 consists of the poorest of those inventoried, with total estate values between zero and £49 at the time of death; group 2 consists of those with estate values between £50 and £225; group 3 consists of those with total estate values between £225 and £490; and the final category, group 4, contains all estates valued at equal to or greater than £491. The £50 division between wealth groups 1 and 2 was close to the median value of all estates in Saint Mary's County until 1730. These group divisions are also valid for the rest of the Chesapeake, because all estates in this category in all counties had similar types of material culture, and the median value of estates in the other counties is close to that found in Saint Mary's County. At the £225 and £490 limits, consumption rates rose dramatically among estates in the colonial Chesapeake. Carr and Walsh determined that these jumps probably identify different groups and are therefore valid wealth group boundaries. These categories appear to represent real clusters of consumption habits.[47]

A commodity price index that demonstrates the proportional differences between prices of specific goods for different years accounts for inflation in a diachronic comparison. An annual price series is derived by collecting annual mean prices of specific goods and then dividing those prices by the mean prices for a base period. "Percentage differences between each number and the base period number provide a measure of price change comparable from one item to another," state Carr and Walsh.[48] The weights used to develop the commodity price index for the lower western shore of Maryland, 1658–1776, is applicable to other Chesapeake areas, including Annapolis and Anne Arundel County (see table 13).[49] The index accounts for both domestic products and imported goods and weighs the relative prices of specific items over time. The product is a relative weight that can be divided into a value of a good, or estate, for a specific year. The relative cost of goods vary from year to year, but with the creation of this new value that takes inflation into account, comparison between time periods are made easier. All estate values are adjusted to the 1700 English pound. The commodity price index is used in this study to arrange the wealth groups for a diachronic comparison.

I examine data sets from Annapolis and surrounding Anne Arundel County to compare the different rates of transmission of the new disciplining and segmenting behavior and the different responses of urban and rural populations to social and economic crises, and to determine how goods shaped and created this new order of behavior. Material and behavioral correlates of this new behavior should appear most dramat-

Table 13. Weights for a Commodity Price Index, Lower Western Shore, 1658–1776

I. Domestically Produced Agricultural Products

$$1659\text{--}99 \quad \frac{(\text{Cow and Calf} \times 4) + \text{Corn}}{5}$$

$$1700\text{--}76 \quad \frac{(\text{Cow and Calf} \times 4) + (\text{Corn} + \text{Wheat}) / 2}{5}$$

II. European Manufactured Goods

$$1659\text{--}99 \quad \frac{\text{Pewter} + (\text{Dowles} + \text{Canvas} + \text{Ozenbridge}) / 3}{2}$$

$$1700\text{--}20 \quad \frac{(\text{Pewter} + \text{Plate}) / 2 + (\text{Dowels} + \text{Canvas} + \text{Ozenbridge}) / 3}{2}$$

$$1721\text{--}76 \quad \frac{(\text{Pewter} + \text{Plate}) / 2 + \text{Ozenbridge}}{2}$$

$$\text{Commodity Price Index} = \frac{\text{I} + \text{II}}{2}$$

Source: Carr and Walsh 1980:100 (and personal communication with Carr 1986).

ically in the 1720s, and again just before the American Revolution. The rural and urban populations were threatened by the social and economic fluctuations and the creation of a more competitive society. Long-term tobacco depressions may have affected planters more than city dwellers, although inflation would have hurt both groups. Urbanization and a dramatic increase in the city's population most likely affected Annapolis to a far greater extent than the surrounding county.

If goods are analyzed in the context of their social and historical meanings, reasons for consumption patterns can be understood. The following is a descriptive analysis of consumption trends from coded probate inventories. The data are coded from 1688 to 1777, and the midpoints of predetermined year groupings are marked on the graphs.[50] (Raw data can be found in the Appendix.)

Items Related to the Segmentation and Measurement of Time and Space

Here I examine the material goods related to the segmentation and measurement of time and space. The items analyzed include clocks for the measurement of time and scientific instruments for the measurement of land, time, and atmosphere. A select few who owned these objects used them to divide and measure their environment. Use of these objects enforced a naturalizing ideology that served to demonstrate the elite's control over nature by dividing it unnaturally but making this division appear to be natural, thus helping to legitimize their power and control. These items were used in the creation and maintenance of a hegemonic relationship in society.[51] They were used implicitly by the elite to naturalize their dominance and to internalize a new disciplined, measured, and exacting behavior. I expect that this internalization occurred before the introduction of other consumption goods that explicitly created and reinforced a disciplined and segmented society. The naturalization of time consciousness created a disciplined person, thereby facilitating the acceptance of mass-produced and individualizing goods that catalyzed and reinforced our modern behavior. The discipline created and reinforced by these clocks is very much part of our lives today.

Clocks and Scientific Instruments

Annapolis.   The only clock that existed in early Annapolis belonged to a member of the third wealth group (fig. 10). All wealth groups increased their ownership of clocks until the 1740s. Wealth groups 2 and 3 had relatively fewer clocks than the wealthiest group by the 1760s and 1770s. The two middle groups followed similar consumption patterns, and ownership peaked during the 1740s. The graph line of group 3 surpassed the wealthiest group only in the 1740s, as members of group 4 did not substantially increase the number of households with clocks after the 1720s. Only during the 1720s and the 1760s and 1770s did the four groups own clocks in proportion to their wealth.

By the turn of the eighteenth century in Annapolis, the wealthiest and third wealthiest groups possessed scientific instruments (fig. 11). The wealthiest group had more estates with scientific instruments than any other group through the 1760s and 1770s. All groups' consumption patterns generally fluctuated through the eighteenth century, except group 3, whose consumption steadily increased through the 1760s and 1770s. Wealth groups 4 and 2 displayed similar fluctuating patterns, whereas the lowest wealth group remained low throughout the entire

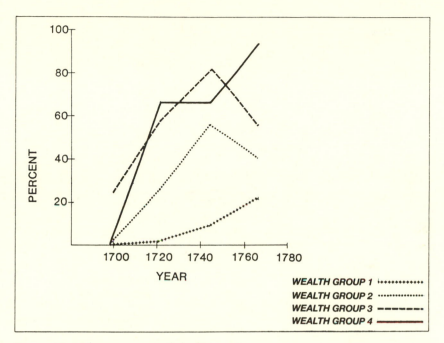

Figure 10. Urban presence of clocks.

period of study. The three wealthiest groups had similar consumption rates in the 1720s, whereas only groups 3 and 4 had similar consumption rates in the 1760s and 1770s. Throughout the period, each group owned scientific instruments in proportion to its position from the 1720s.

Anne Arundel County.   Clocks existed in all wealth groups in Anne Arundel County by the beginning of the eighteenth century (fig. 12). Throughout the study period, the four wealth groups owned clocks in proportion to their wealth. Group 4 had proportionately twice as many estates with clocks as the other groups combined. None of the wealth groups followed similar trends, as group 4 peaked during the 1720s and gradually declined, and group 3 peaked during the 1740s then declined. Wealth group 2 steadily increased its clock ownership throughout the eighteenth century, and by the 1760s and 1770s had a consumption frequency close to that of wealth group 3. Wealth group 1's ownership remained relatively low throughout the entire study period.

Scientific instruments were found only in the wealthiest group at the

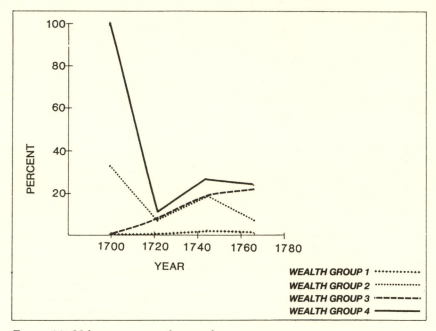

Figure 11. Urban presence of scientific instruments.

turn of the century in Anne Arundel County (fig. 13). All of the groups' consumption patterns fluctuated differently throughout the eighteenth century, but all of the groups owned scientific instruments in proportion to their wealth. Groups 1 and 2 remained relatively low throughout the period examined. Group 4's consumption peaked during the 1740s, and the third group's consumption of scientific instruments peaked in the 1760s and 1770s but was still lower than that of the wealthiest group. During the 1760s and 1770s, there is little difference in consumption of these items between groups 1 and 2 and between groups 3 and 4.

Summary of Clocks and Scientific Instruments

Clocks and scientific instrument consumption patterns in the city tended to be more erratic and less predictable than in rural areas.[52] Whereas in rural areas groups owned these items in proportion to their wealth, in Annapolis this was not the case. In the 1740s the second and third wealth groups had a similar number of estates with clocks, but

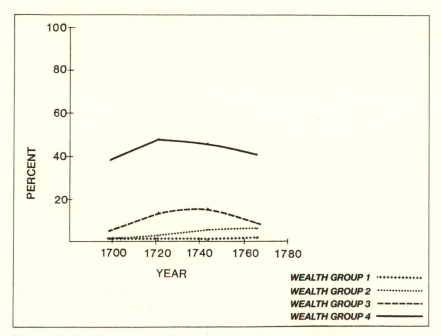

Figure 12. Rural presence of clocks.

wealth group 3 had more estates with clocks than wealth group 4. The urban wealthy did have more clocks in the 1720s, 1760s, and 1770s than the other wealth groups; the ownership of clocks peaked among the rural wealthy in the 1720s. It appears that although clock ownership may have been part of an elite response to social and economic stress, the lower wealth groups responded differently to the socioeconomic instabilities, having little direct use for clocks and scientific instruments.

Clocks and scientific instruments generally are found in larger proportions among the elite. The elite owned the greatest proportion of these items in all time periods, regardless of social and economic stress. In the case of urban and rural clocks, the elite's purchasing pattern increased dramatically during the 1720s, and in all cases the elite owned more clocks by the 1760s and 1770s. The control over time and the measurement of time, space, and atmosphere may have been the elite's attempt to demonstrate control over nature, legitimizing the elite's control over society. In the case of Annapolis, because the elite reestablished firm control over their threatened hierarchy, there may not

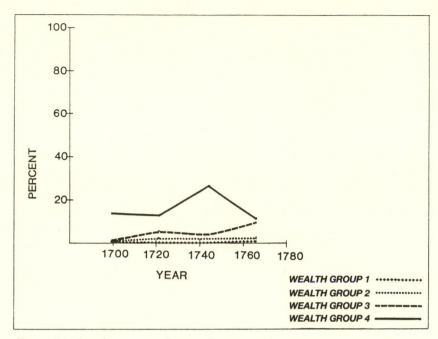

Figure 13. Rural presence of scientific instruments.

have been a need to continue dominance over all items that expressed the naturalization of the hierarchy. When once again threatened in the 1760s and 1770s, the elite regained their domination of objects that licensed their power and control.

Dining Items

The inventoried goods related to dining include, for the purpose of this study, formal and segmenting dining items (i.e., salad dishes, tureens, dish covers, fruit dishes, custard cups, castors, butter boats, and wine glasses); sets of plates; sets of forks; sets of knives; sets of cups and saucers; sets of chairs; and the presence of knives, forks, napkins, and functionally specific tables (such as tea tables and dining tables). Such items were not only indicators of wealth but also of the new behavior associated with dining. They were rare, and in many cases nonexistent, in preindustrial America. During this time a plate, spoons, and drinking vessels were the norm for the table setting, and people typically ate with their hands and sat on benches, trunks, or the edges of beds. As noted previously, as social stress and competition increased in Annapolis and Anne Arundel County, people acquired new disciplining and segmenting objects in greater numbers. This new behavior occurred in Annapolis in the 1710s and 1720s and around the time of the American Revolution. This process was not as dramatic, but was just as extensive, among the rural population.

Formal and Segmenting Dining Items

With the introduction of formal and segmenting dining items came the rejection of the communal behavior associated with premodern eating. Items were introduced to separate the dinner into its many parts. This new behavior led to practices such as having separate dishes for the salad, the main course, and the dessert. These specialized dining items began to separate both the dinner into parts and the diners from one another.

Annapolis.   The earliest Annapolis inventories lacked formal and segmenting dining items (fig. 14). By the 1720s the elite and wealth group 3 increased their consumption of these goods, the wealthy having significantly more. The poorer wealth groups, 1 and 2, did not obtain formal and segmenting dining items until the 1740s. At this point the wealthy decreased their acquisition of these goods and were surpassed by the second and third wealth groups. By the 1760s and 1770s, the wealthy increased their consumption and had relatively more estates with formal and segmenting dining than any other group. In the 1760s and 1770s, only the fourth and second wealth groups had these items. Groups 1, 2, and 3 followed similar patterns.

Anne Arundel County.   In Anne Arundel County, segmenting dining items only appear in wealth group 4 at the turn of the eighteenth century (fig. 15). This group's consumption increased notably in the 1720s, decreased in the late 1740s, and rose again in the 1760s and 1770s. Only in 1700, the 1730s, and the 1760s did group 4 have more segmenting and formal dining items than the other groups. Group 3's consumption grew in the 1720s and surpassed the wealthiest group in the 1740s,

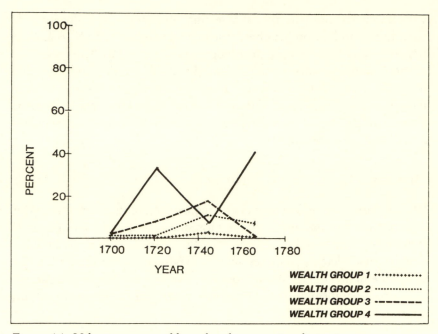

Figure 14. Urban presence of formal and segmenting dining items.

but it decreased in the 1760s and 1770s. Throughout the study period, the first and second groups did not participate in the consumption of these goods.

Sets of Plates

As indicated above, the presence of sets of objects implies that one individual used one item rather than sharing single items with other persons. This pattern of use demonstrates a rejection of the communal tradition and the adaption of a new order of behavior. Although sets of plates are absent from the early archaeological record, plates did appear in material forms other than ceramics, such as wood or pewter. Often the estate appraiser did not distinguish the material and they were recorded simply as "plates" or "dishes."

Annapolis.   Sets of plates are present in only the first and third wealth groups at the turn of the eighteenth century in Annapolis (fig. 16). The

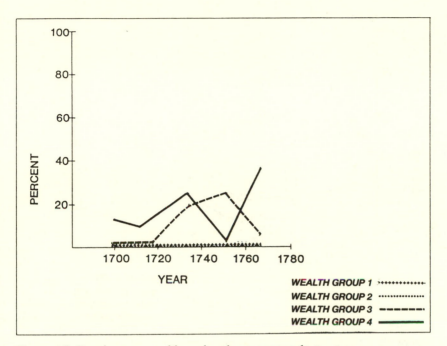

Figure 15. Rural presence of formal and segmenting dining items.

wealthy employed more of these goods than the other wealth groups by the 1720s. The acquisition by all wealth groups leveled off or decreased slightly in the 1740s and increased again in the 1760s and 1770s. The second wealth group gradually increased its consumption rate through the study period. The first and second groups' patterns tended to be more erratic, and the second group surpassed the third group in the 1740s. By the 1760s and 1770s, the four wealth groups owned sets of plates in proportion to their wealth.

Anne Arundel County. At the turn of the eighteenth century in Anne Arundel County, the third wealth group had proportionately more sets of plates than the fourth wealth group, and the first wealth group had more than the second (fig. 17). The wealthy increased their consumption, and from the 1710s to the 1760s, the wealthiest group had more sets of plates than the other groups. From the 1710s until the 1740s, the first and second groups had the same or proportionately more of these

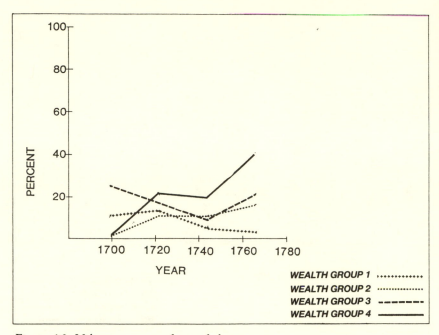

Figure 16. Urban presence of sets of plates.

goods than group 3. From the 1740s through the 1760s all groups owned sets of plates in proportion to their wealth. The first and second groups followed similar patterns of consumption, with the second group consistently having proportionately more sets of plates than the first group from the 1710s.

Sets of Forks and Sets of Knives

Because their acquisition followed similar consumption patterns, knives and forks will be discussed together but graphed separately. The only difference is that knives were found in a slightly greater proportion in the early part of this study, due to their longer tradition. The fork is a somewhat newer instrument, which, for bringing food to the mouth, supplanted the hand and the knife.

With the introduction of the fork into Western society came a new etiquette with rules to govern eating. As a result hands were prohibited from touching food. By the early eighteenth century in French court

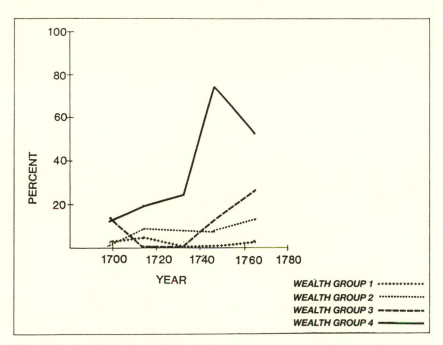

Figure 17. Rural presence of sets of plates.

society, specific rules accompanied the use of the various knives and forks. Sets of forks further implies the break from the premodern tradition, because one person used one fork, thus increasing the segmentation of the dinner process, of the people at the table, and of the standardization of their behavior.

Annapolis. Even though forks appeared in early Annapolis (see the Appendix), there were no sets of forks until the 1720s (fig. 18). During this era all wealth groups owned sets of forks in proportion to their position. This consumption rate changed significantly, however, and by the 1740s the second and third wealth groups had surpassed the consumption rate of the fourth group. By the 1760s and 1770s the third wealth group had slightly more fork sets than the fourth wealth group. None of the wealth groups followed similar patterns of acquisition.

Sets of knives were present only among the second wealth group at the turn of the eighteenth century in Annapolis (fig. 19). The wealth-

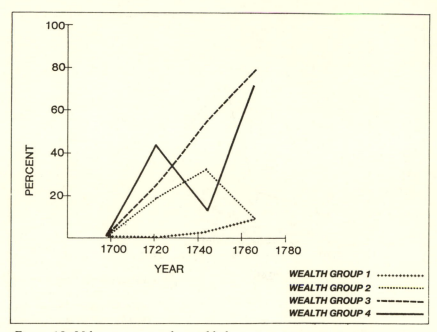

Figure 18. Urban presence of sets of forks.

iest group dramatically increased its consumption in the 1720s, but decreased in the 1740s. During the 1740s groups 2 and 3 surpassed the wealthiest group, and by the 1760s and 1770s, the third group had slightly more households with sets of knives than group 4. The poorest group did not acquire sets of knives until after the 1740s and always owned substantially fewer than the other groups. None of the wealth groups followed similar consumption patterns.

Anne Arundel County.   Only the wealthiest group owned sets of forks in Anne Arundel County (fig. 20). Throughout the study period, the four groups owned sets of forks in proportion to their wealth. Fork sets were nonexistent in group 1. None of the groups followed similar patterns of acquisition.

Sets of knives were found in only the wealthiest group in Anne Arundel County (fig. 21). Throughout the study period, the four groups owned sets of knives in proportion to their wealth. The poorest group

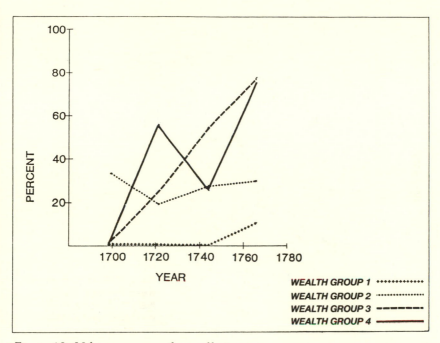

Figure 19. Urban presence of sets of knives.

did not own these items. None of the groups followed similar consumption patterns to each other.

Sets of Cups and Saucers

The presence of cups and saucers signifies the segmentation of daily activities. These objects were usually for coffee, tea, or chocolate, related to leisurely, ritual activities among the elite. Tea, a costly item, had become a fashionable drink among England's elite by the mid-seventeenth century. Tea drinking was synonymous with the upper wealth groups because of the expense of the tea and the cost of the elaborate equipment used. Tea and other exotic drinks, such as coffee and chocolate, were usually part of an elaborate social ceremony that conspicuously displayed the availability of leisure time.[53] Leisure time was now a noticeable part of everyday life. Instead of leading a corporate way of life, people participated in a life emphasizing social segmentation, which this new material culture aided.[54]

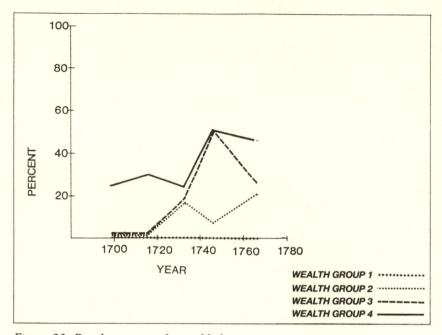

Figure 20. Rural presence of sets of forks.

Annapolis.   Sets of cups and saucers are not present in the earliest Annapolis inventories (fig. 22). By the 1720s wealth groups 2, 3, and 4 had
increased their consumption of these items. All of the groups owned
sets of cups and saucers in proportion to their wealth through the 1740s.
By the 1760s and 1770s, the wealthiest group still has proportionately
more of these items than the other groups, and group 2 slightly surpassed the consumption rate of the third group. The poorest group
owned relatively fewer sets of cups and saucers than other groups and
only began to own more after the 1740s. Wealth groups 2, 3, and 4 followed similar consumption patterns.

Anne Arundel County.   Sets of cups and saucers are not present in any
of the early eighteenth-century Anne Arundel inventories, but the
second wealth group had more of these items than the other groups by
the 1710s (fig. 23). By the 1720s groups 3 and 4 owned sets of cups in
proportion to their wealth, whereas the first and second groups did not

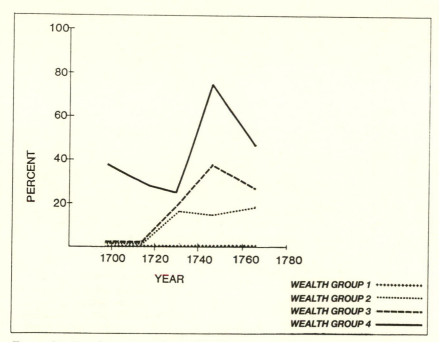

Figure 21. Rural presence of sets of knives.

own any of these goods. By the 1740s the wealthiest group's consumption pattern decreased markedly and was surpassed by the second and third group. By the 1760s and 1770s, all of the wealth groups owned sets of cups in proportion to their wealth. Throughout the entire study period, the poorest group did not own any of these items. None of the groups displayed similar consumption patterns.

Napkins

Napkins are also an item associated with the development of a new dining etiquette. They provided an alternative to the tablecloth and sleeves for cleaning the hands and mouth after eating. The napkin became so important soon after its development that etiquette writers not only specified how to use it but also created rules on how to fold the napkin in order to present an orderly and standardized placement around the table. The development of the napkin is a product of modern Western culture and the dismantling of the preindustrial tradition.

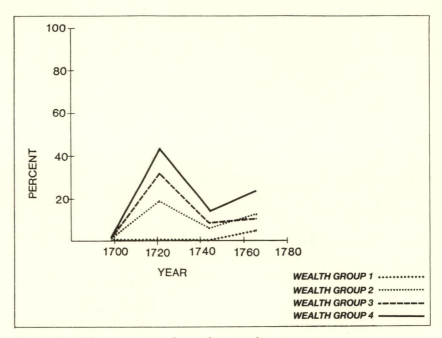

Figure 22. Urban presence of sets of cups and saucers.

Annapolis. At the turn of the eighteenth century in Annapolis, all four groups owned napkins in proportion to their wealth (fig. 24). By the 1720s the wealthy had decreased their consumption rate and were surpassed by wealth group 3. Groups 1, 2, and 3 increased their consumption in the 1720s, and all groups declined in the remaining periods. By the 1740s the second and third groups had more napkins than the wealthiest group. By the 1760s the wealthiest group had proportionately more napkins than the lower groups. The first, second, and third groups displayed similar patterns of consumption.

Anne Arundel County. Napkins were present in greatest proportion among the wealthiest at the turn of the eighteenth century in Anne Arundel County (fig. 25). From the 1710s through the 1760s, the four groups owned napkins in proportion to their wealth. The groups did not show similar consumption patterns.

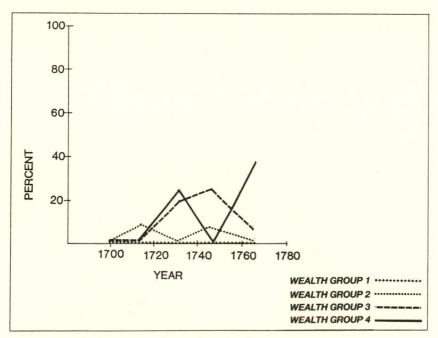

Figure 23. Rural presence of sets of cups and saucers.

Sets of Chairs

Chairs replaced communal benches and trunks for sitting, separating people with a more rigorously defined space and providing an index of individuality. The use of sets of chairs further defines the increasing acceptance of individualized seating furniture.

Annapolis. Sets of chairs first appeared in Annapolis during the 1720s (fig. 26). All groups owned these items in proportion to their wealth. During the 1740s the wealthiest group's proportion decreased dramatically; all the lower groups had more sets of chairs than group 4. By the 1760s and 1770s, the two wealthiest groups had increased their proportion of chair sets, but group 3 still had relatively more. Possession of sets of chairs then decreased among the first and second groups. Wealth groups 1 and 2 had similar consumption patterns, as did groups 3 and 4.

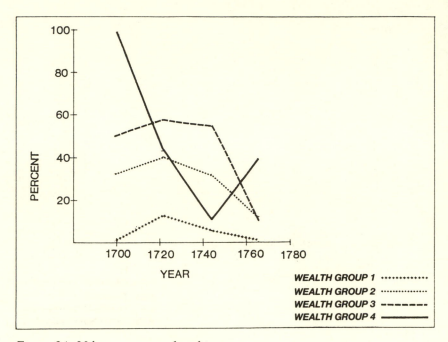

Figure 24. Urban presence of napkins.

Anne Arundel County.   Sets of chairs were nonexistent in Anne Arundel probate inventories until after the 1740s (fig. 27). During the 1760s and 1770s, all groups owned sets of chairs in proportion to their wealth.

Tea Tables

Tea tables were a part of the elaborate ceremony related to tea consumption. Tea became an expensive item when merchants introduced it to England from Holland in 1657, after which it became a drink of the elite.[55] It was a midday beverage and was a way for the upper class to signal to members of other social strata that they were capable of taking time off from their regular activities to socialize, and thus segment their day. Equipment associated with this ceremony included tea, a tea canister, a tea pot, teaware or tea sets, a strainer, tongs, teaspoons, and a specialized table-the tea table. The tea table further segmented a leisure/ceremonial activity from the other activities of the day.

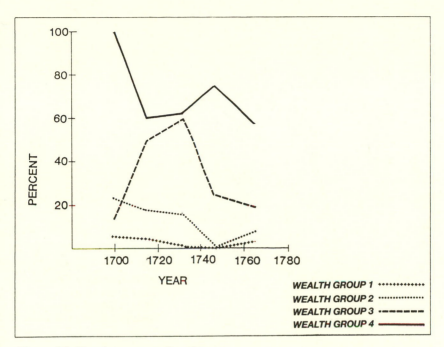

Figure 25. Rural presence of napkins.

Annapolis.   Tea tables were not present in early Annapolis inventories (fig. 28). By the 1720s wealth groups 2, 3, and 4 had similar consumption frequencies. In the 1740s the wealthiest group's consumption jumped drastically but decreased sharply by the 1760s and 1770s, falling below group 2's consumption frequency. The 1740s was the only era in which all groups owned tea tables in proportion to their wealth. Tea tables first appeared in the poorest wealth group after the 1740s, and by the 1760s and 1770s, wealth groups 1, 3, and 4 had similar consumption rates. During this period wealth group 2 had the highest consumption rate.

Anne Arundel County.   Tea tables first appeared in Anne Arundel County inventories shortly after 1700 (fig. 29). Throughout the study period, the wealthy increased their consumption of this item and owned proportionately more of them than any other group. After the 1740s all

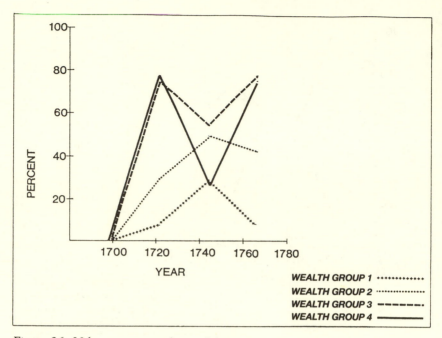

Figure 26. Urban presence of sets of chairs.

groups owned tea tables in proportion to their wealth. Wealth groups 1, 2, and 3 displayed similar patterns of acquisition.

Summary of Dining Items

Generally, urban consumption patterns of goods related to dining activities tended to be more erratic than rural consumption. Complex processes stimulated the consumption of goods. In particular, there appears to have been some relationship between social and economic instability (specifically in the 1710s, 1720s, 1760s, and 1770s) and the acquisition of goods that reinforced new standardizing, exacting, and precise behavior. In some cases there was no correlation between wealth and consumption—except during the 1720s and 1760s. In these decades goods were usually found in proportion to wealth for the majority of artifact categories in both urban and rural areas. In Annapolis nine of ten items were in greatest proportion among the wealthy in the 1720s, and in the 1760s and the 1770s six of ten items were in greatest proportion

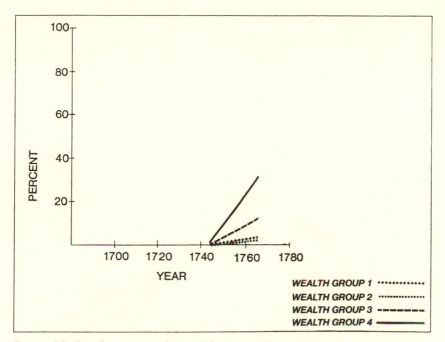

Figure 27. Rural presence of sets of chairs.

among the elite. In Anne Arundel County these goods were in greatest proportion among the wealthy in all items. This consumption pattern may have been a way for the elite to reassert their domination. Also, the wealthiest urban group no longer owned the majority of most dining-related items during the 1740s. This phenomena holds true for only two artifact cases in the rural population. In all cases in Anne Arundel County, residents acquired goods in proportion to their wealth by the 1760s and 1770s. There was some consumption-pattern imitation between groups during specific eras, and for some goods some groups appeared to react in similar fashion for the entire period studied. No groups reacted in a similar fashion to another group for all categories and time periods.

Hygiene and Grooming-related Items

The presence of close stools, chamber pots, handkerchiefs, and grooming-related items (i.e., dressing boxes, dressing tables, dressing glasses,

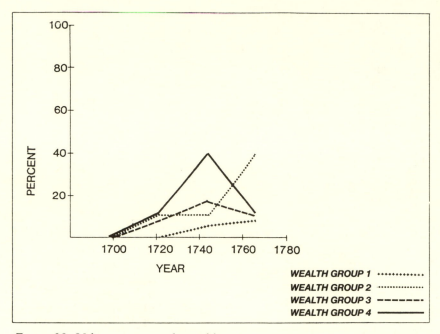

Figure 28. Urban presence of tea tables.

shaving/wash basins, clothes brushes, combs, toothbrushes, and toothpicks) were noted in Annapolis and Anne Arundel County inventories.
These items should not only be considered items of wealth but also objects that helped to create and reinforce the new behavior that aided the
development of the individual. Such items were rare in preindustrial
society, as grooming and recognizable concepts of hygiene existed almost exclusively among members of the nobility. As social competition
increased in response to a growing population and economic crises, people began to acquire these objects in an effort to create expressions of
individual material and physical wealth. This type of consumption was
part of the concern for personal discipline. The expression of individuality also should have occurred during the American Revolution, although I believe that the effects of this and other crises would not have
been as severe in the rural areas. Without keen social competition, the
expression of individuality through hygiene and grooming were not as
widespread.

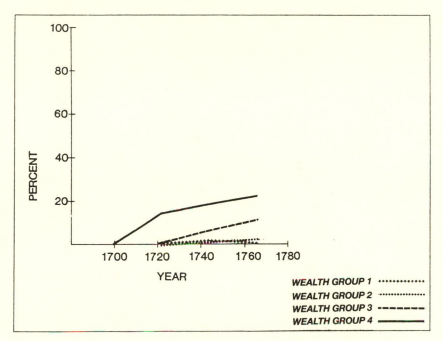

Figure 29. Rural presence of tea tables.

Grooming Items

Grooming-related items are all used in the creation of the individual. In the premodern tradition, the Roman Catholic Church, which was influential in guiding people's behavior, frowned upon grooming because it promoted vanity. Private and public baths were common in premodern Europe, for example, but Catholics and Calvinists thought they brought moral dangers to the community. Washing clothes, the hair, or the teeth aided in the creation of the individual through a personal discipline, segmenting one person from another, either within or between social groups. Public baths declined in the sixteenth and seventeenth centuries, although a few remained. Bathing once again became popular by the late eighteenth century.[56]

Annapolis. Grooming-related items were found only in the second wealth group at the turn of the eighteenth century in Annapolis (fig. 30). By the 1720s both the third and fourth groups had substantially

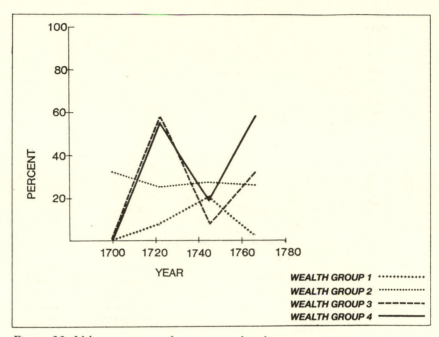

Figure 30. Urban presence of grooming-related items.

increased their consumption of grooming-related items. These groups decreased their consumption rates in the 1740s and increased their rates again by the 1760s and 1770s. The second group's consumption remained relatively constant throughout the period. The first wealth group's consumption rate peaked in the 1740s. During this era both the first and second groups had more estates with grooming-related items than the third and fourth groups. By the 1760s and 1770s, all groups owned these items in proportion to their wealth.

Anne Arundel County.   In Anne Arundel County, wealth group 4 owned more grooming-related items than the other groups in all time periods except at about 1730, when the third wealth group owned slightly more (fig. 31). The first and second wealth groups followed similar consumption patterns throughout the study period, although the first group usually owned slightly more.

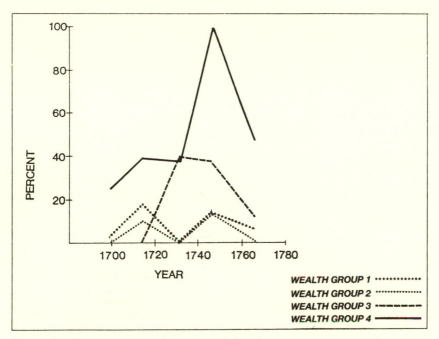

Figure 31. Rural presence of grooming-related items.

Handkerchiefs

Handkerchiefs were items introduced specifically for blowing the nose, a step further from the napkin. No longer was one to use the sleeve, tablecloth, or fingers. Handkerchiefs represented a new etiquette, or new personal discipline, for the individual in his or her presentation of self to society.

Annapolis.   Handkerchiefs were present in the estates of wealth groups 1, 3, and 4 in early Annapolis (fig. 32). The wealthy owned relatively more of them from about 1700 through the 1720s. The first and third groups had more than the second group until the 1730s. By the 1740s the consumption rates had decreased for the first, third, and fourth group, whereas that of the second group increased. During this time period, groups 2, 3, and 4 had similar rates, but in reverse proportion to

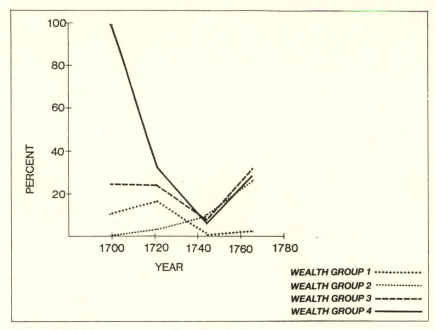

Figure 32. Urban presence of handkerchiefs.

their wealth. By the 1760s and 1770s, these groups' rates of consumption had increased, with the third group owning more. The first group
owned relatively fewer handkerchiefs than the other groups.

Anne Arundel County. In Anne Arundel County, only the first and
fourth wealth groups owned handkerchiefs at the turn of the eighteenth
century, but the wealthiest group had relatively more estates with these
items listed (fig. 33). During the 1710s through the 1730s, all groups
owned handkerchiefs in proportion to their wealth. By the 1740s only
wealth group 4 had these items.

Sanitary Equipment

The use of sanitary equipment—close stools and chamber pots—is another indicator of individualization and privatization. James Deetz demonstrates that the number of chamber pots found in the archaeological
record increased through the eighteenth century.[57] The following data

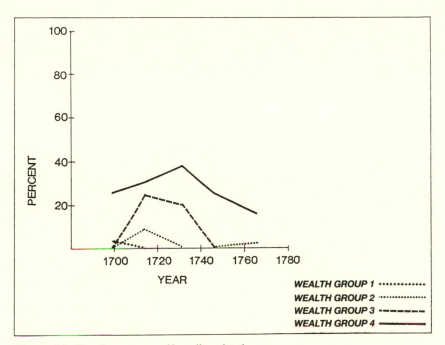

Figure 33. Rural presence of handkerchiefs.

define the acceptance of the use of these objects by wealth groups and trace how the ideas of individuality and privatization through grooming and hygiene spread through society.

Annapolis.   The first and third wealth groups owned chamber pots in early Annapolis (fig. 34). By the 1720s the wealthiest group had increased its possession of chamber pots and owned more than the other groups. By the 1740s all wealth groups acquired chamber pots in proportion to their wealth. By the 1760s and 1770s, the two wealthiest groups had proportionately more chamber pots than the lower groups, although group 3 had more estates with these items than group 4.

Close stools were found among the first and third wealth groups in early Annapolis (fig. 35). By the 1720s group 3 had more than the wealthiest group. In the 1740s group 4 owned relatively more than the third group, and by the 1760s and 1770s, all of the groups owned close stools in proportion to their wealth. Groups 1 and 2 had a relatively lower consumption rate than the wealthier groups, although neither of

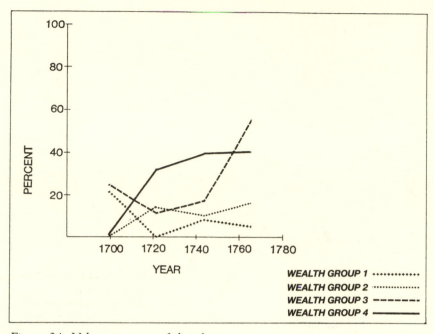

Figure 34. Urban presence of chamber pots.

the poorer groups consistently owned more than the other throughout the study period.

Anne Arundel County. Chamber pots existed in all wealth groups at the turn of the eighteenth century in Anne Arundel County (fig. 36). From the 1720s until the revolution, all groups owned these items in proportion to their wealth. The first and second wealth groups followed similar patterns of acquisition.

Close stools were present in the three wealthiest groups at the turn of the eighteenth century in Anne Arundel County (fig. 37). Throughout the study period, the groups owned close stools in relative proportion to their wealth, although there were very few in the lowest wealth groups. The relative consumption proportion peaked among the wealthiest group during the 1720s.

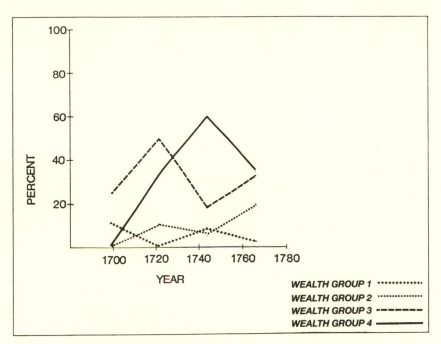

Figure 35. Urban presence of close stools.

Summary of Hygiene and Grooming-related Items

With hygiene and grooming-related items, consumption patterns tended to be less predictable in urban than in rural areas. In both cases use of the chamber pot generally increased through the eighteenth century (fig. 38). In Anne Arundel County, goods related to health and hygiene were acquired in proportion to the wealth of the purchaser more frequently than in Annapolis. The wealthiest groups lost their domination of acquisition of these items more in Annapolis than in the surrounding county. Because the consumption rates appear to have been more erratic in Annapolis, imitation between groups for possession of these items was less prevalent than in the county.

EIGHTEENTH-CENTURY CONSUMPTION PATTERNS

Annapolitans generally acquired goods related to formal dining, grooming, and hygiene during the 1710s and 1720s; consumption leveled off

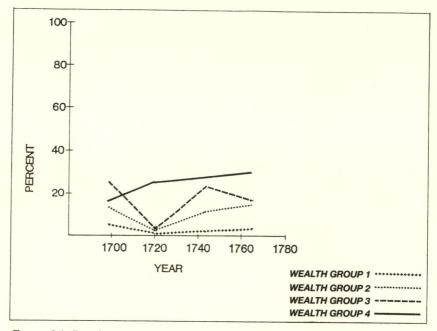

Figure 36. Rural presence of chamber pots.

or decreased in the 1730s and 1740s, then increased again from the 1750s through the 1770s.[58] This pattern was almost nonexistent in the rural population. Instead consumption of these goods generally increased through time, but in a more random fashion. In both areas the different wealth groups often acquired goods at different rates. Depending upon the item, some groups tended to imitate the consumption pattern of their immediately wealthier group. In both Annapolis and Anne Arundel County, for instance, group 1 most often echoed the consumption pattern of group 2. The frequency of consumption imitation among the rural and urban populations were similar.

Items that segment time, land, and space, were usually found in the earliest urban and rural inventories, and were predominantly in the hands of the wealthy. The elite used these goods to consciously or unconsciously internalize a new discipline. Because this new behavior was almost exclusively in the hands of the elite, a foundation was laid for an ideology that perceived this new order as natural. Driven by time discipline, this order allowed for the development of a new type of etiquette

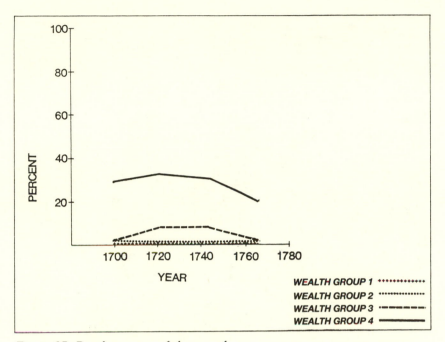

Figure 37. Rural presence of close stools.

that reinforced a stratified society. This new etiquette required an increasing amount of material culture to create and reinforce behavior.

In almost all urban and rural data sets there appears to be some relationship between the socioeconomic fluctuations in the 1720s and the
consumption of dining related goods, scientific instruments, and grooming and hygiene items. During this era of instability, the wealthy acquired more of these items than the lower wealth groups. Eleven of fourteen disciplining items examined were found in greatest proportion
among the elite in Annapolis, and thirteen of these items were found in
greatest proportion among the elite in Anne Arundel County. The relative consumption pattern in Annapolis fluctuated greatly compared to
the rural population. The consumption rate for eight of the fourteen
items found among the wealthiest urban groups falls below the consumption rate of at least one other group during the 1740s. This decrease was a product of either the consumption rates increasing more
dramatically for the lower groups or the lower groups' consumption rates

Figure 38. "The Phrensy of Baltimore Bard," drawn by Alexander Hamilton. John Work Garrett Collection, Johns Hopkins University. A bedroom sketch from the mid-eighteenth century showing a chamber pot under a man's bed.

not decreasing as sharply as that of wealth group 4. This trend was found in only two of the fourteen goods in the rural population.

During social and economic changes in the Chesapeake, and during the reorganization of wealth in Annapolis in the 1720s, a change from planter and craft wealth to merchant and capitalist wealth, material items, and associated behaviors justified the reestablished hierarchy. Ostentation was used most frequently in times of instability.[59] During the 1720s merchants built the earliest brick houses in the city of Annapolis, and the wealthy began to use items associated with the new disciplined behavior more frequently. Clearly there is some relationship between dining items, grooming and hygiene items, scientific instruments, early ostentatious architectures, and socioeconomic fluctuations and the reordering of wealth.

By the 1740s the social order was reestablished and goods related to the new discipline were no longer purchased in greater quantities among the elite. Most Chesapeake historians would agree that the elite had attained a hegemonic relationship with the lower classes, including freed and indentured servants and freed and enslaved blacks, by the 1740s.[60] This relationship did not remain unchallenged as the middle and lower groups and landless common folk questioned the gentry's domination through religious dissention. They challenged the traditional assumptions of established religions and their methods of enforcing the community order. Baptists, who were mostly poor whites and slaves, shaped a negative image of the dominant culture.[61]

In the case of the Annapolis and Anne Arundel County probate inventories, the urban elite appear to have been more seriously challenged than the rural elite in the 1740s. Some of the lower groups purchased more disciplining items than the elite, and it appears that the elite reacted by using ostentatious architecture to explicitly separate themselves. They also became concerned with privatization, as indicated by the increased use of chamber pots and close stools.

In rural areas all fourteen disciplining items were found in proportion to wealth by the 1760s and 1770s, possibly indicating that the order had been well reestablished. This proportionality is evident in less than half of the cases in the urban context, as consumption appears to have been more erratic and less controlled. Before the American Revolution in both rural and urban areas, the elite's position was compromised because they lacked the means to bargain effectively with the British authorities. Their place in the hierarchy was challenged continually by dissenting religions and lower wealth groups. As the distance between social groups narrowed, the elite created a common front with the lower classes to defy the authority of the crown. Material goods furnished symbols of this common front. Some goods, especially those related to the tea ceremony, were found in greatest proportion in the less wealthy groups in Annapolis. This democratization of some goods created a united front among the colonists. While uniting the lower groups, the elite also had to proclaim their domination. One way was to reassert their dominance in the social graces, the "natural" embellishments, which they did through, among other things, the acquisition and use of formal dining items. Another way was to make the accumulation of wealth more difficult for the lower classes. In 1763, 1771, and 1773, the Maryland assembly passed legislation that made it difficult for the middle- and lower-class planters to increase their estate values and tobacco production. Legislators also placed taxes on slave labor.[62] All of these acts were a way for the established planter, who controlled political decisions, to suppress the wealth of newcomers and of less wealthy planters. Without a large work force, wealth could not be accumulated and the established hegemonic relationship could not be threatened.

Goods are often more than an index of wealth. An analysis of probate inventory data from Annapolis and surrounding Anne Arundel County that considers the meaning of these goods is important for understanding patterns in material culture. Populations—urban or rural, wealthy or poor—often reacted differently to the various social and economic fluctuations in the eighteenth century. But in most cases, the wealthiest groups used goods that reinforced a disciplined and modern behavior to create social boundaries.

4. The Long-Term History of Etiquette

A comprehensive analysis of the meanings and uses of goods should consider material culture in the context of long-term history. Long-term history can be discussed in terms of centuries or even millennia.[1] It reveals trends and broad changes and filters out the idiosyncracies of individuals and short-term events. As with individual history and social time, long-term history can contribute to the context of meanings and uses of material goods and provide the broadest temporal view on the ways that goods actively created and reinforced behavior. Specifically, long-term history may explain how groups used goods to create and legitimize power and domination. I use etiquette books and health care guides published in Western Europe from the fifteenth through the nineteenth century to show changes in behavior and group interaction. Beginning in the late medieval era, different behaviors and different material goods increasingly reinforced group differences and came to form part of the social structure of modern industrial capitalist society. I concentrate on behavior related to dining and hygiene to demonstrate how this behavior and new material changed during times of social and hierarchical instability, especially during the development of modern discipline. These etiquette guides are essentially ethnographic descriptions of ideal behavior, which help interpret material in English colonies, including Maryland and the city of Annapolis.

From the medieval to the Renaissance tradition, human behavior be-

came more exacting and precisely measured. The trend reached an ex-
treme peak with late-nineteenth and early twentieth-century "Taylorism" in the workplace in which time-motion studies treated individuals
explicitly as machines.[2] Expectations of precision, though, extended
beyond the workplace and became part of everyday social life. This
changing behavior was not empty formality—it supported interest
groups, institutions, and structures of domination. The trend toward
precisely measured behavior may be linked in part to the heightened
consciousness of time discipline and its relationship to the development
of manners. Time consciousness in Western society is a phenomenon
related to the development of precise rules and behavior and a standardizing material culture. There is a relationship between time consciousness and the formation of a new disciplining and standardizing
etiquette that developed during the Renaissance. I will trace the formation of this new etiquette and its relationship to dining and hygiene
practices in the West. The archaeology of the house lot in Annapolis
and probate inventories from Annapolis and Anne Arundel County
provide context and meaning to the long-term history.

Probate inventories and regional historical context indicates that
time discipline and new forms of etiquette began to penetrate colonial
America by at least the early eighteenth century. Time pieces were
found in a relatively large quantity of the elite's estates during this era.
An increased use of etiquette books correspond to the new acceptance
of precisely measured time. Archaeological analyses of several households shows that even though the elite prescribed to modern discipline
by the early eighteenth century, it took almost a century for it to dissem-
inate fully into most aspects of daily life. Eighteenth-century Annapolitans purchased items that enforced individualizing behavior, such as
many different kinds of plate sizes of varying designs. Not until the early
to mid-nineteenth century did individuals acquire matched sets of
goods that required precise and regular behavior in their manufacture
and reinforced precise and regular behavior in their use.

TIME DISCIPLINE

With the creation of measured time began the development of modern
discipline, which reinforced the internalization of order and regularity.
This seemingly unnatural process became internalized and is now taken

for granted in modern-day Western society.[3] Modern discipline, therefore, did not suddenly arise during the Industrial Revolution. It began sometime in the late medieval period, first in monastic communities, which established a rhythm in daily activities, imposed particular activities, and regulated and reinforced the cycles of repetition. "For centuries," Michel Foucault asserts, "the religious orders had been masters of discipline: they were specialists of time, the great technicians of rhythm and regular activities."[4] Through the late medieval period, time, motion, and human action became more refined and in turn became more accurate, structured, and disciplined. Time became segmented and was divided into quarter hours, minutes, and eventually seconds. With the development and wide acceptance of time came an increased discipline in everyday life that was made to appear part of the natural order.[5]

Foucault notes that a disciplined behavior permits the best use of time and the correct use of the body: "Nothing is to remain idle . . . everything must be called upon to form the support of the act required." Discipline constitutes a type of law levied onto societies, groups, and the individual. Its function is to train through repeated performance. Behavior repeated several times becomes mechanical, yet fluid and natural, and allows for increased efficiency.[6]

Compared to our life today, most aspects of premodern life appear unstandardized. Most units of measurement, for instance, varied from place to place, often originating in people's physical characteristics— the English foot and the French inch (the pouce, measured from the thumb) are examples—and volume standards were derived from containers, such as the bushel, but varied from mill to mill. Even the earliest measurements of time were uneven.[7]

The cycle of nature guided people's daily routines. Work began when the sun rose and ended when the sun set. E. P. Thompson describes this notion of time as task oriented.[8] Task orientation meant that the laborer focused his or her energies upon what was necessary. Little demarcation existed between work life and social life, and the work day expanded or contracted according to the nature of the task. To people accustomed to time discipline, task orientation seems wasteful.

The pattern of work in medieval cities differed slightly from that in rural areas. The craftsman awoke at sunrise and labored as long as natural light permitted. Davis Landes notes, "Productivity, in the sense of output per unit of time, was unknown." Jacques LeGoff argues that agrarian rhythms, which were "free of haste, careless of exactitude, [and] unconcerned by productivity," created a preindustrial economy that was "sober and modest, without enormous appetite, undemanding, and incapable of quantitative efforts."[9] E. P. Thompson notes an example of task-oriented labor in the diary of a small-scale farmer-weaver in eighteenth-century England: "On a rainy day he might weave 8 1/2 or 9 yards; on October 14th he carried his finished pieces, and so wove only 4 3/4 yards; on the 23rd he 'worked out' till 3 o'clock, wove two yards before sunset, 'clouted [mended] my coat in the evening.' On December 24th 'wove 2 yards before 11 o'clock. . . .'"[10]

In medieval Europe the church dominated everyday life and people's attitudes toward time. According to Herbert Applebaum, "The Church rejected the notion of earnings from the mere passage of time, a notion that ruled out interest and credit."[11] The church claimed that eternity was incalculable and unlimited. Merchants had to reject the church's view to capitalize on market expenditures and commercial networks, because merchants relied upon predictable time measurements that could be calculated into profit.

With the development of time discipline, society gradually shifted from task orientation to a more labor-oriented, standardized, and regimented order. The perception of time changed along with the definition of work. Clocks replaced the rhythms of nature. Not only did public life become scheduled and routinized, but so did house life, social life, and the manufacturing process.

The earliest medieval clocks were built in towers and lacked the hands and dials that we now expect. Instead, timers tripped an alarm a few times per day, reminding people of specific times to perform specific tasks. They usually signaled the start of the day, the opening and closing of the market, the closing of the city gates, or curfews.[12] The earliest documented recognition of secular time in Western civilization was a regulation written in 1306 in the town of Sarum, England. It stated that "before the clock of the cathedral has struck one no one person was to purchase or cause to be purchased flesh, fish or other victuals."[13]

Public clocks and church bells were ways to regulate and standardize public life, Landes notes. "A turning hand, specifically a minute hand (the hour hand turns so slowly as to seem still), is a measure of time used, time spent, time wasted, time lost. As such it was . . . [the] key to personal achievement and productivity."[14] Through the centuries clock manufacturing became more precise, and time measurement became more exact. This precision helped to regulate many more aspects of everyday life. Bringing the clock inside helped to order home and work life. This internalization at the immediately private and personal level was a major stimulus to individualism and the advent of modern discipline. Daily routines such as eating or sleeping could now be standardized and measured. An order of everyday life became internalized and was made to appear part of the natural order.

Thompson provides an example of public clocks regulating life: In 1664 a sexton in Workingham, England rang the great bell in town for half an hour. He did this at 8:00 at night and 4:00 in the morning from 10 September to 11 March, "that as many as might live within the sound might thereby induce to a timely going to rest in the evening, and early arising in the morning to the labors and duties of their several callings, things ordinarily attended and rewarded with thrift and proficiency."[15] By the late seventeenth century, clocks had become an important aspect of daily life in England, an era during which British attained preeminence in the field of horology.[16]

The earliest measurements of time during the medieval tradition in Western Europe were based on nature, dividing the night and day into temporal hours, or twelve equal parts. Sundials and water clocks measured the length of the hour, which therefore varied from season to season. In the summer, for example, the hour was longer during the day and shorter during the night. The reverse was true for the winter months. Other forms of dividing the day replaced the temporal hour, especially with the development of the mechanical clock.[17]

As the popularity of clocks increased in the fifteenth and sixteenth centuries, the temporal hour gave way to equal hours, although the hours still varied from place to place and season to season. For example, the Italian hour system divided the day into twenty-four equal parts, beginning at dusk. The twenty-fourth hour was what is today our three o'clock. This meant that midnight was at the bottom of the dial and midday at the top, "thus simulating the apparent motion of the sun." Some parts of Europe used Babylonian hours, or twenty-four hours beginning at sunrise. In sixteenth-century southern Germany, people employed Nuremberg hours, or great clock hours, which were "reckoned according to the length of the period of daylight and were divided into two series of hours of equal length—one series for the period of daylight and another series for the period of darkness."[18] During the summer this clock had sixteen daylight hours and eight night hours. The changing amounts of daylight associated with the changing seasons necessitated the periodic adjustment of the hour lengths. Timekeepers used sophisticated tables to adjust the amount of hours for each series.[19] Whole clock hours divided the day into twenty-four equal parts, and the hour hand revolved around the clock once a day. Some whole clocks divided the day into two twelve-hour segments, but there was still only one revolution of the hour hand every twenty-four hours. This gave way to small clock hours, or French hours. Here the clock was numbered from one to twelve; thus the hour hand had to revolve twice for every twenty-four hours. Most of Europe adopted this system in the seventeenth century, and it became the standard method of time keeping, one that we still use today.[20]

By the sixteenth century, the royal court and, later, the rising class of bourgeois and wealthy merchants had begun to demand ownership of time-measuring devices. During the sixteenth and seventeenth centuries, artisans created many clocks as "universe[s] in miniature," with their "movement supplemented with complicated globes and astrolabic dials to demonstrate astronomical phenomena, with the time telling function reduced to a secondary roll." Rachel Doggett argues that people considered clocks status symbols; the wealthy even posed for portraits with them.[21] But status doesn't tell the whole story. Along with Leone, I suspect that this instrument was not only a reflection of wealth but also had other symbolic meanings.[22] Time-keeping devices became part of a naturalizing process that demonstrated how the elite had control over the systematic measurement of time. The use of early clocks as "universe[s] in miniature" suggests the ability of a select few who owned these devices to control nature by making observations more regular, predictable, and replicable, and by producing regulated behavior. Claiming that their new behavior was fixed in natural law legitimized their control over time and over others. Thompson's research notes the continued control over time in late eighteenth-century England through taxes on all watches, a practice that kept time-keeping devices in the hands of a few wealthy people.[23]

An example of the internalization of time discipline comes from Lord Chesterfield in the eighteenth century. In a letter to his bastard son, who was touring Europe, Chesterfield repeatedly emphasized the importance of time discipline. He wrote, "I recommend you take care of the minutes; for the hours will take care of themselves. I am very sure, that many people lose two or three hours every day, by not taking care of the minutes. Never think any portion of time whatsoever too short to be employed; something or other may always be done in it." In another letter he lectured, "Instead of sitting and yawning . . . take up a book, though even so trifling a one, even down to a jest-book, it is still better than doing nothing."[24] He also wrote:

> I knew a gentle man, who was so good a manager of his time, that he would not even lose that small portion of it, which the calls of nature obliged him to pass in the necessary-house; but gradually went through all Latin Poets, in those moments. He bought, for example, a common edition of Horace, of which he tore off gradually a couple pages, carried them with him to the necessary place, read them first, and then sent them down as a sacrifice to Cloacina: this was so much time fairly gained; and I recommend to you to follow his example.[25]

The new outlook on time discipline not only regulated people's lives but stressed the idea of time efficiency, thus laying the groundwork for internalization. In probate inventories from Annapolis and Anne Arundel County, clocks were found predominantly in the estates of the wealthy, although by the end of the eighteenth century, ownership had increased among the lower wealth groups. Regimentation and precise movement began to become a part of every action and movement in life's daily routines. Primary sources from the Chesapeake region indicate that along with increased use of time came a new discipline in music, landscape, and etiquette.

THE DEVELOPMENT OF COURTESY AND CIVILITY

The formation of a new standardizing behavior in Western culture can be traced through etiquette books, as they provide the prescriptions for changing cultural behavior. Medieval behavior guides were known as courtesy books. The 1952 edition of *The Middle English Dictionary* describes "courtesy" as "the complex of courtly ideals; chivalry, chivalrous conduct, also contextually of these ideals as courtly love, benevolence, kindness, cheerfulness." The word probably originated in the court or court life, where members tried to win the favor of great lords and princes. Courtesy, or increasingly modern behavior for "polite" society, developed during the late Middle Ages. These codes of manners became formulated to regulate behavior and reinforce the hierarchy as being part of the natural order. Extolled in poetry during the Middle Ages, courtesy involved the regulation of outward behavior, such as speech (forms of address and greeting), conduct (action), and thought, and became a code of values. Courtesy consisted of a list of behaviors, and those who did not conform were compared to ill-mannered lowly creatures or peasants.

Because literacy was popular among the elite, the nobility wrote courtesy books for their peers, especially in the last half of the Middle Ages.[26] Education was not available to the lower class because fees were high.[27] This meant that only the elite were able to learn the rules of polite society, which enabled them, through different behavior, to separate themselves from the lower classes.

The development of courtesy in England may be traced in part to an increased need for social regulation initiated by the surge in castle building between 1154 and 1216.[28] Castles were an effective and essential part of an authoritative presence. Henry II, for example, tried to use them to enforce his authority. Castles, under the rule of a baron or regal representative, housed different groups of people in close proximity, necessitating a workable hierarchy. Standards for different groups were adopted to regulate and create a hierarchy for military and social life.[29]

Castles became the center of social life in England during the fourteenth and fifteenth centuries. They transformed from functional garrisons to courtly centers. Parents often boarded young nobles in castles to be educated and to learn courtesy and noble customs. In 1502 Francesco Capello, the Venetian ambassador to England, claimed that this process was a national tradition that lacked affection.[30]

Table manners were a popular topic in medieval courtesy books. Authors devoted much time to this subject because eating had come to be considered one of the most important social functions. It created a break from the work routine and often provided the setting for interactions among larger groups of people, either family or community.[31]

One of the earliest extant courtesy books is *Disciplina Clericals* by Pertus Alfonis, which first appeared in Latin during the early twelfth century. By the early thirteenth century, courtesy books were being written in European vernaculars, although English translations did not appear much before the fifteenth century. This lag in the use of English was mostly because the upper classes spoke French until this time.[32]

John Russell's *Boke of Nurture,* one of the earliest and most popular English courtesy books, was published about the middle of the fifteenth century.[33] Russell listed the duties a servant must perform for his master, including setting the table; serving bread, meat, and wine; and removing the tablecloth. Also included were directions for the preparation of the lord's bed chamber.

In 1478 the *Black Book of Edward IV* proposed ways to train the ideal courtier in the liberal arts, a Renaissance ideal. The book was geared toward young nobles, so that they might

> learne them to ride cleanly and surely, to drawe them also to justes, to lerne them were theyre harneys; to have all curtesy in wordes, dedes and degrees, dilygently to keepe them in rules of goynges and sittiges, after they honour. Moreover to teach them sondry languages and other lernynges vertuous, to herping, to pype, sing, dance, and with other honest and temperate behauling and pacience; and to keepe dayly and wykley with thees children dew convenitz, with correcions in theyre chambers according to such gentlemen; and eche of them to be used to that thinges of vertue that he shal be most apt to learn, with remembraunce dayly of Goddes servyce accustomed.[34]

Thus young nobles learned liberal arts as well as courtesy for daily interaction. This education provided the basis for what nobles needed in their adult life as the social elite.

After the Wars of the Roses, membership in the old nobility dwindled and the new aristocracy grew in numbers and strength. Henry VIII endorsed education and soon thereafter this institution became acceptable among the aristocracy, thus creating a favorable environment for Renaissance ideas. With the development of a new socially competitive upper class, the questions of uniform proper behavior became acute. The establishment of a new hierarchy in England may also explain the acceptance of a new modern behavior. This new hierarchy rejected the feudal order and based itself on mercantile capitalism. As the ancien régime lost power in Enlightenment England, material goods and behavior became associated with the new rich. This new system used modern behavior to reinforce social asymmetry and separate the new mercantile elite from both the feudal-based ancien régime and the lower classes.

With the expressions of the Renaissance, the concept of civility replaced the old order of medieval courtesy. Civility created new relationships with more disciplined human behavior. Moreover, the whole system of behavior in society concerned the new authors of etiquette books. De Callieres, a Renaissance author of an etiquette book, expressed the atmosphere of the Renaissance ideal: "It seemed to me that to acquire what is called the science of the world one must first apply oneself to knowing men as they are in general, and then to gain particular knowledge of those with whom we have to live, that is to say, knowledge of their inclinations and their good and bad opinions, of their virtues and their faults."[35] Authors generally refrained from attaching epithets to people using impolite behavior. They suggested that unpleasant behavior should be pointed out only when one could take a friend aside to tell him or her of his impolite behavior.

The Book of the Courtier by Baldassare Castiglione, originally published in Italian in 1528, was translated into English by Thomas Hoby in 1561.[36] This book was the most popular courtesy book published for several centuries. Rather than list proper behaviors like many of the earlier guides, it provided an account of four evenings of conversation at the court of Urbino, Italy. The conversations defined a universal model of the perfect courtier, who should be urbane, attractive, a sportsman, an accomplished conversationalist, versatile in art, well read, and well educated, among other things. Castiglione went beyond mere description; he also engaged in the "analysis of behavioral situations and the moral problems they posed."[37] This book served for centuries as the guide to the Renaissance ideal of behavior and proper conduct. Western nations reprinted it numerous times, and many authors between the sixteenth and eighteenth centuries copied its style and ideas.

Another, even longer lasting, work on polite behavior was *Il Galateo: or A Treatise on Politeness and Delicacy of Manners,* written by Giovanni della Casa in 1558.[38] This book's popularity was such that it was republished as late as 1811. The contents addressed manners by specific categories, an arrangement that became a trend in courtesy books.[39] This segmentation of the courtesy book may also be an indication of how life was no longer treated as a whole, but rather divided into particular categories of behavior for different social circumstances. The separate topics in Castiglione's book include proper dress, table manners, and polite conversation—even how to blow one's nose. Renaissance ideals were contrasted to unacceptable behaviors, as illustrated in this passage: "Now what shall we think this Bishop, his modest and honest company about him would say, if they saw these whom wee see other while, (like swyne w[ith] their snouts in the wash, all begroined) never lyft up their heads nor look up, much less keepe their hands from the meate, and w[ith] both their cheeks blowne (as if they should sound a trumpet or blowe the fyer) not eat but ravon. . . ."[40]

Desiderius Erasmus also wrote on matters of hygiene and manners, publishing *De Civilitate Morum Puerilium* (On Civility in Children) in 1526. This book, later translated into French, was reprinted more than thirty times within the first six years of publication, thirteen times in the late eighteenth century, and 130 times in all. Although not a radical departure from the premodern tradition, Erasmus's work appears to be a transition between the old and new orders. His descriptions, covering a range of behaviors from table manners to grooming and hygiene, demonstrate the transition of habits as they became more exacting, segmented, and disciplined.

Stefano Guazzo's work, *The Civile Conversation*, was first translated into English in 1581.[41] The book characterized dialogues in a way similar to Castiglione's and many other Renaissance works. Guazzo dictated rules for the polished gentleman just as Castiglione had sought to define the ideal courtier. The importance of Guazzo's work is that it addressed more aspects of daily life than did Castiglione's or della Casa's, including marriage and choosing a wife. He stated that a wise man chooses with his head, not his heart. And he believed that servants should be treated well if one expected them to be faithful.

With the emergence of a gentry class, more behavioral guides were being written for gentlemen. In 1568 John Ball wrote *Instruction of a Gentleman*, claiming that three types of gentlemen existed: the gentle gentle, the gentle ungentle, and the ungentle gentle. The "gentle gentle and the gentle ungentle were perenials, blooming in the well rooted growths of the entrenched gentry. The ungentle gentle could be likened to animals soon, in the true to become perenials."[42] In 1583 Sir Thomas Smith further elaborated on the requirements and characteristics of a gentleman: "For whosoever studieth in the Lawes of the Realme, who studieth in the Universities, who professeth liberal Sciences; and to be short, who can live idly and without manual labor, and will beare the part, change, and countenance of a Gentleman he shall be called Mas-

ter, for that is the Title which men give to Esquires and other Gentlemen."[43]

Other literature, such as *Ludus Literaturius; or The Grammar School by
John Brinsley* written in 1612 and Henry Peachman's *The Complete Gentleman* written in 1622, stressed the importance of a proper upbringing.
Brinsley believed in teaching youth how they ought to behave in all
companies, times, and places. Promptness, or time discipline, became
an important issue, as did polite conversation. Peachman also encouraged a liberal education. He stated that "a gentleman, should know his
universe and his nation" and believed that this training should come
early in life.[44]

Other popular civility books of the seventeenth century include
Richard Brathwaite's *The English Gentleman,* published in 1630, and
Richard Allestree's *The Gentleman's Calling,* originally published in
1660. These books further reinforced the idea of an ordered behavior
that gentlemen should undertake and reiterated the Renaissance ideal
of a liberal education and the ability to compete in sports.[45]

During the seventeenth century, and particularly by the reign of
Louis XIV, France became the acknowledged leader in matters of civility. French authors added to the rules set forth by della Casa. Antoine
de Courtin wrote one of the more popular French seventeenth-century
books, titled *Nouveau Traité de la Civilité que se pratique en France, parmi
les honnestes gens* (The Rules of Civility; or Certain Ways of Deportment
Observed in France, Amongst All Persons of Quality).[46] The twenty-
four chapters deal with topics such as manners in the presence of others,
manners in church, the elegances of conversation, table manners, and
letter writing. The chapter on letter writing, the longest in the book,
prescribes rules for correct salutations, conclusions, size of paper, and
space. The section on table manners dictates rules of offering and ac-
cepting wine, proper table conversation, and some of the earliest evidence for a well-defined, segmented dinner.

By the late seventeenth century, the ideas prescribed in contempor-
ary rules of behavior found in civility books had not thoroughly penetrated the upper echelon in England. This is also true of the Chesapeake. The aristocracy there lacked rigid forms of civility, as evidenced
by the absence of material goods often associated with modern discipline from probate inventories. An example of the lack of Western civility can be seen in the behavior of the Restoration poet Sir Charles

Sedley, who "defecated into the street from a balcony while drunk and thus made history of a sort by establishing what is apparently the first recorded case of indecent exposure as a common law offensive. Upon receiving a lenient sentence of one week in jail and a fine of '2000 marks,' Sedley declared he believed himself to be 'the first man that paid for shiting.'"[47]

During the early decades of the eighteenth century, the English were still not considered to be a society of high decorum governed by precise rules of behavior. The "eighteenth century began with the English as ill-behaved as ever," declares Esther Aresty, "particularly those who comprised the froth, often indistinguishable from the dregs." Queen Anne failed to inspire English polite behavior when she took the throne in 1702, and George I despised court life and lacked the material goods and social behavior often found in the French court. George II also did little to encourage etiquette. It appears that etiquette books were being read by the growing merchant class and that several generations passed before the crown participated fully in the new order of civility, beginning with the reign of George III.[48]

By the end of the first half of the eighteenth century, the English court produced profound alterations to the rules related to civility. Behavior became more intricate and precise and changed beyond recognition what it had been in the seventeenth century. Aresty notes that the increasing preciseness of rules was an attempt by members of the upper class to prevent the upward mobility of the lower classes, to which end they "evolved a code of manners—regulations really—modeled on those that governed court life, but composed also of numerous private ceremonials observed in certain cliques and sets. Each ceremonial was an invisible bar against intruders and by the end of the century these had been codified into rules of etiquette."[49]

Western society began to publish more courtesy books with the middle class in mind in the eighteenth century. These works include Adam Petrie's *Rules of Good Deportment* in 1720, Sir John Barnard's *A Present for an Apprentice: or, A Sure Guide to Gain Both Esteem and Estate with Rules for his Conduct to his Master and in the World* in 1741, and James Burgh's *The Art of Speaking*, published in 1758.[50] This orientation toward the middle class was an attempt to regiment, discipline, and order the behavior of the majority of the population.

New and increasingly disciplined behavior served to segment populations living in the same area and also to separate the urban from the rural populations. Joseph Addison's description of the contrasts between early eighteenth-century Englishmen in the city and country illustrates the explicit differences: "If we look on the People of the Mode of the Country, we find in them the manners of the last Age. They have no sooner fetched themselves up to the Fashion of the Polite World, but the Town has dropped off them, and are nearer to the first State of Nature than to those Refinements which formerly reigned in the Court, and still prevailed in the Country."[51]

By the middle of the eighteenth century, precise and highly structured ideals of behavior replaced the broad, general rules of the civility books. Lord Chesterfield, who belonged to one of the leading aristocratic families in England, contributed significantly to this. Chesterfield had visited the most important courts in Europe, including that of Louis XIV, known for its decorum and impeccable manners. He played a major role in "modernizing" English politics and government, and in 1752 introduced to England the Georgian calendar, which the rest of Europe had used since the fifteenth century.[52]

Many consider Lord Chesterfield's volume of letters, originally published in 1776, the most influential English work of its time. This volume consisted of a collection of letters to his son, who was touring Europe. Throughout this work he emphasized the ideas of proper dress, time discipline, and polite conversation. His ideals concerned not only common civility but also outstanding manners and distinguished politeness. Chesterfield wrote that "good breeding . . . does not consist in low bows and formal ceremony; but in an easy, civil and respectful behavior."[53]

When George III became monarch in 1760, the new modern discipline swept into most English households. In contrast to George I and George II, the new reigning king and his court exhibited the "polite behavior" found in the high courts of France. With the ever-increasing power and influence of the entrepreneurial class, "etiquette became the banner word of the social side of the Industrial Revolution and dominated the lives of all socially ambitious families."[54] As noted previously, industrial goods associated with precise regimentation of manufacturing became increasingly important in the everyday lives of Annapolitans by the late eighteenth and early nineteenth centuries. Ceramic deposits from several Annapolitan sites indicate the penetration of industrial culture to an increasing number of people.

The above information on rule making in Western Europe was gleaned from a wide span of time and a wide range of countries. Renaissance Italy was the center of high culture from approximately the fourteenth to seventeenth centuries, France from the last half of the seventeenth century and the first half of the eighteenth, and England from the last half of the eighteenth century. Most of the new literature on the changing and increasingly precise rules of civility was written in the language of the center of high culture. The new aristocracy translated the most popular civility books into English and used them as behavioral guides. These behavioral guides written in foreign languages in the late seventeenth century were translated into English more rapidly than the books of the fifteenth and sixteenth centuries had been. For example, although the English took thirty-three years to translate Castiglione's *The Book of the Courtier,* originally published in Italian in 1528, de Courtin had his *Nouveau Traité de la Civilité* published in France in 1670 and translated into English only one year later. The elite assimilated and internalized these books.

Etiquette books were found in the libraries of the Annapolis elite as early as the 1720s. Associated with these etiquette books were new types of material goods, such as leisurely dining items, sets of objects, and grooming-related objects. No etiquette books appear in the early Anne Arundel County inventories. It was the new and growing merchant and professional classes in Annapolis, comprised of people such as Amos Garret, Thomas Bladen, and Thomas Bordley, that first consumed items associated with modern discipline.

Manners, ways of behavior, and material goods often support structures of domination. During the rise of a new aristocracy in England, the elite manipulated new rules and behavior to support the new hierarchical order. Renaissance behaviors changed drastically compared to those of the medieval court. The medieval courtier's behavior seemed crude and unmentionable even in Renaissance children's etiquette books. Changing behaviors and material cultures associated with a formal and segmented dining, and objects associated with the development of personal appearance and hygiene, provide a context for the uses of meanings associated with these objects.

Behavior Associated with Formal and Segmenting Dining

Data were collected from a variety of behavioral guides dating from the fifteenth through the eighteenth centuries. Presented are the rules and social contexts of the uses of specific goods. This information reveals a general trend toward regimentation, segmentation, and individualization, all components of a modern discipline, from the medieval to Renaissance traditions. Rules associated with dining were probably the first to become standardized, because this daily activity was considered to be one of the most important in court society.

Although not everyone read etiquette books, the guides serve as general measurements of accepted codes of behavior. Socialization through teaching and the use of everyday material goods played a major role in learning the rules of "proper conduct." Useful for this analysis is Bourdieu's concept of *habitus*, discussed earlier, which recognizes how people read objects' meanings to provide an understanding of social and material strategies of power. It is the seemingly trivial, everyday objects that often express meaning in the everyday world and contain symbolic power. It is the ability to read material goods and social circumstances that determines how one should act.

Some of the most basic modern-day behaviors associated with eating were awkward in the premodern tradition but seen in the Renaissance as being natural and therefore unchallengeable. Rules became more standardized and exacting throughout the Renaissance. Premodern dining customs differed greatly from those of today. Until the sixteenth century, a table setting usually consisted of knives, plates, and goblets. People helped themselves from a communal dish, often using hands to take solids. Diners frequently drank liquids from ladles or spoons and sometimes used a communal glass. There were no special implements for different foods; rather, diners used the same knife or spoon for all foods. People drank soups and sauces from plates and dishes lifted to the mouth. It was not uncommon to have two or more diners eating from the same plate or trencher.[55]

Medieval courtesy tended to be concerned with external behavior. Behavioral guides often presented a list of permitted and prohibited behaviors. An example of this can be found in the *Boke of Nurture:*

> And sup not loud of thy pottage, no time in all thy life.
> Dip not thy meat in the salt cellar, but take it with a knife.

> When thou hast eaten thy pottage, do as I shall thee wish;
> Wipe clean thy spoon and leave it not in thy dish,
> Lay it down before thy trencher, there of be not afraid;
> And take heed who taketh it up, lest it be conveyed [stolen].[56]

In an anonymous manuscript, the *Babees Book,* the discipliner cautions, "Cut your bread with your knife and break it not. Lay a clean trencher before you, and when your pottage is brought, take your spoon and eat quietly; and do not leave your spoon in the dish, I pray you. . . . Do not hang your head over your dish, or in anywise drink with a full mouth. Keep from picking your nose, your teeth, your nails at mealtime—so we are taught." The concern for hygiene in communal drinking was also mentioned: "When ye shall drink, wipe your mouth clean with a cloth, and your hands also, so that you shall not in any way soil the cup, for then shall none of your companions be loth to drink with you."[57]

And in *Stans Puen In Mensan* (The Boy Standing at the Table): "Pare clean thy nails, and wash thy hands also, / Before thy meat and when thou dost arise." Later in the book, the author notes, "It is not decent to poke your fingers into your ears or eyes, as some people do, or to pick your nose while eating. These three habits are bad."[58] In Russell's *Boke of Nurture,* he noted that one should be sure that "you have enough napkins, spoons and cups for your lord's table." Also, explicit instructions were given on how to fold a napkin. Rules for table decorum stated: "Do not have the habit of squirting or spouting with your mouth, or gape, or yawn, or point. And do not lick a dish with your tongue to get out dust."[59]

In general, premodern manners were prohibitions rather than prescriptions. They included directions to wash the hands, and prohibitions against dipping food in the salt cellar and cleaning teeth with a knife. Medieval manners prohibited spitting over the table and returning pieces of food that were in the mouth to the communal dish. Behavioral guide books also emphasized wiping lips and restraining gluttony. As these ideas became internalized, or perceived as "natural," greater regimentation and complexity relating to behavior and objects were introduced. This served to create greater formality in eating. The increased regimentation and exactness, specifically in dining, became learned as though they were natural, or part of the laws of nature.

By the time of Erasmus's *De Civilitate Morum Puerilium* in 1530, the premodern tradition of courtesy among the elite was near its end. Regarding behavior at the table, Erasmus required that one should remove one's hat in the presence of socially superior people. He explained that the knife and goblet should be clean and placed to the right, whereas the bread should be placed to the left. Erasmus claimed, "Some people put their hands in the dishes the moment they have sat down. Wolves do that. . . . If you are offered something liquid, taste it and return the spoon, but first wipe it on your serviette. To lick greasy fingers or to wipe them on your coat is impolite. It is better to use the tablecloth or the serviette."[60]

Napkin use became popular for those participating in courteous behavior during the late premodern tradition. Often diners used the nearest available object, such as a tablecloth or napkin, to clean one's hands or to blow one's nose. The napkin was originally for cleaning hands after a meal. With the introduction of the fork, hands did not get dirty as easily, thus the napkin lost its functional use and became an ornament and object of ceremony. Charles II created an "Officer of the Mouth," and left intricate instructions on twenty-six different methods for folding napkins.[61] During the reign of George III, napkins and tablecloths were no longer considered fashionable. Instead finger bowls and dessert doilies were provided for cleaning the fingers.

With the introduction of the fork into Western culture, the eating process became increasingly segmented and individualized. The earliest documented use of the fork was in Venice, when a Doge married a Greek princess in the early eleventh century. She clearly had used the fork in Byzantium, her homeland, but in Venice its use was considered excessive and vain and was frowned upon by the church, which called upon God to punish her. Shortly afterward she became deathly ill with the plague, as did a large percentage of the population. Saint Bonaventure declared her illness a punishment from God.[62]

The first documentation of the fork being used in England was in 1601 by Thomas Coryate, a squire of Odcombe in the county of Somerset. Returning from his grand tour of Europe, he described a new way of eating that he had found in Italy. He explained that the hands should not touch the food during the eating process, because the fork now held the meat while cutting and bringing food to the mouth. This innovation was not well received as he was "rebuked from the pulpit for his impiety."[63] Coryate's wrote:

The Italian and also most strangers that are commorant in Italy, doe alwaise at their meales use a little forke when they cut their meat. For while with their knife which they hold in one hand they cut the meate out of the dish, they fasten their fork which they hold in their other hand upon the same dish, so that whatsoever he be that sitting in the company of any others at meale, should unadvisedly touch the dish of meate with his fingers from which all the table do cut, he will give occasion of offence unto the company, as having transgressed the lawes of good manners, in so much that for his error he shall be at least browbeaten, if not reprehended in wordes. This form of feeding is generally used in all places of Italy, their forkes being for the most part made of yron or steele, and some of silver, but those are used only by Gentlemen. The reason of this their curiosity is, because the Italian cannot by any means indure to have his dish touched with fingers, seeing all mens fingers are not alike cleane. Hereupon I myself thought good to imitate the Italian fashion by this forked cutting of meate, not only while I was in Italy but also in Germany and often times in England since I came home.[64]

The earliest known surviving fork in England, marked by an unknown London maker, is dated "1632/3" on the handle and includes the crests of two families. This is the same year that marriage united these two families, and the fork and design symbolized this event.[65] This suggests that this implement and its associated behavior penetrated to at least a portion of the upper class within several decades of its introduction. In this case it was probably considered a prestigious item and was therefore used as a symbol in a rite of passage.

With the introduction of the fork in France, cleanliness, especially of the hands, became mandatory. Increasing demand for cleanliness can be found in Antoine de Courtin's *Nouveau Traité de la Civilité*:

It is very impolite to touch anything greasy, a sauce or syrup, etc., with your fingers, apart from the fact that it obliges you to commit two or three more improper acts. One is to wipe your hands frequently on your serviette and to soil it like a kitch cloth, so that those who see you wipe your mouth with it feel nauseated. Another is to wipe your fingers on your bread, which again is very improper. The third is to lick them, which is the height of impropriety.[66]

The condemnation of the premodern tradition in late seventeenth-century France was further reinforced by de Courtin. He claimed: "Formerly one was permitted . . . to dip one's bread into the sauce, provided only that one had not already bitten it. Nowadays that would be a kind of rusticity. Formerly one was allowed to take from one's mouth what one could not eat and drop it on the floor, provided it was done skillfully. Now that would be very disgusting."[67] The meal became increasingly segmented. The gentry frowned upon the sharing of utensils. No longer was a person able to use his spoon to take food from the serving dish. De Courtin wrote a manners guide for the use by a friend, and only other "well bred people." He wrote from the court society of Louis XIV and therefore was popular among the upper class. He stated, "And even, if you are at the table of very refined people, it is not enough to wipe your spoon; you should not use it but ask for another. Also, in many places, spoons are brought in with the dishes, and these serve only for taking soup and sauce."[68]

Braudel explains that *Les Délices de la Campagne* (The Pleasure of the Countryside), written by Nicholas de Bonnefons in 1654, is characteristic of the changing formalization and segmentation found among the upper class regarding etiquette.[69] Bonnefons claimed that place settings should be spaced the distance of one chair's width. The author prescribed the number of courses to be served, the changing of plates after each course, and the replacement of napkins after every two courses. Bonnefons also expresses the importance of variety and claims, "Nothing pleases people more than diversity, and the French especially have particular inclination towards it. That is why you should try as much as you can to diversify what you are preparing and make them distinct in both taste and appearance."[70]

In 1691 Massialot, in *Le Cuisinier Roial et Bourgeous*, described which dishes should be served as entrées and which as hors d'oeuvres. He even specified how a dinner for twelve should be laid out. It was to consist of three services, each with a central dish, four lesser dishes, and four hors d'oeuvres. The following is a description of the three services.

First service:
—two soups (one of pigeon, one of chicken and vegetables).
—two entrees (a hot partridge pie and poularde aux truffess).
—grande entrées—two sorts of roast beefs and four hors d'oeuvres (paupetons de pigeon, braised quails, chicken stuffed with mushrooms, partridge with sauce espagnole).
Second service:
—two roasts (turkey, partridge, chicken, lamb).

—four entrenets (cream tart, two sorts of ham).
—four hors d'oeuvres (including salad).
Third service:
—fruit and confectionery. [71]

Publishers frequently reissued Massialot's book, and in 1712 and in 1730 he wrote a second and third volume.

An anonymous work, *Civilité Française* published in 1714, further reinforced the idea of segmentation and the use of a new object, the fork, to regiment and create a new discipline. The manuscript notes: "It is against propriety to give people meat to smell, and you should under no circumstances put meat back into the common dish if you have smelled it yourself. If you take meat from a common dish, do not choose the best pieces. Cut with the knife, holding still the piece of meat in the dish with the fork, which you will use to put it on your plate the piece you have cut off; do not therefore, take the meat with your hand." [72]

In 1729 La Salle also described the changing disciplined and segmented dinner. He prescribed the use of three different utensils for the table, a plate instead of a trencher, and a napkin. La Salle defined the rules associated with the knife, the spoon, and the fork. The following is La Salle's description of the table and the rules for specific utensils:

> At the table you should use a serviette, a plate, a knife, a spoon, and a fork. It would be entirely contrary to propriety to be without any of these things while eating.
>
> It is for the person of highest rank in the company to unfold his serviette first, and the others should wait until he has done so before unfolding theirs.
>
> It is improper to use the serviette to wipe your face; it is far more so to rub your teeth with it, and it would be one of the grossest offenses against civility to use it to blow your nose. . . . The use you may and must make of the serviette when at the table is for wiping your mouth, lips, and fingers when they are greasy, wiping the knife before cutting bread, and cleaning the spoon and fork after using them.
>
> When the fingers are very greasy, wipe them first on a piece of bread which should be then left on the plate, before cleaning them on the serviette, in order not to soil it too much.
>
> When the plate is dirty, you should be sure not to scrape it with the spoon or fork to clean it, or to clean your plate or the bottom of any dish with your fingers; that is very impolite. Either they should not be touched

or, if you have the opportunity of exchanging them, you should ask for another.

It is also very impolite to put a piece of bread into your mouth while holding the knife in your hand; it is even more so to do this with the point of the knife.

It is against propriety to hold the fork or spoon with the whole hand, like a stick; you should always hold them between your fingers.

You should not use your fork to lift liquids to the mouth. . . . It is the spoon that is intended for such uses.

It is polite always to use the fork to put meat into your mouth, for propriety does not permit the touching of anything greasy with the fingers.

In 1774 La Salle's rules for dining were still being reprinted, but in a more direct tone. In a revised edition he stated, "The spoon is intended for liquids, and the fork for solid meats."[73]

Summary

There are some basic trends that can be observed in these courtesy and civility books. The most obvious is the change from a communal to an individual lifestyle. Erasmus's and Calviac's works in the sixteenth century noted a change in medieval courtesy at the dinner table.[74] They arranged the table with bread, glass, and knife, but the fork was only used for lifting food from a common dish. The napkin and handkerchief, also symbols of transition to a modern discipline, appeared to be optional rather than necessary. If a person owned a handkerchief, it was to be used rather than the tablecloth to clean the fingers. If a napkin was present, Erasmus said that it should be placed over the shoulder. "One hundred and fifty years later," asserts Norbert Elias, "both napkins and handkerchiefs are, like the fork, more or less indispensable utensils in the courtly class."[75]

By the 1670s dining among King Louis XIV's court and the gentry in France had become very regimented and segmented, and precise rules for the use of eating implements had appeared. These segmenting rules separated the dinner and the behavior around the table into its many parts. People no longer ate soup out of a common dish, but poured it into their own dish. Most of the gentry no longer wiped their spoons after dipping them into common bowls. One was no longer permitted to dip a spoon into the common dish, but told to ask for a clean one. It appears that everyone had his or her own plate and spoon. The soup service had its own implement, probably a dipper, for a specialized container or a tureen. Elias notes that "eating had acquired a new style corresponding to the new necessities of social life."[76]

Also found in early behavioral guides was the use of similes in phrases denoting undesirable behavior, such as "like a pig," "like wolves," and "like peasants." These similes indicate that guide writers considered civility in late medieval times to be a naturally human phenomenon among the elite. Contrary behavior was likened to subhuman behavior (i.e., animals and peasants). The way some of these guides were written, however, indicates that this new ordered behavior was not internalized, as it had to be stated as rules and reinforced. Training and repeated performance eventually made this behavior mechanical yet fluid, and "natural," allowing for an increased efficiency of behavior.[77]

These developing and seemingly natural processes increasingly segmented and standardized this new social behavior in dining. Elias writes:

> Nothing in table manners is self-evident or the product, as it were, of a "natural" feeling of delicacy. The spoon, fork and napkin are not invented by individuals as technical implements with obvious purposes and clear direction for use. Over centuries, indirect social intercourse and use, the functions are gradually defined, their forms sought and consolidated. Each custom in the changing ritual, however minute, establishes itself infinitely slowly, even forms of behavior that to us seem quite elementary or simply "reasonable," such as the custom of taking liquids only with the spoon. Every movement of the hand—for example, the way in which one holds and moves knife, spoon, or fork—is standardized only step by step.[78]

Dining rules became more precise from the late medieval times through the Renaissance, so that by the Renaissance, the medieval courtier's behavior seemed crude. With this changing behavior came an increase in the forms of material culture, prescribed with a set of increasingly complex rules to actively produce a stratified society. Individual drinking vessels and plates replaced shared goblets and trenchers. Several forks, knives, and spoons were added to the single knife and, possibly, ladle at the table. Elaborate meals created a need for formal dining items.

Etiquette writers had begun to write for the middle classes by the mid-eighteenth century in England, although it was not until the reign of George III that the court fully prescribed to civility. Apparently, instead of courtesy trickling down from the courts to the gentry and middle classes, the court of George III emulated the growing and powerful mercantile class.

The patterns of growth of new and varying material goods related to dining in Annapolis and Anne Arundel County were similar, in some ways, to that found among the mercantile classes Western Europe. The types of material goods, such as sets of dining items and grooming-related objects, that indicate a form of individuality are found in both regions. The difference is that these prescribed behaviors found in courtesy books do not appear in the Chesapeake until about the 1710s and 1720s. The later introduction of this new behavior may be explained in part by poor transportation. But other explanations are possible and more comprehensive. The introduction of modern discipline in the Chesapeake, based on the presence of etiquette books and new disciplining material goods, appeared suddenly during a time of social and economic instability. The elite used this new material culture and modern discipline to reaffirm their position in the hierarchy. Primary references indicate that citizens of the region believed this behavior to be embedded in human nature.

Behavior Associated with Hygiene and Personal Appearance

Aspects of individuality also conveyed through etiquette books regard appearance, clothing, and oral hygiene. During premodern times, personal appearance and hygiene and care for the human body were not considered important. The church taught that it was sinful to gaze at another person. Grooming or care for the body made a person attractive and was therefore frowned upon. Thus Western European premodern society considered hygiene unnecessary.[79]

During the Renaissance there was a shift from a family and community-oriented society to an individual-oriented society.[80] With this new awareness of the person, some aspects of creating individuality, such as outward appearance, hygiene, and a new ordered behavior, became increasingly prominent in the West.

The handkerchief, invented in Renaissance Italy, became a prestigious item. Prior to the introduction of the handkerchief, noses usually were blown on a sleeve, coat, or the fingers. In medieval Europe, Bonvesin de la Riva wrote, "When you blow your nose or cough, turn around so that nothing falls on the table."[81] Later in the fifteenth century, a common rule was not to blow one's nose with the same hand used to hold one's meat.[82] This rule implies the increased concern for keeping your eating hand free of unsightly substances.

The handkerchief developed individuality by emphasizing a clean outward appearance. With this came a new set of rules to follow, to standardize the behavior of all those who could afford to own and use a handkerchief. Della Casa noted that "you should not offer your handkerchief to anyone unless it has been freshly washed."[83] He also noted, "And when thou hast blown thy nose, use not to open thy handkerchief, to glare upon thy snot, as if you hadst pearles and rubies fallen from your braynes."[84] Later, Richard Weste wrote:

> Nor imitate with Socrates
>   to wipe thy snivelled nose
> upon thy cap, as he would do
>   nor yet upon thy clothes.
> But keep it clean with handkerchief
>   provided for the same. . . .[85]

La Salle discussed the growing awareness of cleanliness and appearance associated with the creation of disciplined behavior. He wrote, "It is vile to wipe your nose with your bare hand, or to blow it on your sleeve or your clothes. It is very contrary to decency to blow your nose with two fingers and then to throw the filth onto the ground and wipe your fingers on your clothes, which should always be very clean."[86]

The handkerchief in the sixteenth and seventeenth centuries was usually placed in the front shirt or coat pocket to be visible to all. The gentry displayed their wealth and indicated their awareness of the latest codes of behavior. Few handkerchiefs existed in the late sixteenth century; even Henry IV owned only five. It is not until the reign of Louis XIV that there was an abundance of handkerchiefs in court society. The handkerchief helped this court develop and reinforce a strong hierarchy.[87] As Elias notes, "The dependence of the upper class also explains the dual aspect which the behavior patterns and instruments of civilization have at least in this formative stage. They express a certain measure of compulsion and renunciation, but they also immediately became a weapon against social inferiors, a means of distinction."[88]

Personal appearance and cleanliness became a concern in late medieval etiquette books. The following is a list of rules written by John Russell in the *Boke of Nurture* for the office of chamberlain to follow in order to make his lord suitable for public appearance. Russell noted:

> The duty of chamberlain is to be diligent in office, neatly clad, his clothes not torn, hands and face well washed and head well kempt.
>
> See that your lord has a clean shirt and hose . . . his hose well brushed . . . his shoes and slippers as brown as a water leach.
>
> In the morning, against your lord shall rise, take care that his linen be clean. . . .
>
> You must attend busily to your lords wardrobe, to keep the clothes well, and to brush them cleanly.[89]

About 150 years later Richard Weste wrote:

> Let thy apparel not exceed
>   to pass for sumptuous cost,
> Nor altogether be too base,
>   for so thy credits lost.
> Be modest in thy wearing it,
>   and keep it neat and clean,
> For spotted, dirty or the like
>   is loathsome to be seen.[90]

As noted earlier, etiquette around the table was probably the most important aspect of social life. Therefore appearance at the table was equally important. Erasmus believed that comfort and health in dining should also be considered. He wrote, "Sit not down until thou have washed, but let thy nails be prepared before, and no filth stick in them, lest thou be called sloven and a great nigard. Remember the common saying, and before making water, and if need require, ease thy belly, and if thou be gird too tight, to unloose they girdle is wisdom, which to do at table is same."[91] Shortly afterward della Casa also emphasized the development and importance of the creation of individuality by emphasizing cleanliness at the table. He noted, "Let a man then take hede, he doe not begrease his fyngers so deep, yt he befyles the napkins to much: for it is an yll sight to see it: neither is it good maner, to rub your greasie fyngers uppon bread you must eat."[92]

In the mid-eighteenth century, Lord Chesterfield, who spent long periods of time in the high court of Louis XIV, emphasized the importance of proper grooming and a dress code. To him, dress was symbolic of a person's social standing. In a letter he condemns the dress of the youths in England:

> . . . others go in brown frock, leather britches, great oaken crudgels in their hands, their hat uncocked, and their hair unpowdered; and imitate grooms, stage coachmen, and country bumkins so well in their outside, that I do not make the least doubt of their resembling them equally into their insides. A man of sense carefully avoids any particular character in his dress; he is accurately clean for his own sake; but all the rest is for other people. He dresses as, and in the same manner, as the other people of sense and fashion of the place where he is.[93]

According to Chesterfield, the highest and most precise rules for decorum are to be found in socially competitive places. He wrote to his son, "I love capitals extremely; it is in capitals that the best company is always to be found; and consequently, the best manners to be learned. The very best provincial places have some awkwardness, that distinguishes their manners from those of the metropolis."[94] Chesterfield's contemporaries who resided in Annapolis, Alexander Hamilton and William Eddis, held similar views. They believed that Annapolitans displayed the highest of social graces, whereas those living in the countryside lacked any knowledge of polite behavior. Probate inventory analyses indicate a difference between urban Annapolis and rural Anne Arundel County: the former had a proportionately greater amount of estates with grooming and hygiene-related items.

Oral hygiene played a role in the presentation and creation of the individual. As early as the fifteenth century, Russell in his *Boke of Nurture* wrote, "Do not pick your teeth, or grind, or gnash them, or with puffing and blowing cast fowl breath upon your lord." Della Casa was concerned with the cleanliness and odors of the mouth. He wrote, "When a man talketh with one, it is no good maner to come so neere, that he must needes breath in his face; for there be many that can not abyde to feele the ayer of another mans breathe, albeit there come no yll sour from him."[95]

Erasmus also concerned himself with the teeth and with oral hygiene as a whole. He explained:

Cleanliness of the teeth must be cared for, but whiten them with powder does for girts. To rub the gum with salt or alum is injurous. . . . If anything sticks to the teeth, you must get it out, not with a knife, or with your nails after the maner of dogs and cats, or with your napkin, but with a toothpick, or a quill of small bone taken from tibias of cocks or hens. To wash the mouth in the mourning with pure water is both manerly and healthful; to do it often is foolish.[96]

Attitudes had changed little about one hundred years later, as Richard Weste wrote:

> Keep white thy teeth and wash thy mouth
>   with water pure and clean;
> And in that washing, mannerly
>   observe and keep a mean.[97]

Pierre Fachard, who many consider to be the founder of dentistry, recommended in 1728 that the toothbrush not be used to clean the teeth. He claimed that the bristles would damage the gums. Instead, a small sponge should be used.[98]

Lord Chesterfield wrote to his son, "Do you take care to keep your teeth very clean, by washing them constantly every morning, and after every meal? This is very necessary, both to preserve your teeth a great while, and to save you a great deal of pain. Mine have plagued me long, and are now falling out, merely from want of care when I was your age."[99]

Later in the eighteenth century, the toothbrush became a popular instrument in oral hygiene.[100] With the regular use of the toothbrush, precise rules were established. By the nineteenth century, health guides advised people to brush their teeth after every meal, before bedtime, and upon rising in the morning.[101] From the seventeenth- and eighteenth-century probate data collected from Annapolis and Anne Arundel County, only Amos Garret's probated estate of 1728 had toothbrushes, although archaeological deposits from the Reynolds Tavern site in Annapolis indicate that toothbrushes became accepted starting in the late eighteenth century and grew more popular by the mid-nineteenth century. A late eighteenth-century newspaper even advertised the dentist's arrival in town and prescribed good oral hygiene habits. Grooming and hygiene became an essential component to the creation of the individual in late eighteenth-century Western society.

SUMMARY

Etiquette and material goods served more than formality or display. They became integrally related to guiding human relations and also became part of the larger political and social systems. Manners supported special interests, created hierarchy and structured domination. Medieval courtesy books often provided directions for everyday activities, such as eating, sleeping, urinating, defecating, and copulating. The separation from premodern norms became dictated by new "exacting standards," or modern discipline, which became internalized and used as a natural guide for behavior. These new rules became enforced by the "internalization of prohibitions and [the development of] exquisite sensitivity to embarrassment, shame, and guilt."[102]

Several topics concerning items and behavior associated with dining and hygiene have been examined in scales of long-term history. The increasing and changing rules of behavior had new material and cultural implications. By the late seventeenth century, many premodern traditions that supported communality had been replaced by new rules prescribing exacting, precise, standardizing, and segmenting behavior. In Western Europe this new behavior was gradually advanced with the introduction of town clocks. As time measurement became more precise, so did many other aspects of daily life, including dining, health, and hygiene. By the late seventeenth century, it was improper for a member of the Western European gentry to share dishes and goblets, eat food directly with a knife, or blow the nose in the tablecloth. New material goods had new rules for their use, which required exacting and precise behavior. One plate for one person became the norm for the gentry. Rules associated with the use of handling utensils also became important. The rules were never static; they changed constantly, and as consumerism became democratized in the eighteenth century, rules for their use changed more rapidly and became more detailed. The elite introduced these new goods into society and often changed the rules for the goods' use. As the social hierarchy became threatened by a new emerging group, the rules changed to exclude outsiders and protect the established hierarchy.

The influx of new material goods into the Chesapeake is part of this broad change and is no accident of technological innovation. These goods did not operate in a system that relied on traditional rules and behaviors; new dining practices and an increasing concern for appearance, including hygiene, accompanied the new material culture.

5. The Historical Meanings of Consumption

A study of the long-term history of Western society demonstrates dramatic material and behavioral change from the fifteenth through the nineteenth century. An examination of social time in the Chesapeake reveals the sudden appearance of particular consumer goods in the 1720s and the 1760s as a result of the wealthy defining their position in a modernizing society. Archaeological materials from particular sites representing shorter time periods exemplify the increasing segmentation and standardization of life among various groups with the introduction of mass-produced goods. Generally, the three scales of history—individual, social, and long-term—provide different perspectives of consumerism as purchasing patterns changed substantially over the centuries.

Various explanations exists for the birth of the consumer revolution.[1] McKendrick, Brewer and Plumb provide an outline for the historical development of consumption and claim that consumerism was integrally related to the English Industrial Revolution.[2] They explain that production could not have changed without altering the tastes of the population, and that the desire for new goods was an "irresistible drug." Consumer demand became possible because of new innovations in marketing and style obsolescence that developed during the eighteenth century.[3] Rosalind H. Williams's work demonstrates that Louis XIV's court experimented with consumption. Louis XIV controlled his subordinate nobles by making them accelerate their consumption. Voltaire believed that this pattern of consumption would aid the development of Western civilization, whereas others, such as Rousseau, argued the contrary. Williams describes the symbolic power of goods as they became an instrument of Louis XIV's power and control. New symbolic strategies become evident with the new consumer society.[4] Chandra Mukerji claims that the new consumer culture arose in fifteenth- and sixteenth-century Europe and precipitated the rise of capitalism.[5] She proposes that goods have meanings that helped form modern Western civilization.

Borrowing from Grant McCracken's work, I believe it is necessary to examine the history of consumption and the consumer boom of late sixteenth-century Western Europe to understand the history of the meaning and uses of material goods in the West. This examination can bring insight to the changing patterns in the eighteenth-century Chesapeake.

In late sixteenth-century England, Elizabeth I began to spend money with great enthusiasm on items such as housing, hospitality, and clothing. Her rate of consumption far exceeded that of earlier Tudors. Apparently Elizabeth drew her inspiration from the Italian Renaissance courts. Fernand Braudel describes the courts' new expenditures as "a sort of parade, a theatrical spectacle . . . [and, with luxury] a means of government."[6] Faced with internal and external political difficulties, Elizabeth created extravagant consumption patterns and new material symbols to justify her power. She initiated a system by which the nobility footed most of the bill. No longer were favors passed from intermediaries to nobility—they now came from her directly. This meant that nobles had to leave their country seats and come to court to ask for the queen's favor. Elizabeth showed great favor for those who participated in the courtly ceremonies. This in turn left the nobility in financial ruin and forced them to become dependent upon their queen. Gentry spending amplified as competition between peers increased.[7] The new consumption patterns restructured the reciprocal patterns in the nobles' communities. When the nobles began to spend more time away from their communities, they suspended the process of largess as they had less to spend on the subordinates. McCracken states that "the nobleman began in effect to withdraw from the reciprocal relationships he and his ancestors had established with the locality. Contemporaries called this development the death of hospitality."[8]

Some material goods that had little or no symbolic meaning during times of unquestioned social order were transformed to create meaning and reinforce the unstable hierarchy. As production of goods increased and consumption became more democratized, the elite desired to reestablish differences between themselves and the lower groups.[9] New goods, new behaviors, and new social actions were necessary for the wealthy to keep their social distance from the lower groups. The elite achieved this by controlling the access to knowledge about goods much in the same way their own behavior was controlled at court.

The shift in consumer behavior created radical differences between subordinates' and superordinates' life-styles. Both groups now wanted different things and uniformity of life-style disappeared. "Differences in social location were becoming differences in style, aesthetic preference, and attitude," McCracken asserts.[10] The growing social distance also created a reciprocal bargain between the groups. Despite the growing schism, the elite still shaped the attitudes toward consumer goods.

A consumer explosion characterized the eighteenth century. There were growing opportunities for purchasing various goods. What was once a luxury became a decency, and what many had considered a decency became a necessity.[11] The practice of purchasing goods for self rather than for family or community emerged. Goods developed as an emblem of status and fulfilled new social and cultural needs: the reinforcement of hierarchy. New marketing devices became a major force in the consumer revolution, and their affects were widespread, including Europe's colonies. The desire for fashion affected an increasing number of social groups. Newly defined necessities were introduced, such as frequent bathing and meticulous grooming. Goods initiated and reinforced differentiation and expressions of the self.[12]

Some historians have traced the new marketing techniques developed in the early eighteenth century.[13] For example, the fashion doll served as the elite's guide to clothing. In the early eighteenth century, this guide benefitted only court society. The elite were encouraged to participate in consumption because they needed to acquire symbols similar to those of their peers in order to maintain their position in society. Throughout the eighteenth century, the fashion doll was controlled by merchants and served the mass consumer market. Previously, sumptuary laws restricted democratic consumption behavior and reinforced social separateness. With the fashion doll in the hands of entrepreneurs, the entrepreneurs encouraged fashion change and persuaded a growing number of social groups to participate. Fashion magazines gained popularity in the early eighteenth century, and by the end of the century, entrepreneurs were systematically printing them. In 1777 John Trusler in *The Way to be Rich and Respectable* described the trickle-down of goods from the higher ranks: "The infection of the first class soon spread among the second; a taste for elegances spread itself through all ranks and degrees of men."[14] The *British Magazine* of 1763 wrote that "the present rage of imitating the manners of high life hath spread itself so far among the gentle folks of lower life, that in a few years we shall probably have no common folk at all."[15]

From Trusler to the social scientists at the turn of the twentieth century,[16] through today, material culture change has often been explained by the trickle-down concept, as one group's desire for another group's objects. However, the trickle-down, or emulation, theory often ignores the probable conflict between groups and implies that lower wealth groups readily accepted change and followed the lead of the upper groups. This concept denies the fact that lower groups had the power and desire to change and struggle for control. The struggle for the establishment of a group's identity can be created by co-opting goods used by the dominant group and either manipulating them in the same way and emulating a higher status level or creating different symbolic meanings. The fact that the eighteenth-century probate data indicate that the poor in Anne Arundel County and Annapolis did not have the same material goods as the wealthy may be explained in part by their lack of purchasing power. But it might also have been a product of the lower groups trying to maintain their own identities. The archaeological record shows us that by the nineteenth century both rich and poor owned mass-produced ceramics. Therefore the poorer segment of the population no longer participated in communal-like eating activities, although other material differences separated these two groups.

To understand the forces of subordinate ideology, archaeologists have increasingly turned to Gramsci's concept of hegemony.[17] Hegemony is not necessarily specific to any particular interest group or class, although it usually refers to dominant cultural ideals. According to Gramsci, subordinate groups with common interests create a complex of associations to resist and possibly overthrow the dominant group. The subordinate group builds influence and takes over "a wide variety of elements within a society prior to any formal overthrow of the state."[18]

From the premodern era through the Industrial Revolution in Western society, goods were used to justify hegemonic differences, although the meanings of the goods changed radically between these two eras. During the preindustrial era, it often was not only the type but also the age of the object that legitimized status. As objects became "minutely dented, chipped, oxidized, and worn away, they began to take on a 'patina.'" Patina authenticated status as it marked the longevity of a family's position in society. Goods with patina demonstrated that gentry-related objects were in the family for several generations, and therefore the family could claim to be part of the old gentry, thus inflating their social standing. Lack of patina meant that the wealth was new and therefore the status was new and less respected.[19] In premodern times patina, not consumption, played a major role in group dynamics. This preindustrial concept began to lose legitimacy during the consumer revolution.

Capitalism could not sustain itself without the consumer revolution. During the democratization of consumerism, goods acquired new meaning and created groups in new ways. Consumerism in an industrializing society creates a way to reestablish control, and in a threatened hierarchy it is a way to express domination. Consumer choice is usually more than a function of wealth or access to resources. Consumer choice is to a large extent dependent upon the symbolic value of goods. Members of the same group will choose similar symbols and thereby construct the group's social boundaries.

McCracken describes several ways that material goods may be accepted by the dominant culture. First, the new meanings given to goods and their related meanings must be associated with established cultural categories.[20] The accompanying ideology must declare that these meanings are inevitable and have always existed. For example, today we are convinced that time discipline is natural and inevitable, but this concept is only several centuries old. Second, new goods and meanings may be enforced by "opinion leaders," whom a community holds in highest esteem. This is the way Josiah Wedgwood successfully developed and sold "Queensware" to the middle class.[21] Third, sometimes radical reformers change the systems of meaning. Western industrial societies constantly undergo systematic change, sometimes stimulated by marginal groups. In modern times peripheral groups would include the hippies of the 1960s and early 1970s, and the punkers of the late 1970s and early 1980s.[22] These innovative groups had the same ability to participate in the hegemonic process to supply new meanings to goods. "If the sources of meaning are more dynamic and numerous," notes McCracken, "so are the agents who gather this meaning up and accomplish its transfer to consumer goods."[23]

Consideration of the social context of goods takes into account strategies of power and domination and the related manipulation of new and modern discipline. Regional and local socioeconomic stress in the Chesapeake, and more specifically in Annapolis, stimulated mechanisms of social stratification. On the broader scale, global issues such as the quest for surplus influenced the development of Annapolis.[24] The Chesapeake region had an economy based on tobacco and was strongly affected by the world's demand for this product, creating a boom or bust economy. On a local scale, the city's social composition was influenced by its growth, the concentration of wealth, and the development of a naturalizing ideology. All of these factors played an influential role in contributing to the creation of overt expressions of material culture and differences between groups. A hegemonic process naturalized the domination of a few over the majority of people by claiming control over natural laws. This process laid the groundwork for the beginning of a modern disciplined society, which the lower wealth groups adapted or had imposed on them, creating distinct social categories.

By interpreting goods in the Chesapeake in their symbolic context we can create an understanding of meaning that is far more comprehensive than an understanding based solely on an index of wealth. It is the understanding of the recursive, or socializing, quality of material culture and how it is manipulated in social circumstances that is particularly important here.

In a consumer society, goods tend to become diversified; groups develop a finely tuned perception of the meaning of these goods. When competition becomes keen, as it was in the Chesapeake during the social and economic tensions of the 1720s and the questioning of the political and social order in the 1760s, disciplined behavior and standardization of goods emerge. The closer one is to a competitive center, the more important standardization and precise behavior become and the

more significant, and detrimental, deviation becomes. Regions under-
going the greatest socioeconomic stress develop a more competitive
base. This competition standardizes behavior and fosters overt expressions using material culture, creating distinct groups and justifying negative reciprocity among groups through naturalizing ideology. Etiquette
and the goods associated with it become a growing part of the social
strategy of power and domination.

These ideas regarding competition and socioeconomic stress may
contribute to a satisfying interpretation for the changing consumption
patterns and the creation of a hierarchical society in the Chesapeake.
The social and economic tensions of the 1720s and the 1760s affected
the Chesapeake in general, as well as Anne Arundel County and Annapolis. In response the elite's consumption patterns changed, further
separating them from the threatening lower group. Before large-scale
changes could take place in the form of overt material expressions, however, a naturalizing ideology must have been in place. As Leone explains, goods with the ability to measure land, time, and atmosphere (as
well as musical instruments for measuring sound) were in the hands of a
few, who thus understood the laws of nature through direct observation.[25]

Measured time, first found in the monastic orders of the late medieval
era, is one feature of the control over nature by a small group of people.
Eventually, the control of time and the manipulation of time discipline
became a tool of power and domination controlled by the aristocracy.
The way people used objects in a disciplining and segmenting fashion
can be understood in a broad context by observing the behavior associated with them through behavioral guide books beginning in the
twelfth century. Eric Wolf describes the early stages of this era as Europe's first attempts to harness wind and water power, technology that
enabled greater production of surplus.[26] This new technology allowed
tribute-taking overlords to enhance the military class and move toward
political consolidation by creating a central kingship. Nichols notes a
correlation between this era of conflict and consolidation and the building of castles.[27] Increased rules of behavior, or discipline, were created
to stratify, order, and control people within the confined environment
of the castle as it became the center of social intercourse. In the late
medieval and early Renaissance period, rules of behavior became more
artifact-specific, and disciplined, guiding each move and behavior. In

the Chesapeake, written documents pertaining to the meaning of these objects are rare, if not nonexistent, before the 1740s, but the use of these objects were probably similar to that in Europe. Based on the probate data, it appears that Annapolitans were participating in this new order of behavior by at least the 1720s. Although the majority of the Anne Arundel County elite lacked some of the disciplining items that their counterparts in Annapolis had, by the 1760s both the urban and rural elite had substantially more of these goods than the lower groups.

Lord Chesterfield's letters in the mid-eighteenth century stressed the importance of time discipline and productivity to his son. Time management was a necessity in the eyes of Chesterfield, for not one moment should one stay "idle and yawning."[28] The idea of productivity, regimentation, and precise behavior became internalized and was made to appear natural, especially in urban areas. In 1711 Joseph Addison of England stated that the "polite world" of the city was far more advanced in the category of manners than the country.[29] Voltaire wrote in 1733 in a dedication of his *Zaire* to an English merchant, "Politeness is not in the least an arbitrary matter, . . . but is a law of nature."[30]

In 1746 the *Maryland Gazette* proclaimed that nature provided the basis for good taste (a measure of true taste included, by this time, how a man efficiently used his leisure hours) and that formal and segmented dining was "good taste."[31] It is certain that people in Annapolis were subscribing to the etiquette of "polite behavior." That same year Dr. Alexander Hamilton in his traveler's guide explained his uneasiness about dining with some poor farmers who ate from a communal dish and lacked tablecloth, knives, spoons, and forks.[32] Hamilton was eager to avoid this premodern lifeway when invited by this family to join them at supper. He escaped the invitation because he felt repulsed by the manner in which the farmers ate, cramming down whole fish, scales, head and all. This once natural way of behavior seemed now rather unnatural and unappealing. Such a change in attitude was part of the development of the naturalization of a modern discipline.

When probate data are examined for Annapolis and Anne Arundel County, a relationship appears between the socioeconomic fluctuations of the 1720s and the consumption of dining items, scientific instruments, and grooming and hygiene items. This correlation was more evident in the city of Annapolis than in rural Anne Arundel County. It seems likely that material goods associated with the creation of a modern discipline played a role in establishing the hierarchy in Annapolis. Dr. Hamilton's reaction to the poor farmers' etiquette supports the idea that some form of modern discipline existed in Annapolis, although the probate data does not follow conventional wisdom that the wealthy automatically increased their consumption of disciplining items. Rather, it appears that there may have been a struggle for the use and consumption of these disciplining items. In most cases groups other than the wealthiest own more of these items by the 1740s. Such an anomaly requires further exploration and a careful look at the social context of Annapolis. I have hypothesized, along with Barbara Little, that during the social and economic instability of the 1720s the wealthy consolidated their economic and social power.[33] The elite built the earliest brick houses in a successful attempt at ostentation. Dining and personal hygiene items used by the elite may also have served the same purpose. This argument follows the lead of Braudel and Leone, who note that ostentation is most useful during times of instability.[34] During the 1730s and 1740s in Annapolis, the hierarchy appears to have been stable, and material goods may not have been needed to reinforce the hierarchy. It is not until the 1760s, when the elite's authority was again threatened, that the wealthy once more owned a greater proportion of these goods than the lower groups.

Tracing the consumption patterns from probate inventory data of the urban and rural contexts demonstrates different acquisition rates between these two areas. Disciplining items played a greater role among the urban elite than among the rural elite. This is not to deny that the rural elite were not active in creating a hegemonic dominance over the rural poor. Rather, the rural elite used different approaches—legislation that restrained the rights of slaves, indentured servants, and freed indentured servants, for example—to gain control over their subordinates. The rural elite's explicit use of material goods to demonstrate their authority over the poor became more rampant in the mid-eighteenth century. Most prevalent was the elite's use of mathematical proportions to design their houses and formal gardens. As noted in the *Maryland Gazette*, these proportions were believed to be a natural phenomena, and it was the elite who possessed the knowledge to construct their environment using them. Many of the elite no longer constructed their dwellings out of wood with window placement based on the need for lighting. Instead balance, order, symmetry, and ostentation were important.

So far there are only three sites analyzed in Annapolis that have undisturbed stratigraphic layers dating to the 1720s. As noted above, there were few or no mass-produced ceramic plates made during this time. Therefore, conclusions relating to discipline and the segmentation of society cannot be made based on the archaeological record of this time. We do not find large quantities of ceramics in Annapolis until the second half of the eighteenth century, but ceramics found in the probate data of households dating to this time may have served ideological rather than utilitarian purposes. Ceramics were much more expensive earlier in the century than later, and they therefore may have been ostentatiously displayed, relaying messages of social position and status in society, a function Deetz acknowledges as sociotechnic. By the late eighteenth century, ceramics actively segmented and disciplined behavior, thereby continuing their social function, although in essentially different ways.

Variation in ceramic plate sizes, as well as increasing functional diversity, signify the segmentation of dining as well as the separation of people around the table. This phenomenon occurred increasingly from the 1770s to the 1780s. In Annapolis the wealthiest sites contained the highest variation throughout time, although lower wealth groups had increased their variation to similar proportions by the early nineteenth century. By the mid-nineteenth century, the wealthy once again had proportionately greater amounts of segmenting dining items.

Both social behavior and the workplace were subject to the disciplining process. Toothbrushes serve as an indicator of how a personal discipline was created through both hygiene and activity in the workplace. The manufacture of the toothbrush became increasingly standardized through time. Through this mass manufacturing process, they became cheaper and were adopted by a larger portion of society. Generally, toothbrushes were used in Annapolis to a greater degree beginning in the early nineteenth century. The rules observed in the production of the individual were also observed in the production of goods.

A consumer revolution in the Chesapeake in the 1710s to 1720s introduced a shift in consumption patterns among the wealthy and the poor. More and better means of transportation and production can to a large extent explain the advent of consumerism in the Chesapeake, but it is necessary to establish the social context to understand the acceptance of material and behavioral change. During periods of socio-economic stress, a newly formed gentry, who based their wealth on mercantile capitalism, began to compete against the old guard. This unstable order was reordered by providing a new meaning to consumer goods. The concept of patina, once used to justify the hierarchy, was replaced by a concept of consumerism. New and fashionable goods became the goal of consumption. Associated with these goods was a new behavior that encouraged discipline, regimentation, and segmentation. Although members of lower wealth groups acquired these goods, the wealthy, as an exclusionary tactic, created the rules for using them.

Scholars of material culture must pay attention to the significant interdependencies between culture and consumption. Consumer goods, McCracken notes, "express cultural categories and principles, cultural ideals, create and sustain lifestyles, construct notions of self, and create social change."[35] To understand the patterns of consumption, it is important to understand the social context in which goods are desired, used, and, eventually, fall out of favor. When examining archaeological assemblages in historical and symbolic contexts, questions asked of the data must consider that goods can be more than passive objects reflecting relative wealth. A vessel analysis may indicate more than the types of foods consumed—it also may be a reflection of how goods created and reinforced behaviors and establish social groups.

Historical archaeology need not be confined to describing and reconfirming what we already know. It is important that we participate in the growing interest in historical anthropology. The rediscovery of historical perspectives in the field of anthropology has helped archaeologists realize that culture change is not an evolutionary but a historical process. Change is persistent, but the direction is often unknown.[36] In historical contexts, change is in large part the struggle for power and domination. Power is very much involved in the daily relations between people and groups. To ignore this aspect of culture is to deny a vital aspect of everyday life.[37] Understanding the historical and social context of goods, etiquette, and workplace and time discipline helps put modern life into perspective.

Appendix:
Data for Disciplining Items

Table A1.   Presence of Clocks in Rural Anne Arundel County

Wealth in Pounds	Years											
	1688–1709			1710–32			1733–54			1755–77		
	C	N	%	C	N	%	C	N	%	C	N	%
000–49	129	1	01	124	0	00	91	1	01	109	2	02
50–225	124	2	02	107	3	03	139	9	06	122	9	07
226–490	38	2	05	35	5	14	86	14	16	91	8	09
491+	29	11	38	46	22	48	68	31	46	86	35	41

C = Total number of cases
N = Presence of item
% = Percentage of cases

Table A2.   Presence of Scientific Instruments (Globes, Spy Glasses, Barometers, and Sundials) in Rural Anne Arundel County

Wealth in Pounds	Years											
	1688–1709			1710–32			1733–54			1755–77		
	C	N	%	C	N	%	C	N	%	C	N	%
000–49	129	0	00	124	0	00	91	0	00	109	1	01
50–225	124	0	00	107	3	03	139	2	01	122	3	03
226–490	38	0	00	35	2	06	86	4	04	91	5	10
491+	29	4	14	46	6	13	68	18	27	86	10	12

C = Total number of cases
N = Presence of item
% = Percentage of cases

Table A3.   Presence of Compasses in Rural Anne Arundel County

Wealth in Pounds	Years																	
	1697–1699			1713–15			1730–32			1745–47			1761–64			1775–77		
	C	N	%	C	N	%	C	N	%	C	N	%	C	N	%	C	N	%
000–49	33	0	00	21	0	00	10	0	00	13	0	00	27	0	00	9	0	00
50–225	21	0	00	11	0	00	12	0	00	13	1	08	36	0	00	12	0	00
226–490	7	0	00	4	1	25	5	1	20	8	1	13	15	1	07	11	0	00
491+	8	0	00	10	0	00	8	2	25	4	1	25	19	1	05	13	0	00

C = Total number of cases
N = Presence of item
% = Percentage of cases

Table A4. Presence of Formal and Segmenting Dining Items (Salad Dishes, tureens, Dish Covers, Fruit Dishes, Custard Cups, Castors, Butter Boats, Wine Glasses) in Rural Anne Arundel County

Wealth in Pounds	Years																	
	1697–1699			1713–15			1730–32			1745–47			1761–64			1775–77		
	C	N	%	C	N	%	C	N	%	C	N	%	C	N	%	C	N	%
000–49	33	0	00	21	0	00	10	0	00	13	0	00	27	0	00	9	0	00
50–225	21	0	00	11	0	00	12	0	00	13	0	00	36	0	00	12	0	00
226–490	7	0	00	4	0	00	5	1	20	8	2	25	15	1	07	11	0	00
491+	8	1	13	10	1	10	8	2	25	4	0	00	19	7	37	13	0	00

C = Total number of cases
N = Presence of item
% = Percentage of cases

Table A5. Presence of Sets of Plates in Rural Anne Arundel County

Wealth in Pounds	Years																	
	1697–1699			1713–15			1730–32			1745–47			1761–64			1775–77		
	C	N	%	C	N	%	C	N	%	C	N	%	C	N	%	C	N	%
000–49	33	1	03	21	1	05	10	0	00	13	0	00	27	1	04	9	0	00
50–225	21	0	00	11	1	09	12	1	08	13	1	08	36	5	14	12	2	17
226–490	7	1	14	4	0	00	5	0	00	8	1	13	15	4	27	11	1	09
491+	8	1	13	10	2	20	8	2	25	4	3	75	19	10	53	13	4	31

C = Total number of cases
N = Presence of item
% = Percentage of cases

Table A6.   Presence of Knives in Rural Anne Arundel County

| Wealth in Pounds | Years | | | | | | | | | | | |
| | 1688–1709 | | | 1710–32 | | | 1733–54 | | | 1755–77 | | |
	C	N	%	C	N	%	C	N	%	C	N	%
0–49	129	9	07	124	8	06	91	17	19	109	38	35
50–225	124	10	08	107	19	18	139	60	43	122	87	71
226–490	38	6	16	35	14	35	86	59	69	91	63	69
491+	29	19	66	46	29	63	68	59	87	86	72	84

C = Total number of cases
N = Presence of item
% = Percentage of cases

Table A7.   Presence of Forks in Rural Anne Arundel County

| Wealth in Pounds | Years | | | | | | | | | | | |
| | 1688–1709 | | | 1710–32 | | | 1733–54 | | | 1755–77 | | |
	C	N	%	C	N	%	C	N	%	C	N	%
0–49	129	6	05	124	8	06	91	15	16	109	38	35
50–225	124	4	03	107	16	15	139	59	42	122	85	70
226–490	38	4	11	35	14	40	86	57	66	91	63	69
491+	29	12	41	46	38	82	68	58	85	86	71	83

C = Total number of cases
N = Presence of item
% = Percentage of cases

Table A8. Presence of Sets of Forks in Rural Anne Arundel County

Wealth in Pounds	Years																	
	1697–99			1713–15			1730–32			1745–47			1761–64			1775–77		
	C	N	%	C	N	%	C	N	%	C	N	%	C	N	%	C	N	%
0–49	33	0	00	21	0	00	10	0	00	13	0	00	27	0	00	9	0	00
50–225	21	0	00	11	0	00	12	2	17	13	1	08	36	8	22	12	2	17
226–490	7	0	00	4	0	00	5	1	20	8	4	50	15	4	27	11	4	11
491+	8	2	25	10	3	30	8	2	25	4	2	50	19	9	47	13	3	23

C = Total number of cases
N = Presence of item
% = Percentage of cases

Table A9. Presence of Sets of Knives in Rural Anne Arundel County

Wealth in Pounds	Years																	
	1697–99			1713–15			1730–32			1745–47			1761–64			1775–77		
	C	N	%	C	N	%	C	N	%	C	N	%	C	N	%	C	N	%
000–49	33	0	00	21	0	00	10	0	00	13	0	00	27	0	00	9	0	00
50–225	21	0	00	11	0	00	12	2	17	13	2	15	36	7	19	12	2	17
226–490	7	0	00	4	0	00	5	1	20	8	3	38	15	4	27	11	4	36
491+	8	3	38	10	3	30	8	2	25	4	3	75	19	9	47	13	3	23

C = Total number of cases
N = Presence of item
% = Percentage of cases

Table A10.   Presence of Sets of Cups in Rural Anne Arundel County

Wealth in Pounds	Years																
	1697–99			1713–15			1730–32			1745–47			1761–64			1775–77		
	C	N	%	C	N	%	C	N	%	C	N	%	C	N	%	C	N	%
000–49	33	0	00	21	0	00	10	0	00	13	0	00	27	0	00	9	0	00
50–225	21	0	00	11	1	09	12	0	00	13	1	08	36	0	00	12	0	00
226–490	7	0	00	4	0	00	5	1	20	8	2	25	15	1	07	11	0	00
491+	8	0	00	10	0	00	8	2	25	4	0	00	19	7	37	13	0	00

C = Total number of cases
N = Presence of item
% = Percentage of cases

Table A11.   Presence of Napkins in Rural Anne Arundel County

Wealth in Pounds	Years																
	1697–99			1713–15			1730–32			1745–47			1761–64			1775–77		
	C	N	%	C	N	%	C	N	%	C	N	%	C	N	%	C	N	%
000–49	33	2	06	21	1	05	10	0	00	13	0	00	27	1	04	9	0	00
50–225	21	5	24	11	2	18	12	2	17	13	0	00	36	3	08	12	0	00
226–490	7	1	14	4	2	50	5	3	60	8	2	25	15	3	20	11	4	36
491+	8	8	100	10	6	60	8	5	63	4	3	75	19	11	58	13	2	15

C = Total number of cases
N = Presence of item
% = Percentage of cases

Table A12.   Presence of Sets of Chairs in Rural Anne Arundel County

Wealth in Pounds	Years																	
	1697–99			1713–15			1730–32			1745–47			1761–64			1775–77		
	C	N	%	C	N	%	C	N	%	C	N	%	C	N	%	C	N	%
000–49	33	0	00	21	0	00	10	0	00	13	0	00	27	1	04	9	0	00
50–225	21	0	00	11	0	00	12	0	00	13	0	00	36	1	03	12	1	08
226–490	7	0	00	4	0	00	5	0	00	8	0	00	15	2	13	11	4	36
491+	8	0	00	10	0	00	8	0	00	4	0	00	19	6	32	13	7	54

C = Total number of cases
N = Presence of item
% = Percentage of cases

Table A13.   Presence of Tea Tables in Rural Anne Arundel County

Wealth in Pounds	Years											
	1688–1709			1710–32			1733–54			1755–77		
	C	N	%	C	N	%	C	N	%	C	N	%
0–49	129	0	00	124	0	00	91	2	02	109	0	00
50–225	124	0	00	107	0	00	139	1	01	122	2	02
226–490	38	0	00	35	0	00	86	6	07	91	11	12
491+	29	0	00	46	7	15	68	13	19	86	20	23

C = Total number of cases
N = Presence of item
% = Percentage of cases

Table A14.   Presence of Grooming-related Items (Dressing Boxes, Dressing Tables, Dressing Glasses, Shaving/Wash Basins, Combs, Toothbrushes, Clothes Brushes, Toothpicks) in Rural Anne Arundel County

Wealth in Pounds	Years																	
	1697–99			1713–15			1730–32			1745–47			1761–64			1775–77		
	C	N	%	C	N	%	C	N	%	C	N	%	C	N	%	C	N	%
000–49	33	1	03	21	4	19	10	0	00	13	2	15	27	2	07	9	0	00
50–225	21	0	00	11	1	09	12	0	00	13	2	15	36	0	00	12	0	00
226–490	7	0	00	4	0	00	5	2	40	8	3	38	15	2	13	11	2	18
491+	8	2	25	10	4	40	8	3	38	4	4	100	19	9	47	13	3	23

C = Total number of cases
N = Presence of item
% = Percentage of cases

Table A15.   Presence of Handkerchiefs in Rural Anne Arundel County

Wealth in Pounds	Years																	
	1697–99			1713–15			1730–32			1745–47			1761–64			1775–77		
	C	N	%	C	N	%	C	N	%	C	N	%	C	N	%	C	N	%
000–49	33	1	03	21	0	00	10	0	00	13	0	00	27	0	00	9	0	00
50–225	21	0	00	11	1	09	12	0	00	13	0	00	36	1	03	12	0	00
226–490	7	0	00	4	1	25	5	1	20	8	0	00	15	0	00	11	0	00
491+	8	2	25	10	3	30	8	3	38	4	1	25	19	3	16	13	0	00

C = Total number of cases
N = Presence of item
% = Percentage of cases

Table A16. Presence of Chamber Pots in Rural Anne Arundel County

| Wealth in Pounds | Years | | | | | | | | | | | |
| | 1688–1709 | | | 1710–32 | | | 1733–54 | | | 1755–77 | | |
	C	N	%	C	N	%	C	N	%	C	N	%
000–49	129	8	06	124	1	01	91	3	03	109	5	05
50–225	124	17	14	107	3	03	139	16	12	122	20	16
226–490	38	10	26	35	1	03	86	21	24	91	16	18
491+	29	4	14	46	12	26	68	19	28	86	27	31

C = Total number of cases
N = Presence of item
% = Percentage of cases

Table A17. Presence of Close Stools in Rural Anne Arundel County

| Wealth in Pounds | Years | | | | | | | | | | | |
| | 1688–1709 | | | 1710–32 | | | 1733–54 | | | 1755–77 | | |
	C	N	%	C	N	%	C	N	%	C	N	%
000–49	129	1	01	124	0	01	91	1	01	109	1	01
50–225	124	2	02	107	1	01	139	1	01	122	1	01
226–490	38	1	03	35	3	09	86	8	09	91	2	02
491+	29	6	29	46	15	33	68	21	31	86	18	21

C = Total number of cases
N = Presence of item
% = Percentage of cases

Table A18.   Presence of Clocks in Annapolis

Wealth in Pounds	Years											
	1688–1709			1710–32			1733–54			1755–77		
	C	N	%	C	N	%	C	N	%	C	N	%
000–49	9	0	00	24	1	04	33	3	09	33	5	22
50–225	3	0	00	27	7	26	18	10	56	30	12	40
226–490	4	1	25	12	7	58	11	9	82	9	5	56
491+	1	0	00	9	6	67	15	10	67	17	16	94

C = Total number of cases
N = Presence of item
% = Percentage of cases

Table A19.   Presence of Scientific Instruments (Globes, Spy Glasses, and Sundials) in Annapolis

Wealth in Pounds	Years											
	1688–1709			1710–32			1733–54			1755–77		
	C	N	%	C	N	%	C	N	%	C	N	%
000–49	9	0	00	24	0	00	33	1	03	33	0	00
50–225	3	1	33	27	2	07	18	3	18	30	2	07
226–490	4	0	00	12	1	08	11	2	18	9	2	22
491+	1	1	100	9	1	11	15	4	27	17	4	24

C = Total number of cases
N = Presence of item
% = Percentage of cases

Table A20.   Presence of Compasses in Annapolis

	Years											
Wealth in Pounds	1688–1709			1710–32			1733–54			1755–77		
	C	N	%	C	N	%	C	N	%	C	N	%
000–49	9	0	00	24	0	00	33	0	00	33	0	00
50–225	3	0	00	27	0	00	18	0	00	30	0	00
226–490	4	0	00	12	0	00	11	0	00	9	0	00
491+	1	1	100	9	2	22	15	0	00	17	0	00

C = Total number of cases
N = Presence of item
% = Percentage of cases

Table A21.   Presence of Formal and Segmenting Dining Items (Salad Dishes, Tureens, Dish Covers, Fruit Dishes, Custard Cups, Castors, Butter Boats, Wine Glasses) in Annapolis

	Years											
Wealth in Pounds	1688–1709			1710–32			1733–54			1755–77		
	C	N	%	C	N	%	C	N	%	C	N	%
000–49	9	0	00	24	0	00	33	1	03	33	0	00
50–225	3	0	00	27	0	00	18	2	11	30	2	07
226–490	4	0	00	12	1	08	11	2	18	9	0	00
491+	1	0	00	9	3	33	15	1	07	17	7	41

C = Total number of cases
N = Presence of item
% = Percentage of cases

Table A22. Presence of Sets of Plates in Annapolis

| Wealth in Pounds | Years | | | | | | | | | | | |
| | 1688–1709 | | | 1710–32 | | | 1733–54 | | | 1755–77 | | |
	C	N	%	C	N	%	C	N	%	C	N	%
000–49	9	1	11	24	3	13	33	2	06	33	1	03
50–225	3	0	00	27	3	11	18	2	11	30	5	17
226–490	4	1	25	12	2	17	11	1	09	9	2	22
491+	1	0	00	9	2	22	15	3	20	17	7	41

C = Total number of cases
N = Presence of item
% = Percentage of cases

Table A23. Presence of Forks in Annapolis

| Wealth in Pounds | Years | | | | | | | | | | | |
| | 1688–1709 | | | 1710–32 | | | 1733–54 | | | 1755–77 | | |
	C	N	%	C	N	%	C	N	%	C	N	%
000–49	9	0	00	24	2	08	33	8	24	33	10	30
50–225	3	1	33	27	13	48	18	8	44	30	14	47
226–490	4	1	25	12	8	67	11	10	91	9	7	77
491+	1	0	00	9	7	78	15	12	80	17	17	100

C = Total number of cases
N = Presence of item
% = Percentage of cases

Table A24.   Presence of Knives in Annapolis

Wealth in Pounds	Years											
	1688–1709			1710–32			1733–54			1755–77		
	C	N	%	C	N	%	C	N	%	C	N	%
000–49	9	2	22	24	2	08	33	8	24	33	10	30
50–225	3	2	67	27	13	48	18	9	50	30	14	47
226–490	4	3	75	12	7	58	11	10	91	9	7	77
491+	1	0	00	9	7	78	15	13	87	17	17	100

C = Total number of cases
N = Presence of item
% = Percentage of cases

Table A25.   Presence of Sets of Forks in Annapolis

Wealth in Pounds	Years											
	1688–1709			1710–32			1733–54			1755–77		
	C	N	%	C	N	%	C	N	%	C	N	%
000–49	9	0	00	24	0	00	33	1	03	33	3	09
50–225	3	0	00	27	5	19	18	6	33	30	3	10
226–490	4	0	00	12	3	25	11	6	55	9	7	78
491+	1	0	00	9	4	44	15	2	13	17	12	71

C = Total number of cases
N = Presence of item
% = Percentage of cases

Table A26.   Presence of Sets of Knives in Annapolis

Wealth in Pounds	Years											
	1688–1709			1710–32			1733–54			1755–77		
	C	N	%	C	N	%	C	N	%	C	N	%
000–49	9	0	00	24	0	00	33	0	00	33	3	11
50–225	3	1	33	27	5	19	18	5	28	30	4	30
226–490	4	0	00	12	3	25	11	6	55	9	7	78
491+	1	0	00	9	5	56	15	4	27	17	13	76

C = Total number of cases
N = Presence of item
% = Percentage of cases

Table A27.   Presence of Sets of Cups and Saucers in Annapolis

Wealth in Pounds	Years											
	1688–1709			1710–32			1733–54			1755–77		
	C	N	%	C	N	%	C	N	%	C	N	%
000–49	9	0	00	24	0	00	33	0	00	33	2	06
50–225	3	0	00	27	5	19	18	1	06	30	4	13
226–490	4	0	00	12	4	33	11	1	09	9	1	11
491+	1	0	00	9	4	44	15	2	13	17	4	24

C = Total number of cases
N = Presence of item
% = Percentage of cases

Table A28.   Presence of Napkins in Annapolis

Wealth in Pounds	Years											
	1688–1709			1710–32			1733–54			1755–77		
	C	N	%	C	N	%	C	N	%	C	N	%
000–49	9	0	00	24	3	13	33	2	06	33	0	00
50–225	3	1	33	27	11	41	18	6	33	30	4	13
226–490	4	2	50	12	7	58	11	6	55	9	1	11
491+	1	1	100	9	4	44	15	2	13	17	7	41

C = Total number of cases
N = Presence of item
% = Percentage of cases

Table A29.   Presence of Sets of Chairs in Annapolis

Wealth in Pounds	Years											
	1688–1709			1710–32			1733–54			1755–77		
	C	N	%	C	N	%	C	N	%	C	N	%
000–49	9	0	00	24	2	08	33	10	30	33	3	09
50–225	3	0	00	27	8	30	18	9	50	30	13	43
226–490	4	0	00	12	9	75	11	6	55	9	7	78
491+	1	0	00	9	7	78	15	4	27	17	13	76

C = Total number of cases
N = Presence of item
% = Percentage of cases

Table A30.   Presence of Tea Tables in Annapolis

	Years											
Wealth in Pounds	1688–1709			1710–32			1733–54			1755–77		
	C	N	%	C	N	%	C	N	%	C	N	%
000–49	9	0	00	24	0	00	33	2	06	33	3	09
50–225	3	0	00	27	3	11	18	2	11	30	12	40
226–490	4	0	00	12	1	08	11	2	18	9	1	11
491+	1	0	00	9	1	11	15	6	40	17	2	12

C = Total number of cases
N = Presence of item
% = Percentage of cases

Table A31.   Presence of Grooming-related Items (Dressing Boxes, Dressing Tables, Dressing Glasses, Shaving/Wash Basins, Combs, Toothbrushes, Clothes Brushes, Toothpicks) in Annapolis

	Years											
Wealth in Pounds	1688–1709			1710–32			1733–54			1755–77		
	C	N	%	C	N	%	C	N	%	C	N	%
000–49	9	0	00	24	2	08	33	7	21	33	1	03
50–225	3	1	33	27	7	26	18	5	28	30	8	27
226–490	4	0	00	12	7	58	11	1	09	9	3	33
491+	1	0	00	9	5	56	15	3	20	17	10	59

C = Total number of cases
N = Presence of item
% = Percentage of cases

Table A32.   Presence of Handkerchiefs in Annapolis

| Wealth in Pounds | Years | | | | | | | | | | | |
| | 1688–1709 | | | 1710–32 | | | 1733–54 | | | 1755–77 | | |
	C	N	%	C	N	%	C	N	%	C	N	%
000–49	9	1	11	24	4	17	33	0	00	33	1	03
50–225	3	0	00	27	1	04	18	2	11	30	8	27
226–490	4	1	25	12	3	25	11	1	09	9	3	33
491+	1	1	100	9	3	33	15	1	07	17	5	29

C = Total number of cases
N = Presence of item
% = Percentage of cases

Table A33.   Presence of Chamber Pots in Annapolis

| Wealth in Pounds | Years | | | | | | | | | | | |
| | 1688–1709 | | | 1710–32 | | | 1733–54 | | | 1755–77 | | |
	C	N	%	C	N	%	C	N	%	C	N	%
000–49	9	2	22	24	0	00	33	3	09	33	2	06
50–225	3	0	00	27	4	15	18	2	11	30	5	17
226–490	4	1	25	12	4	12	11	2	18	9	5	56
491+	1	0	00	9	3	33	15	6	40	17	7	41

C = Total number of cases
N = Presence of item
% = Percentage of cases

Table A34.   Presence of Close Stools in Annapolis

Wealth in Pounds	1688–1709			1710–32			1733–54			1755–77		
	C	N	%	C	N	%	C	N	%	C	N	%
000–49	9	1	11	24	0	00	33	3	09	33	1	03
50–225	3	0	00	27	3	11	18	1	06	30	6	20
226–490	4	1	25	12	6	50	11	2	18	9	3	33
491+	1	0	00	9	3	33	15	9	60	17	6	35

C = Total number of cases
N = Presence of item
% = Percentage of cases

Notes

INTRODUCTION

1. Eric Wolf, *Europe and the People Without History* (Berkeley: Univ. of California Press, 1982).
2. Bruce Trigger, "Distinguished Lecture in Archaeology: Constraints and Freedom," *American Anthropologist* 93, no. 3 (1991): 551–69.
3. Robert Paynter, "The Archaeology of Equality and Inequality," *Annual Review of Anthropology* 18 (1989): 369–99.
4. Wolf, "Distinguished Lecture in Archaeology: Facing Power," *American Anthropologist* 92, no. 3 (1990): 586–96.
5. Michel Foucault, *Discipline and Punish* (New York: Vintage Books, 1979).
6. Paynter, "Steps to an Archaeology of Capitalism: Material Change and Class Analysis," in *The Recovery of Meaning: Historical Archaeology in the Eastern United States,* ed. Mark P. Leone and Parker B. Potter (Washington, D.C.: Smithsonian Institution Press, 1988), 414.
7. Mark P. Leone, Parker B. Potter, Jr., and Paul A. Shackel, "Toward a Critical Archaeology," *Current Anthropology* 28, no. 3 (1987): 283–302.
8. Paynter, "Archaeology of Capitalism," 407–8.
9. Ibid., 407–10.
10. James Deetz, *In Small Things Forgotten: The Archaeology of Early American Life* (New York: Doubleday, 1977). Henry Glassie, *Folk Housing in Middle Virginia: A Structural Analysis of Historic Artifacts* (Knoxville: Univ. of Tennessee Press, 1975). Leone, "The Georgian Order as the Order of Mercan-

tile Capitalism in Annapolis, Maryland," in *The Recovery of Meaning*, 235–61.

11. Fernand Braudel, Preface to *La Méditerranée et al Monde Méditerranéen à l'eporque de Phillipp II*, rpt. in Fernand Braudel, *On History*, trans. Sarah Matthews (Chicago: Univ. of Chicago Press, 1980), 3 ff.

12. Exceptions are Norbert Elias, *The Civilizing Process* 1, *The History of Manners*, trans. Edmund Jephcott (New York: Pantheon Books, 1978), and John Kasson, *Rudeness and Civility: Manners in Nineteenth-Century Urban America* (New York: Hill and Wang, 1990).

13. See Braudel, Preface to *La Méditerranée*.

14. See, for instance, Daniel Miller, *Material Culture as Mass Consumption* (New York: Basil Blackwell, 1987); Neil McKendrick, John Brewer, and J. H. Plumb, *The Birth of a Consumer Society: The Commercialization of Eighteenth-Century England* (Bloomington: Indiana Univ. Press, 1982).

15. Mary Douglas and Baron Isherwood, *The World of Goods* (New York: Basic Books, 1979).

16. Miller, *Material Culture as Mass Consumption*.

17. Ibid., 136.

18. Leone, "The Georgian Order."

19. Leslie C. Stewart-Abernathy, "Urban Farmsteads: Household Responsibilities in the City," *Historical Archaeology* 20, no. 2 (1986): 5–15.

20. See, for instance, Ian Hodder, *Archaeology as Long-Term History* (Cambridge: Cambridge Univ. Press, 1987).

21. For recent works that provide examples of archaeological and historical data, see Barbara J. Little, *Text-Aided Archaeology* (Boca Raton, Fla.: CRC Press, 1992); Mary C. Beaudry, *Documentary Archaeology in the New World* (Cambridge: Cambridge Univ. Press, 1988).

22. Robert L. Schuyler, "The Spoken Word, the Written Word, Observed Behavior and Preserved Behavior: The Contexts Available to the Archaeologist," in *Historical Archaeology: A Guide to Substantive and Theoretical Contributions*, ed. Robert Schuyler (Farmingdale, N.Y.: Baywood Publishing, 1978), 269–77.

23. Miller, "The Limits of Domination," in *Domination and Resistance*, ed. Daniel Miller, Michael Rowlands, and Christopher Tilley (London: Unwin Hyman, 1989), 76.

24. Daniel Miller and Christopher Tilley, "Ideology, Power and Prehistory: An Introduction," in *Ideology, Power, and Prehistory*, ed. Miller and Tilley (Cambridge: Cambridge Univ. Press, 1984), 1–15.

25. Martin Wobst, "Stylistic Behavior and Information Exchange," *Univ. of Michigan, Museum of Anthropology Anthropological Papers* 61 (1977): 317–42.

26. Mary Braithwaite, "Decoration as Ritual Symbol: A Theoretical Proposal and an Ethnographic Study in Southern Sudan," in *Symbolic and Structural Archaeology*, ed. Ian Hodder (Cambridge: Cambridge Univ. Press, 1987), 80–88; Hodder, *Symbols in Action: Ethnoarchaeological Studies of Material Culture* (Cambridge: Cambridge Univ. Press, 1982); Hodder, *Reading the Past* (Cambridge: Cambridge Univ. Press, 1986); Michael Shanks and Christopher Tilley, *Social Theory and Archaeology* (Albuquerque: Univ. of New Mexico Press, 1987); Miller, *Artifacts as Categories: A Study of Ceramic Variability in Central India* (London: Cambridge Univ. Press, 1985).

27. Leone, "Symbolic, Structural and Critical Archaeology," in *American Archaeology Past and Future*, ed. D. Meltzer, D. Fowler, and J. Sabloff (Washington, D.C.: Smithsonian Institution Press, 1986), 416.

28. Shanks and Tilley, *Social Theory and Archaeology*, 79–116, 89.

29. Hodder, "Theoretical Archaeology: A Reactionary View," in *Symbolic and Structural Archaeology*, 7; Hodder, "Economic and Social Stress and Material Culture Patterning," *American Antiquity* 44, no. 3 (1979): 447.

30. Hodder, "Economic and Social Stress," 449.

31. Douglas and Isherwood, *The World of Goods*, 5, 72, 66.

32. Ibid., 66–68.

33. Grant McCracken, *Culture and Consumption: New Approaches to the Symbolic Character of Consumer Goods and Activities* (Bloomington: Indiana Univ. Press, 1988), 94.

34. Elias, *The Court Society* (New York: Random House, 1983), 85.

35. Ibid., 103.

36. Douglas and Isherwood, *The World of Goods*, 36.

37. Ibid., 65.

38. Elias, *The Court Society*, 65.

39. Shanks and Tilley, *Social Theory and Archaeology*, 102.

40. Foucault, *Discipline and Punish*; Louis Althusser, "Ideology and the State Apparatuses," in *Lenin and Philosophy and the Other Essays* (London: New Left Books, 1971).

41. Foucault, "Truth and Power," in *Power and Knowledge*, ed. C. Gordon (Hassock, England: Harvester, 1980).

42. Michel Foucault, *The History of Sexuality* 1, *An Introduction*, trans. R. Hurley (Harmondsworth: Penguin Press, 1981); Foucault, "Truth and Power."

43. Miller and Tilley, "An Introduction," 1–15.

44. Tilley, "Michel Foucault: Towards an Archaeology of Archaeology," in *Reading Material Culture: Structuralism, Hermeneutics and Post-Structuralism*, ed. Tilley (London: Basil Blackwell, 1990), 287–88.

45. Miller and Tilley, "An Introduction," 6.
46. For an additional discussion of power, see Charles E. Orser, Jr., "Toward a Theory of Power for Historical Archaeology: Plantations and Space," in *The Recovery of Meaning,* 314–43.
47. Foucault, *The History of Sexuality,* 93.
48. Tilley, "Michel Foucault," 286.
49. Foucault, "Truth and Power," 119.
50. Foucault, *Discipline and Punish;* Foucault, "Of Other Space," *Diacratics* 16 (1986): 22–23. Tilley, "Michel Foucault," 309.
51. Foucault, *Discipline and Punish,* 228.
52. Tilley, "Michel Foucault," 311.
53. Foucault, *Power and Knowledge,* 149.
54. Tilley, "Michel Foucault," 317; Foucault, *Discipline and Punish,* 22–26.
55. Pierre Bourdieu, *Outline of a Theory of Practice* (Cambridge: Cambridge Univ. Press, 1977).
56. Miller, Rowlands, and Tilley, Introd. to *Domination and Resistance,* 1–26.
57. Bourdieu, *Outline of a Theory of Practice.*
58. Miller, Rowlands, and Tilley, Introd. to *Domination and Resistance,* 15.
59. Bourdieu, *Outline of a Theory of Practice.*
60. Miller, Rowlands, and Tilley, Introd. to *Domination and Resistance,* 16.
61. Miller, "The Limits of Domination."
62. Ibid., 63.
63. Bourdieu, *Outline of a Theory of Practice;* Miller, *Material Culture as Mass Consumption.*
64. M. Mauss, *The Gift* (London: Cohen and West, 1954).
65. Bourdieu, *Outline of a Theory of Practice,* 3–9.
66. Miller, *Material Culture as Mass Consumption,* 3–9.
67. Ibid., 105.
68. Miller, "The Limits of Domination," 72.
69. See, for instance, Bourdieu, *Outline of a Theory of Practice.*
70. See A. Appadurai, "Introduction: Commodities and the Politics of Value," in *The Social Life of Things: Commodities in Cultural Perspective,* ed. A. Appadurai (Cambridge: Cambridge Univ. Press, 1986), 12 ff.
71. McCracken, *Culture and Consumption;* Hodder, *Symbols in Action;* Leone, "Symbolic, Structural and Critical Archaeology," 415–38.
72. See Miller, *Material Culture as Mass Consumption.*

Chapter 1. Individual Time

1. McKendrick, Brewer, and Plumb, *Birth of a Consumer Society,* 122 ff.
2. The Victualling Warehouse, 77 Main Street, Annapolis, Maryland,

18AP14, was excavated in the summer and fall of 1982 and the summer of 1983 under the supervision of Constance A. Crosby (Univ. of California, Berkeley). The crew consisted of the field school sponsored by the Univ. of Maryland, College Park under the direction of Mark P. Leone. Funding for work and analysis was provided by the Univ. of Maryland, College Park; Historic Annapolis, Inc.; the Maryland Humanities Council; and the Maryland Commission of the Capital City.

3. Anne Arundel County Deeds, 1747, RB 1: 23, p. 48, Maryland State Archives, Annapolis.

4. *Maryland Gazette,* 27 May 1784.

5. Ibid., 6 Oct. 1763.

6. Ibid., 17 Mar. 1768; Marlys J. Pearson, "Archaeological Excavations at 18AP14: The Victualling Warehouse Site, 77 Main St., Annapolis, Maryland 1982–84," (Annapolis: Historic Annapolis Foundation, 1991).

7. Edward C. Papenfuse, *In Pursuit of Profit: The Annapolis Merchant in the Era of the American Revolution, 1763–1805* (Baltimore: Johns Hopkins Univ. Press, 1975), 93.

8. Pearson, "Archaeological Excavations at 18AP14."

9. *Maryland Gazette,* 5 Feb. 1807.

10. Anne Arundel County Deeds, 1810, NH 15: 628, Maryland State Archives, Annapolis.

11. Constance A. Crosby, "Excavations at the Victualling Warehouse, AN 14, 1982: Preliminary Report" (Annapolis, Md.: Historic Annapolis, 1983), 14.

12. Barbara Liggett, "Preliminary Archaeological Investigations at 43 Pinkney Street and the Victualling Warehouse" (Annapolis, Md.: Historic Annapolis, 1977).

13. Pearson, "Archaeological Excavations at 18AP14."

14. Crosby, "Excavations at the Victualling Warehouse," 20.

15. The Thomas Hyde House, 193 Main Street, 18AP44, was excavated in three different sessions under my supervision. This work was generally sponsored by Archaeology in Annapolis, a cooperative project between the Univ. of Maryland and the Historic Annapolis Foundation. The initial work was to test the parking lot area where Mr. Paul Pearson, a local developer, and his associates were to construct a small shopping and business mall. Work was performed December 1985 through January 1986, a total of six weeks, with a crew of five. Mr. Pearson generously provided funding for this project. Because of the success of this initial testing program, further funding was provided by the Maryland Humanities Council. This work was part of a larger program that used as many as eight Univ. of Maryland-College Park students. Dorothy Humph directed the

work. Additional funding was sought in the winter of 1986 to test the inside of the Playhouse Theater, adjacent to the parking lot. The Maryland Commission for the Capital City provided this funding. Excavations proceeded for three weeks employing four Univ. of Maryland-College Park students. Additional work was performed during the summer of 1987 with four Univ. of Maryland-College Park field school students and directed by Eileen Williams.

16.   *Maryland Gazette,* 1 June 1769; *Maryland Gazette,* 4 June 1767.
17.   Jane McWilliams and Edward Papenfuse, eds., *Final Report: Appendix F, Lot Histories and Maps,* 1971, NEH Grant H 69–0–178, Maryland State Archives, Annapolis; Anne Arundel County Wills, 1795, JG 1: 487, Maryland State Archives, Annapolis; Papenfuse, *In Pursuit of Profit,* 10–81.
18.   McWilliams and Papenfuse, *Final Report.*
19.   The first two seasons at the Jonas Green Print Shop site were directed by Constance A. Crosby and assisted by Donald Creveling. In 1985 Barbara J. Little assisted Crosby, and in the summer of 1986 Little directed the field season at the site. Members of the Archaeology in Annapolis Project conducted the excavations, and the site served as the location for the Univ. of Maryland-College Park's field school for the four summers from 1983 to 1986.
20.   McWilliams and Papenfuse, *Final Report.*
21.   Little, *Ideology and Media: Historical Archaeology of Printing in 18th-Century Annapolis, Maryland* (Ann Arbor, Mich.: Univ. Microfilms International, 1987), 118–29.
22.   Ibid., 138–44.
23.   Ibid., 155–62.
24.   Ibid., 168–69.
25.   Ibid.
26.   The initial work at Reynolds Tavern was undertaken by Archaeology in Annapolis during the summer of 1982 under the direction of Anne E. Yentsch. Work continued the following year under the direction of Richard J. Dent. All artifacts were washed and labelled at the Historic Annapolis Foundation laboratory in Annapolis and catalogued at this location as well as at the Univ. of Maryland-College Park lab.
27.   Historic Annapolis, "Historic Sites Report: Reynolds Tavern, Church Circle, Annapolis, Maryland" (Annapolis, Md.: Historic Annapolis, 1979), app. A.
28.   Anne Arundel County Deeds, 1772, L.B., p. 359, Maryland State Archives, Annapolis.
29.   Historic Annapolis, "Historic Sites Report: Reynolds Tavern."

30. *Maryland Gazette,* 19 May 1785.
31. Ibid., 29 June 1786, 23 Mar. 1786.
32. Historic Annapolis, "Historic Sites Report: Reynolds Tavern."
33. *Maryland Gazette,* 27 May 1790.
34. Historic Annapolis, "Historic Sites Report: Reynolds Tavern," app. A.
35. Historic Annapolis, "Historic Sites Report: Reynolds Tavern."
36. See Pearson, "Archaeological Excavations at 18AP14."
37. Paynter, "Archaeology of Capitalism," 407–33.
38. Shackel, *A Historical Archaeology of Personal Discipline* (Ann Arbor, Mich.: Univ. Microfilms International, 1987).
39. Miller, "Classification and Economic Scaling of 19th-Century Ceramics," *Historical Archaeology* 14 (1980): 1–40.
40. Wilma Motley, *Ethics, Jurisprudence and History for the Dental Hygienist* (Philadelphia: Lea and Febiger, 1983), 102.
41. Ibid., 103.
42. Desiderius Erasmus, *La Civilité Puerile Par Erasmede Rotterdam, Traduction Nouvelle, Texte Latin an Regard, Precedée D'Une Notice Sur Les Livres de Civilité Dupuis le XVI Siecle, por Alcide Bonneau,* trans. of *De Civilitate Morum Puerilium* (1526; rpt. Paris: I. Liseux, 1877).
43. Fernand Braudel, *Civilization and Capitalism: 15th-18th Century 3, The Perspectives of the World* (New York: Harper and Row, 1984).
44. Motley, *Dental Hygienist.*
45. Ibid., 104.
46. Michael R. Snow, *Brushmaking: Craft and Industry* (Oxford: Oxford Polytechnic Press, 1984), 39.
47. Ibid., 17–24.
48. Albert Tebbs, *Brushmaking by Hand* (London: Wheatland Journals, 1949).
49. Snow, *Brushmaking: Craft and Industry,* 27–28.
50. Fred Kidd, *Brushmaking Materials* (London: British Brush Manufacturers Research Association, 1957), 142; William Kiddier, *The Old Trade Union: From Unprinted Records of the Brushmakers* (London: Allen and Unwin, 1931), 73.
51. Snow, *Brushmaking: Craft and Industry,* 39.
52. Ibid., 65; Mervyn Gordon Jones, *The Story of Brushmaking: A Northfork Craft* (Northfork, England: Briton Chadwick, 1974), 6.
53. Snow, *Brushmaking: Craft and Industry,* 84.
54. Ibid., 69.
55. Jones, *Story of Brushmaking,* 10; Kiddier, *Records of the Brushmakers,* 78.
56. Leone and Shackel, "The Georgian Order in Annapolis, Maryland," *Maryland Archaeologist* 26, nos. 1 and 2 (1990): 69–84.

57.   Paynter, "Archaeology of Capitalism," 407–8.
58.   Ibid., 414.

Chapter 2. Social Time

1.   Stanley Gray and V. J. Wycoff, "The International Tobacco Trade in
      the Seventeenth Century," *Southern Economic Journal* 7 (1940): 1–26;
      John J. McCusker and Russell R. Menard, *The Economy of British Amer-*
      ica: 1607–1789 (Chapel Hill: Univ. of North Carolina Press, 1985),
      120; see, for instance, Robert Polk Thomas, "The Tobacco Export of
      the Upper James River District, 1773–75," *William and Mary Quarterly*
      18 (1961): 393–401.
2.   McCusker and Menard, *Economy of British America*.
3.   Russell R. Menard, Lois Green Carr, and Lorena S. Walsh, "A Small
      Planter's Profits: The Cole Estate and the Growth of the Early Chesa-
      peake Economy, *William and Mary Quarterly* 40 (1983): 171–96.
4.   Wycoff, "Land Prices in Seventeenth-Century Maryland," *American*
      Economic Review 27 (1938): 82–88.
5.   McCusker and Menard, *Economy of British America*, 120–23; also see
      Menard, "The Tobacco Industry in the Chesapeake colonies, 1617–
      1730: An Interpretation," *Research in Economic History* 5 (1980): 157–
      61.
6.   John M. Hemphill II, *Virginia and the English Commercial System 1689–*
      1733 (New York: Garland Publishing, 1985).
7.   Allan Kulikoff, *Tobacco and Slaves: The Development of Southern Culture*
      in the Chesapeake, 1680–1800 (Chapel Hill: Univ. of North Carolina
      Press, 1986), 77; Carville V. Earle, *The Evolution of a Tidewater Settle-*
      ment System: All Hallow's Parish, Maryland, 1650–1783 (Research paper
      no. 170, Univ. of Chicago, Dept. of Geography, 1975), 14–18; Charles
      Wetherall, "'Boom and Bust' in the Colonial Chesapeake Economy,"
      Journal of Interdisciplinary History 15 (1984): 185 ff.
8.   Lois Green Carr, P. M. G. Harris, and Russell Menard, "The Develop-
      ment of Society in the Colonial Chesapeake: Final Report to the Na-
      tional Endowment for Humanities," 1980, Grant RS-23687–76–431,
      Maryland Hall of Records, Annapolis, 15; Carr and Walsh, "Invento-
      ries and the Analysis of Wealth and Consumption Patterns in St. Mary's
      County, Maryland, 1658–1777," *The Newberry Papers in Family and*
      Community History (Chicago: Newberry Library, 1977), paper 77–46,
      p. 39; McCusker and Menard, *Economy of British America*, 127.
9.   Kulikoff, *Tobacco and Slaves*, 40.

10. James A. Henretta, *The Evolution of American Society 1700–1815: An Interdisciplinary Analysis* (Toronto: D.C. Heath, 1973), 63.

11. William Kilty, *The Laws of Maryland* 1 (Annapolis, Md.: Frederick Green Printer, 1799), chap. 4, B, no. 5, (1728), 203.

12. Kulikoff, *Tobacco and Slaves*, 273–74.

13. Ibid., 79.

14. Earle *Tidewater Settlement System;* Menard, "The Tobacco Industry."

15. Kulikoff, *Tobacco and Slaves*, 92 n. 21.

16. Ibid., 104.

17. John C. Rainbolt, "The Absence of Towns in Seventeenth-Century Virginia," *Journal of Southern History* 25 (1969): 343–60; Edward M. Riley, "The Town Acts of Colonial Virginia," *Journal of Southern History* 16 (1950): 306–23.

18. Kulikoff, *Tobacco and Slaves*, 104–5.

19. Hemphill, *English Commercial System.*

20. Rainbolt, "The Absence of Towns"; Riley, "Town Acts."

21. Kulikoff, *Tobacco and Slaves*, 107.

22. Ibid., 107–10.

23. Ibid., 113.

24. Ibid., 114; Earle, *Tidewater Settlement System,* 24–27.

25. For a detailed description of the commodity price index, see Carr and Walsh, "Inventories and the Analysis of Wealth and Consumption Patterns in St. Mary's County, Maryland, 1658–1777," *Historical Methods* 13, no. 2 (1980): 81–104.

26. Carr, Harris, and Menard, "Society in the Colonial Chesapeake"; Carr and Walsh, "Analysis of Wealth" (1977).

27. Carr and Walsh, "Analysis of Wealth" (1977), 14.

28. Ibid., 14.

29. Kulikoff, *Tobacco and Slaves*, 119.

30. Ibid., 119; also see Kulikoff, "The Economic Growth of the Eighteenth-Century Chesapeake Colonies," *Journal of Economic History* 39 (1979): 282 ff.

31. Brinley Thomas, "The Rhythm of Growth in the Atlantic Economy of the Eighteenth Century," *Research in Economic History* 3 (1979): 19 ff.

32. Kulikoff, *Tobacco and Slaves*, 263.

33. Ibid., 263.

34. Ibid., 289; Henretta, *Evolution of American Society,* 77.

35. Rhys Isaac, *The Transformation of Virginia; 1740–1790,* (Chapel Hill: Univ. of North Carolina Press, 1982), 73–75.

36. Ibid., 37–38, 303, 305.

37. Ibid., 256–66.
38. Timothy H. Breene, "The Meaning of Things: Consumer Culture of Eighteenth-Century America and the Coming Revolution" (Paper presented at Conference of Accumulation and Display, Newark, Del., 7–8 Nov. 1986).
39. Leone, "Interpreting Ideology in Historical Archaeology: Using the Rules of Perspective in the William Paca Garden in Annapolis, Maryland," in *Ideology, Power and Prehistory,* 25–35.
40. Constance Werner Ramirez, *Urban History for Preservation Planning: The Annapolis Experience* (Ann Arbor, Mich.: Univ. Microfilms International, 1975), 33.
41. Papenfuse, *In Pursuit of Profit,* 8.
42. Elihu Riley, *The Ancient City: A History of Annapolis, in Maryland 1649–1887* (Annapolis, Md.: Record Printing Office, 1887), 54–58.
43. Papenfuse, *In Pursuit of Profit,* 9.
44. John W. Reps, *Tidewater Towns: City Planning In Colonial Virginia and Maryland* (Williamsburg, Va.: Colonial of Williamsburg Foundation, 1972), 121.
45. Ibid., 123.
46. Ibid., 123.
47. Ibid., 125.
48. Ramirez, *Urban History,* 38–40.
49. Papenfuse, *In Pursuit of Profit,* 5–34.
50. Ebinezer Cook, "The Sot-Weed Factor, or, A Voyage to Maryland," in *Early Maryland Poetry,* ed. Bernard C. Steiner (1708; rpt. Baltimore: Maryland Historical Society, 1900), 24–30.
51. Walsh, "Annapolis as a Center of Production," in *Annapolis and Anne Arundel County, Maryland, A Study of Urban Development in a Tobacco Economy, 1649–1776,* ed. Walsh, 1983, NEH Grant RS-20199–81–1955, Historic Annapolis, 4.
52. Ibid., 1–5, 5, 6.
53. Ibid., 1.
54. Nancy Baker, "Annapolis, Maryland 1695–1730," *Maryland Historical Magazine* 81, no. 3 (1986): 208.
55. Carr and Walsh, "Analysis of Wealth" (1977), 14.
56. Jean Russo, "Economy of Anne Arundel County," in *Annapolis and Anne Arundel County,* 3; Shackel, *A Historical Archaeology;* Leone and Shackel, "Forks, Clocks and Power," in *Mirror and Metaphor,* ed. Daniel Ingersoll and Gordon Bronitski (Latham, Md.: American Press, 1987).
57. Russo, "Economy of Anne Arundel County."

58. Archives of Maryland, qtd. in Baker, "Annapolis, Maryland 1695–1730," 201.

59. Baker, "Annapolis, Maryland, 1695–1730," in *Annapolis and Anne Arundel County*, 5, 9.

60. In 1771 New York City had a population of 21,900; in 1790, 33,400. See Nan A. Rothschild, *New York City Neighborhoods: The Eighteenth Century* (New York: Academic Press, 1990).

61. Walsh, "Anne Arundel County Population," 6; Papenfuse, *In Pursuit of Profit*, 14–15.

62. Shackel, "Town Plans and Everyday Material Culture: An Archaeology of Social Relations in Colonial Maryland's Capital Cities," in *The Historic Chesapeake: Archaeological Contributions*, ed. Paul A. Shackel and Barbara J. Little (Washington, D.C.: Smithsonian Institution Press, 1993).

63. Russo, "Economy of Anne Arundel County," app.

64. Papenfuse, *In Pursuit of Profit*, 16–17, 15.

65. As qtd. in Aubry Land, ed., *Letters From America by William Eddis* (Cambridge: Harvard Univ. Press, 1969), 49.

66. Kulikoff, *Tobacco and Slaves*, 220.

67. Eddis, qtd. in Land, *Letters From America*, 13.

68. Ibid.

69. Papenfuse, *In Pursuit of Profit*, 136.

70. Ibid., 154.

71. Ibid., 133.

72. Gregory Stiverson, *Poverty in a Land of Plenty: Tenancy in Eighteenth-Century Maryland* (Baltimore: Johns Hopkins Univ. Press, 1977), 99.

73. Harriet Anderson to Mrs. Mary Grafton Ridout, 1791, Ridout Gift Collection, D 504–4, folder 634, Maryland State Archives, Annapolis.

74. Papenfuse, *In Pursuit of Profit*.

75. Carr and Walsh, "Analysis of Wealth" (1977); Hemphill, *English Commercial System*; Kulikoff, *Tobacco and Slaves*; McCusker and Menard, *Economy of British America*.

76. Carr and Walsh, "Analysis of Wealth" (1977).

77. Russo, "Economy of Anne Arundel County"; Shackel, *A Historical Archaeology*; Leone and Shackel, "Forks, Clocks and Power."

78. Voltaire, qtd. in Elias, *History of Manners* 1: 103.

79. *Maryland Gazette*, 26 Aug. 1746.

80. Ibid.

81. Ibid., 4 June 1748.

82. Ibid., 18 Apr. 1793, 2 May 1793.

83. Horatio Sharpe to John Ridout, 1780, Ridout Gift Collection, D 358–9, D 371–4, folder 99, Maryland State Archives, Annapolis.

84. H. Ogle to Mrs. Anne Ogle, 1790, Ridout Gift Collection, D 504–4, folder 626, Maryland State Archives, Annapolis.

85. B. Bladen to Mrs. Anne Ogle, 1765, Ridout Gift Collection, D358–9, D317–4, folder 14, Maryland State Archives, Annapolis.

86. T. Ridout to John Ridout, 1793, Ridout Gift Collection, D 504–4, folder 645, Maryland State Archives, Annapolis.

87. H. Ogle to Mrs. Anne Ogle.

88. Elizabeth Ridout Ward to Samuel Ridout, 1793, Ridout Gift Collection, D 504–4, folder 645, Maryland State Archives, Annapolis.

89. Land, *Letters From America,* xvi.

90. Carroll, qtd. in Land, *Letters From America,* xvi; Eddis, qtd. in Land, *Letters From America,* xv, 58.

91. Land, *Letters From America,* 20.

92. *St. Johns Board of Visitors and Governors Minutes: 1786–1826,* J22, box 5, 5633–53, p. 35, Maryland State Archives, Annapolis.

93. Ibid., 35, 39, 39–40.

94. Ibid., 136.

95. Ibid.

96. Ibid., 3.

97. Carl Bridenbaugh, *Gentleman's Progress: The Itinerarium of Dr. Alexander Hamilton; 1744* (Westport, Conn.: Greenwood Press, 1973), 8.

98. Bridenbaugh, *Gentleman's Progress,* 134.

99. Ibid., 93, 42.

100. Kulikoff, *Tobacco and Slaves.*

101. Elaine G. Breslaw, ed., *Records of the Tuesday Club of Annapolis: 1745–56* (Urbana: Univ. of Illinois Press, 1988), xx.

102. Ibid., 156.

103. Ibid., 282.

CHAPTER 3. PROBATE DATA AND SOCIAL TIME

1. For a complete bibliography of probate inventory studies, see Peter Benes, ed., *Early American Probate Inventories: The Dublin Seminar for New England Folklife Annual Proceedings 1987* (Boston: Boston Univ., 1989); for a study on furnishings, see L. Baumgarten, "The Textile Trade in Boston, 1650–1700," in *Arts of the Anglo-American Community in the Seventeenth Century,* ed. Ian Quimby (Charlottesville: Univ. Press of Virginia, 1975), 219–73; for a study in ceramics, see B. Teller, "Ceramics in

Providence, 1750–1900," *Antiques* 94, no. 4 (1968): 570–77; for a study in clothing, see Patricia Trauman, "Dress in Seventeenth-Century Cambridge, Massachusetts: An Inventory Based Reconstruction," in *Early American Probate Inventories*, 51–73; for a study of fireplace equipment, see Richard M. Candee, "First-Period Architecture in Maine and New Hampshire: The Evidence of Probate Inventories," in *Early American Probate Inventories*, 97–120.

2. For examples on research on changing life-styles, see Gloria Main, "Inequality in Early America: Evidence from Probate Records of Massachusetts and Maryland," *Journal of Interdisciplinary History* 7, no. 4 (1977): 559–81; Carr and Walsh, "Lifestyles and Standards of Living in the British Colonial Chesapeake" (Paper presented at International Economic History Association Meeting, Bern, Switzerland, 1986; Carr and Walsh, "Analysis of Wealth" (1977); Carol Shamas, "The Domestic Environment in Early Modern England and America," *Journal of Social History* 14, no. 1 (1980): 1–24; K. Sweeney, "Furniture and the Domestic Environment in Wethersfield, Connecticut, 1639–1800," in *Material Life in America, 1600–1860*, ed. Robert Blair St. George (Boston: Northeastern Univ. Press, 1988), 262–90; for studies in vernacular architecture, see Abbott Lowell Cummings, "Inside the Massachusetts House," in *Common Places: Readings in American Vernacular Architecture*, ed. Dell Upton and John Vlatch (Athens: Univ. of Georgia Press, 1986), 219–39); for studies on functional uses of space, see Robert Blair St. George, "'Set Thine House in Order': The Domestication of the Yeoman in Seventeenth-Century New England," in *Common Places*, 336–64; Deetz et al., "Plymouth Colony Room-by-Room Inventories, 1633–1684" (Paper presented at the Dublin Seminar for New England Folklife, Early American Inventories, 11–12 July 1987.

3. See Gary Wheeler Stone, "Ceramics in Suffolk County Massachusetts, Inventories, 1680–1775, A Preliminary Study, with Diverse Comments Theron, and Sundry Suggestions," *The Conference on Historic Site Archaeology Papers 1968* 3, no. 2 (1970): 73–90; Deetz, *In Small Things Forgotten*.

4. Marley Brown, "Ceramics from Plymouth, 1621–1800: The Documentary Record," in *Ceramics in America*, ed. Quimby (Charlottesville: Univ. Press of Virginia, 1973), 41–74; Joanne Bowen, "Probate Inventories: An Evaluation from the Perspective of Zooarchaeology and Agricultural History at Mott Farm," in *Historical Archaeology: A Guide*, 149–59.

5. Beaudry, "Words for Things: Linguistic Analysis of Probate Inventories," in *Documentary Archaeology*, 43–50; Beaudry, *"Or What Else You Please to*

Call It" Folk Semantic Domains in Early Virginia Probate Inventories (Ann Arbor, Mich.: Univ. Microfilms International, 1980); Beaudry et al., "A Vessel Typology for Early Chesapeake Ceramics: the Potomac Typological System," *Historical Archaeology* 17, no. 1 (1983): 18–43.

6. Anne E. Yentsch, "Farming, Fishing, Whaling, Trading: Land and Sea as Resource on Eighteenth-Century Cape Cod," in *Documentary Archaeology,* 138–60; Yentsch, *Expressions of Cultural Diversity and Social Reality in Seventeenth-Century New England* (Ann Arbor, Mich.: Univ. Microfilms International, 1980); Kathleen Bragdon, "The Material culture of the Christian Indians of New England, 1650–1775," in *Documentary Archaeology,* 43–50.

7. Steven Pendery, *Symbolism of Community: Status Differences and the Archaeological Record in Charlestown, Massachusetts, 1630–1760* (Ann Arbor, Mich.: Univ. Microfilms International, 1987); Pendery, "Consumer Behavior in Colonial Charlestown, Massachusetts, 1630–1760," *Historical Archaeology* 26, no. 3, (1992): 57–72.

8. Little, *Ideology and Media;* Little, "'She was . . . an Example to her Sex'; Possibilities for a Feminist Archaeology in the Historic Chesapeake," in *The Historic Chesapeake: Archaeological Contributions.*

9. Shackel, "Probate Inventories in Historical Archaeology: A Review and Alternatives," in *Text-Aided Archaeology,* 205–16; Shackel, *A Historical Archaeology;* Shackel, "Modern Discipline: Its Historical Context in the Colonial Chesapeake," *Historical Archaeology,* 26, no. 3, (1992): 73–84; Shackel, "Consumerism and the Structuring of Social Relations: A Historical Archaeological Perspective," in *Digging into Popular Culture: Theories and Methodologies in Archeology, Anthropology and Other Fields,* ed. Ray B. Browne and Pat Browne (Bowling Green, Ohio: Bowling Green State Univ. Popular Press, 1991), 36–47.

10. Carr and Walsh, "Analysis of Wealth" (1977), 2.

11. Main, "Probate Records as a Source for Early American History," *William and Mary Quarterly* 32 (1970); Carr, conversation with author, 1 May, 6 Nov. 1986.

12. Ellie Vallette, *The Deputy Commissary's Guide Within the Province of Maryland* (Annapolis, Md.: Anne Katherine Green and Son).

13. Carr and Walsh, "Analysis of Wealth" (1977), 4.

14. Carr and Walsh, "Analysis of Wealth" (1980), 82; Daniel Scott Smith, "Underregistration and Bias in Probate Records: An Analysis of Data From Eighteenth-Century Hingham, Massachusetts," *William and Mary Quarterly* 32 (1975): 100–112.

15. Vallette, *Deputy Commissary's Guide,* 107.

16. Carr and Walsh, "Analysis of Wealth" (1977), 4.
17. Vallette, *Deputy Commissary's Guide*, 40–1.
18. Carr, conversation with author, 1 May, 6 Nov. 1986.
19. Carr and Walsh, "Analysis of Wealth" (1980), 83.
20. Carr and Walsh, "Analysis of Wealth" (1977), 3.
21. Carr and Walsh, "Analysis of Wealth" (1980), 81; Carr and Walsh, "Analysis of Wealth" (1977), 1.
22. Carr, "Methodological Procedures for Inventory Analysis," in *Annapolis and Anne Arundel County.*
23. Smith, "Underregistration and Bias."
24. Carr and Walsh, "Lifestyles and Standards of Living"; Carr and Walsh, "Changing Lifestyles and Consumer Behavior in the Colonial Chesapeake," MS on file, Maryland Hall of Records, St. Mary's City Commission, Annapolis.
25. Carr and Walsh, "Changing Lifestyles and Consumer Behavior," 5.
26. Carr and Walsh, "Analysis of Wealth" (1977), 31.
27. Ibid., 32.
28. Ibid., 34, 33–36.
29. Carr and Walsh, "Lifestyles and Standards of Living," 5; Carr and Walsh, "Analysis of Wealth" (1977), 38–39; Carr and Walsh, "Changing Lifestyles and Consumer Behavior," 23–25.
30. Carr and Walsh, "Lifestyles and Standards of Living," 7–8.
31. Carr and Walsh, "Changing Lifestyles and Consumer Behavior," 44.
32. Hodder, *Symbols in Action*, 12, 85.
33. Qtd. in Norbert Elias, *The Civilizing Process 2, Power and Civility*, trans. Edmund Jephcott (New York: Pantheon Books, 1983), 100.
34. Douglas and Isherwood, *The World of Goods*; Little, *Ideology and Media.*
35. Leone and Shackel, "Forks, Clocks and Power," 46; Leone, "Symbolic, Structural and Critical Archaeology," 415; Douglas and Isherwood, *The World of Goods*, 5, 72.
36. Shanks and Tilley, *Social Theory and Archaeology*, 131.
37. Hodder, "Postprocessual Archaeology," in *Advances in Archaeological Methods and Theory* 8, ed. Michael B. Schiffer (New York: Academic Press, 1985), 5.
38. Douglas and Isherwood, *The World of Goods*, 118, 144, 180.
39. Ibid., 145; Amos Rapoport, *The Meaning of the Built Environment: A Nonverbal Communication Approach* (London: Sage Publications, 1982), 183.
40. Douglas and Isherwood, *The World of Goods*, 140.
41. Ibid., 118.

42. Hodder, *Symbols in Action;* Hodder, "Economic and Social Stress and Material Culture Patterning," *American Antiquity* 44, no. 3 (1979): 446–54; Hodder, *Symbols in Action,* 187.

43. F. Barth, ed., *Ethnic Groups and Boundaries* (London: Allen and Unwin; Edward Spicer, "Persistent Cultural Systems," *Science* 174, no.4011 (1971): 795–800; also see Randell H. McGuire, "The Study of Ethnicity in Historical Archaeology," *Journal of Anthropological Archaeology* 1 (1982): 159–78.

44. Hodder, *Symbols in Action;* Douglas and Isherwood, *The World of Goods;* Miller, *Material Culture as Mass Consumption.*

45. Miller, "A Tenant Farmer's Tableware: Nineteenth-Century Ceramics from Tabb's Purchase," *Maryland Historical Magazine* 69, no. 2 (1974): 208.

46. Time and fiscal constraints prevented a more in-depth sampling method. If these results are provocative, further research can examine a complete population of probate inventories.

47. Carr and Walsh, "Lifestyles and Standards of Living"; Carr and Walsh, "Analysis of Wealth" (1980); Carr and Walsh, "Analysis of Wealth" (1977).

48. Carr and Walsh, "Analysis of Wealth" (1980), 97.

49. Carr, Harris, and Menard, "Society in the Colonial Chesapeake."

50. Although most of the data sets consist of reliable sample sizes, some of the seventeenth-century Annapolis and Anne Arundel County aggregates contain less than ten cases and should be viewed cautiously.

51. Leone, "The Georgian Order," 235–61; Leone and Shackel, "Forks, Clocks and Power."

52. There is the possibility that the urban data set is more variable than the countryside data, because some of this information is based upon a sample interval of twelve years. Such samples can be smoother and the intervening years may show variation.

53. Braudel, *Civilization and Capitalism* 1: 250–55.

54. Shackel, "Conspicuous Consumption and Class Maintenance: A Case Example from the Nicoll Site," in *The Historical Archaeology of Long Island* 1, *The Sites,* ed. Gaynell Stone and Donna Ottusch-Kianka (St. James, N.Y.: Braun-Brumfield, 1987), 156–70.

55. Braudel, *Civilization and Capitalism* 3: 251.

56. Ibid. 1: 328–33.

57. Deetz, *In Small Things Forgotten.*

58. Because some of the late seventeenth-century data consists of relatively small data sets, generalities for this era should be taken cautiously.

59. Braudel, *Civilization and Capitalism* 3: 48 ff.

60. Timothy H. Breene and Stephen Innes, *"Myne Owne Ground," Race and Freedom on Virginia's Eastern Shore, 1640–1676* (Oxford: Oxford Univ. Press, 1980), 120; Isaac, *Transformation of Virginia*, 137.

61. Breene and Innes, *"Myne Owne Ground"*; Isaac, "Evangelical Revolt: The Nature of the Baptist Challenge to the Traditional Order in Virginia, 1765 to 1775," *William and Mary Quarterly* 31 (1974): 345–48; Isaac, *Transformation of Virginia*.

62. William Kilty, *The Laws of Maryland* 1, chap. 38, Lib HS (1763), 520; chap. 7, Lib RG (1771), 107; chap. 14, Lib RG, (1773), 258.

CHAPTER 4. THE LONG-TERM HISTORY OF ETIQUETTE

1. See, for instance, Braudel, *Civilization and Capitalism* 1, 2, and 3; Wolf, *People Without History*.

2. Hugh G. J. Aitken, *Taylorism at Watertown Arsenal: Scientific Management in Action, 1908–1915* (Cambridge: Harvard Univ. Press, 1960); Harry Braverman, *Labor and Monopoly Capital; The Degradation of Work in the Twentieth Century* (New York, Monthly Review Press, 1975).

3. Davis S. Landes, *Revolution in Time: Clocks and the Making of the Modern World* (Cambridge: Harvard Univ. Press, 1983); 2–5, 25.

4. Foucault, *Discipline and Punish*, 149, 150.

5. E. P. Thompson, "Time, Work-Discipline, and Industrial Capitalism," *Past and Present* 38 (1967): 56–97; Leone, "The Georgian Order," 235–61.

6. Foucault, *Discipline and Punish*, 152, 170, 176, 222.

7. Landes, *Revolution in Time*, 77–78.

8. Thompson, "Time, Work-Discipline," 60.

9. Landes, *Revolution in Time*, 25; Jacques LeGoff, "Labor Time in the 'Crisis' of the Fourteenth Century: From Medieval Time to Modern Time," in *Time, Work and Culture in the Middle Ages*, ed. Jacques LeGoff (Chicago: Chicago Univ. Press, 1980), 44.

10. Thompson, "Time, Work-Discipline," 71.

11. Herbert Applebaum, "Theoretical Introduction," in *Work in Non-Market and Transitional Societies*, ed., Herbert Applebaum (Albany: State Univ. of New York Press, 1989), 17.

12. Landes, *Revolution in Time*, 72.

13. C. F. C. Beeson, *English Church Clocks, 1280–1850* (London: Antiquarian Horological Society, 1971), 16.

14. Landes, *Revolution in Time*, 89.

15. Qtd. in Thompson, "Time, Work-Discipline," 63.
16. Carlo M. Cipolla, *Clocks and Culture: 1300–1700* (New York: W. W. Norton, 1978), 69; Rachel Doggett, Introd. to *Time the Great Innovator: Timekeeping and Time Consciousness in Early Modern Europe*, ed. Rachel Doggett (Washington, D.C.: Folger Shakespeare Library, 1986), 19.
17. Doggett, *Time the Great Innovator*, 105.
18. Ibid., 105, 105–6.
19. Ibid., 106.
20. Ibid.
21. Doggett, Introd. to *Time the Great Innovator*, 17.
22. Leone, "Interpreting Ideology in Historical Archaeology"; Leone, "Material Culture of the Georgian Order" (Paper presented at the Colonial Experience: The Eighteenth-Century Chesapeake, Baltimore, 13–14 Sept. 1984); Leone, "The Georgian Order in Annapolis" (Paper presented at Eastern States Archaeological Federation meeting, Annapolis, 1984); also see Leone and Shackel, "Forks, Clocks and Power."
23. Thompson, "Time, Work-Discipline," 67–68.
24. Philip Dormer Stanhope Chesterfield, *Letters to His Son*, ed. Leigh (1776; rpt. London: M. Walter Dunne, 1901), 33, 31.
25. Chesterfield, *Letters to His Son*, 37.
26. Nicholas Orme, *English Schools in the Middle Ages* (London: Methuem, 1973).
27. Sylvia L. Thrupp, *The Merchant Class of Medieval London: 1300–1500* (Chicago: Univ. of Chicago Press, 1948).
28. See, for instance, R. Allen Brown, "A List of Castles 1155–1216," *English Historical Review* 74 (1959): 249–80; Brown, "Royal Castle-Building in England, 1154–1226," *English Historical Review* 70 (1955): 353–99.
29. Jonathan Nicholls, *The Matter of Courtesy: Medieval Courtesy Books and the Gawaioa-Poet* (Bury St. Edmunds, Suffolk: St. Edondsbury Press, 1985), 43.
30. Ibid., 47–48.
31. Also see Douglas, "Standard Social Use of Food: Introduction," in *Food in the Social Order: Studies in Food and Festivities in Three American Communities*, ed. Mary Douglas (New York: Russell Sage Foundation, 1984).
32. Nicholls, *Matter of Courtesy*.
33. John Russell, "The Boke of Nurture, Folowyng Englondis Gise, by Me

John Russell, Sum Time Servande with Duke Vmfrey of Glowcetur,"
rpt. in *The Babes Book: Medieval Manners for the Young Done Into Modern
English From Dr. Furnivall's Texts by Edith Richert* (c. 1450; rpt. New
York: Cooper Square Publishers, 1966).

34. As qtd. in Nicholls, *Matter of Courtesy*, 48.
35. De Callieres qtd. in Elias, *History of Manners* 1: 78.
36. Baldassare Castiglione, *The Book of the Courtier*, trans. Sir Thomas
Hoby (1528; rpt. New York: AMS Press, 1967).
37. Wayne A. Rebhorn, *Courtly Performance: Masking and Festivity in Castiglione's Book of the Courtier* (Detroit: Wayne State Univ. Press, 1978),
13.
38. Esther B. Aresty, *The Best Behavior: The Course of Good Manners From
Antiquity to the Present-As Seen Through Courtesy and Etiquette Books*
(New York: Simon and Schuster, 1970), 69.
39. Giovanni della Casa, *Il Galateo: or A Treatise on Politeness and Delicacy of
Manners* (1558; 1576 ed., *Il Galateo; or A Treatise of the Manners and
Behaviours*, rpt. as *A Treatise of the Manners and Behaviours* [Amsterdam,
N.Y.: Da Capo Press, 1969]).
40. Della Casa, qtd. in Elias, *History of Manners* 1: 90.
41. Stefano Guazzo, *The Civile Conversation of M. Steeven Guazzo*. The first
three books were translated by George Pettie in 1581 and the fourth by
Brath Young in 1586. (New York: Knopf, 1925).
42. Ball qtd. in Aresty, *The Best Behavior*, 88.
43. Sir Thomas Smith *The Commonwealth of England and Manner of Government Thereof. With New Additions of the Cheefe Court in England, the Offices There of, and Their Several Functions, by Sayd Author, Never Before
Published* (1583; rpt. London: Imprinted by J. Windef for G. Seton,
1589); Smith, qtd. in Aresty, *The Best Behavior*, 88.
44. John Brinsley, *Ludus Literarius; or, The Grammer School by John Brinsley*,
ed. E. T. Campagnac (1612; rpt. London: The Univ. Press, 1917);
Henry Peachman, *The Complete Gentleman* (1622; rpt. New York: Da
Capo Press, 1968), 21.
45. Richard Brathwaite, *The English Gentleman* (London: Printed by John
Haverland, 1630); Richard Allestree, *The Gentleman's Calling* (1660;
rpt. London: Printed for R. Pawlet, 1660).
46. Antoine de Courtin, *The Rules of Civility; or Certain Ways of Deportment
Observed in France, Amongst All Persons of Quality, Upon Several Occasions* (1670; rpt. London: Printed for J. Martyn at the Bell in St. Paul's
Church-Yard, and John Starkey at the Mitre in Fleet-Street, New Tem-
ple Bar, 1671).

47.   Aresty, *The Best Behavior*, 105.

48.   Ibid., 129–30, 129–31.

49.   Ibid., 129.

50.   Adam Petrie, *Rules of Good Deportment or Good Breeding* (1720; rpt. Edinburgh: Privately printed, 1877); Sir John Barnard, *A Present for an Apprentice: or, A Sure Guide to Gain Both Esteem and Estate with Rules for His Conduct to His Master and in the World* (1741; rpt. London: Jeffcoat, 1953); James Burgh, *The Art of Speaking* (1758; rpt. Boston: Printed by Thomas Hall for James White and Ebenezer Larkin, 1795).

51.   Joseph Addison, *The Spectator* (1711; rpt. London: J. M. Dent, 1907), vol. 1: 135–36.

52.   Aresty, *The Best Behavior*, 144–46.

53.   Chesterfield, qtd. in John Edward Mason, *Gentlefolk in the Making: Studies in the History of English Courtesy Literature and Related Topics From 1531 to 1774* (New York: Octagon Books, 1971), 286.

54.   Aresty, *The Best Behavior*, 151.

55.   Elias, *History of Manners*, 67.

56.   Rhode, "Book of Nurture and School of Good Manners," rpt. in *The Babee's Book*, 134.

57.   Rhode, "The Babee's Book," in *The Babee's Book*, 6, 6–7.

58.   Ibid., 27; as qtd. in Elias, *History of Manners*, 88.

59.   Russell, "Boke of Nurture," 57.

60.   As qtd. in Elias, *History of Manners*, 89–90.

61.   Charles Cooper, *The English Table in History and Literature* (London: Sampson Low, Marston and Co., 1929).

62.   Judith Martin, *Common Courtesy: In Which Miss Manners Solves the Problem that Baffled Mr. Jefferson* (New York: Athenaeum Press, 1985).

63.   Thomas Coryate, *Coryate's Crudities* (1611; rpt. Macmillan and Co., 1901, 236.

64.   Ibid., 236–37.

65.   Charles Cooper, *The English Table*, 236–37.

66.   As qtd. in Elias, *History of Manners*, 236–37.

67.   Ibid., 92.

68.   Ibid.

69.   Braudel, *Civilization and Capitalism* 1: 203–9.

70.   Nicholas de Bonnefons, qtd. in Stephen Mennell, *All Manners of Food: Eating and Taste in England and France from the Middle Ages to the Present* (Glasgow: Bell and Bain, 1985), 73.

71.   Massialot, qtd. in Mennell, *All Manners of Food*, 73.

72.   As qtd. in Elias, *History of Manners*, 94–95.

73. Ibid., 95–96.

74. Ibid., 106–8.

75. Ibid., 107.

76. Ibid.

77. Foucault, *Discipline and Punish*, 170, 176, 222.

78. Elias, *History of Manners*, 107–8.

79. Motley, *History for the Dental Hygienist*, 102.

80. Donald M. Lowe, *History of Bourgeois Perception* (Chicago: Univ. of Chicago Press, 1982), 86.

81. De la Riva, qtd. in Elias, *History of Manners*, 143.

82. Ibid., 144.

83. Ibid., 145.

84. Della Casa, *A Treatise of the Manners and Behaviours*, 8.

85. Richard Weste, "The School of Virtue, The Second Part, Or The Young Scholar's Paradise: A Digression for Children How They Ought to be Instructed," rpt. in *The Babee's Book*, 164.

86. Elias, *History of Manners*, 147.

87. Ibid., 149–51.

88. Ibid., 151.

89. Russell, "Boke of Nurture," 63–66.

90. Weste, "School of Virtue."

91. Erasmus, qtd. in Aresty, *The Best Behavior*, 79.

92. Della Casa, *A Treatise of the Manners and Behaviours*, 13.

93. Chesterfield, *Letters to His Son*, 35–36.

94. Ibid., 193.

95. Russell, "Boke of Nurture," 57; Della Casa, *A Treatise of the Manners and Behaviours*, 14–15.

96. Erasmus, qtd. in Aresty, *The Best Behavior*, 78.

97. Weste, "School of Virtue," 168.

98. William J. Gies, *Dental Education in the United States and Canada* (New York: The Carnegie Foundation for the Advancement of Teaching, 1926), 27.

99. Chesterfield, *Letters to His Son*, 180.

100. A. J. Asgis, "History of the Toothbrush," *Dental Digest* 35 (1929): 307–13.

101. Jane Taylor, *Wouldst Know Thyself or the Outline of Human Physiology: Designed for Youth of Both Sexes* (New York: George F. Cooledge and Brother, 1858).

102. John Kasson, *Rudeness and Civility: Manners in Nineteenth-Century Urban America* (New York: Hill and Wang, 1990), 11.

Chapter 5. The Historical Meanings
of Consumption

1. For a more detailed discussion, see McCracken, *Culture and Consumption*, 4–11.
2. McKendrick, Brewer, and Plumb, *Birth of a Consumer Society*.
3. Ibid., 10. McCracken, *Culture and Consumption*, 6, notes that the annual fashion was very much part of Elizabethan England.
4. Rosalind H. Williams, *Dream Worlds: Mass Consumption in Late Nineteenth-Century France* (Berkeley: Univ. of California Press, 1982), 28–54.
5. Chandra Mukerji, *From Graven Images: Patterns of Modern Materialism* (New York: Columbia Univ. Press, 1983).
6. In McCracken, *Culture and Consumption*, 11.
7. Ibid.
8. Ibid., 14.
9. Miller, *Material Culture as Mass Consumption*.
10. McCracken, *Culture and Consumption*, 14–15.
11. McKendrick, Brewer, and Plumb, *Birth of a Consumer Society*, 1.
12. Kasson, *Rudeness*, 43; McCracken, *Culture and Consumption*, 16–21.
13. See, for instance, McKendrick, Brewer, and Plumb, *Birth of a Consumer Society*.
14. As qtd. in McKendrick, Brewer, and Plumb, *Birth of a Consumer Society*, 51.
15. Ibid., 53.
16. See, for instance, George Simmel, "Fashion," *Interdisciplinary Quarterly* 10: 130–55; Thorstein Veblen, *The Theory of the Leisure Class* (New York: Macmillan, 1904).
17. See, for instance, Little, *Ideology and Media*; Antonio Gramsci, *Selections from the Prison Notebooks of Antonio Gramsci*, ed. and trans. Q. Hoare and G. Smith (New York: International Publishers, 1971).
18. Miller, Rowlands, and Tilley, Introd. to *Domination and Resistance*, 11.
19. McCracken, *Culture and Consumption*, 32.
20. Ibid., 80–81; Roland Barthes, *The Fashion System*, trans., Matthew Ward and Richard Howard (New York: Hill and Wang, 1983).
21. Stuart Flemming, "Josiah Wedgwood: A Potter of Fashion," *Archaeology Magazine* 39, no. 3 (1986): 70–81; McKendrick, Brewer, and Plumb, *Birth of a Consumer Society*.
22. Paul Blumberg, "The Decline and Fall of the Status Symbol: Some Thoughts on Status in a Post-Industrial Society," *Social Problems* 21 (1974): 480–98.

23. McCracken, *Culture and Consumption*, 81.
24. Wolf, *People Without History*; Immanuel Wallerstien, *The Modern World-System*, 3 vols. (New York: Academic Press, 1974);
25. Leone, "The Georgian Order," 235–61.
26. Wolf, *People Without History*.
27. Nicholls, *Matter of Courtesy*.
28. Chesterfield, *Letters to His Son*; Chesterfield, *The Modern Chesterfield: A Selection of Chesterfield's Letters to His Son*, ed. Robert McMundy (1776; rpt. Boston: R. G. Badger, 1917).
29. Addison, *The Spectator* 1: 135–6.
30. Elias, *History of Manners* 1.
31. *Maryland Gazette*, 26 Aug. 1746.
32. Bridenbaugh, *Gentleman's Progress*.
33. Little and Shackel, "Scales of Historical Anthropology: An Archaeology of Colonial Anglo-America," *Antiquity* 63, no. 240 (1989): 495–509.
34. Braudel, *Civilization and Capitalism* 3: 489 ff; Leone, "Rule by Ostentation: The Relationship between Space and Sight in 18th-century Landscape Architecture in the Chesapeake Region of Maryland," in *Method and Theory for Activity Research*, ed. Susan Kent (New York: Columbia Univ. Press, 1987), 604–33; also see Leone and Shackel, "Plane and Solid Geometry in Colonial Gardens in Annapolis, Maryland," in *Earth Patterns: Essays in Landscape Archaeology*, ed. William M. Kelso and Rachel Most (Charlottesville: Univ. Press of Virginia, 1990), 164.
35. McCracken, *Culture and Consumption*, xi.
36. Paynter, "Archaeology of Equality and Inequality," 369–99.
37. Although gender and race relations were not the focus of this book, they are important and socially relevant issues that are now being addressed by archaeologists in the Archaeology in Annapolis project.

Selected Bibliography

Aitken, Hugh G. J. *Taylorism at Watertown Arsenal: Scientific Management in Action, 1908–1915*. Cambridge: Harvard Univ. Press, 1960.

Althusser, Louis. "Ideology and the State Apparatuses." In *Lenin and Philosophy and the Other Essays*. London: New Left Books, 1971.

Appadurai, A., ed. *The Social Life of Things: Commodities in Cultural Perspective*. Cambridge: Cambridge Univ. Press, 1986.

Aresty, Esther B. *The Best Behavior: The Course of Good Manners From Antiquity to the Present-As Seen Through Courtesy and Etiquette Books*. New York: Simon and Schuster, 1970.

Baker, Nancy. "Annapolis, Maryland 1695–1730." *Maryland Historical Magazine* 81, no. 3 (1986): 191–209.

Beaudry, Mary C. *Documentary Archaeology in the New World*. Cambridge: Cambridge Univ. Press, 1988.

———. *"Or What Else You Please to Call It" Folk Semantic Domains in Early Virginia Probate Inventories*. Ann Arbor, Mich.: Univ. Microfilms International, 1980.

Benes, Peter, ed. *Early American Probate Inventories: The Dublin Seminar for New England Folklife Annual Proceedings 1987*. Boston: Boston Univ., 1989.

Bourdieu, Pierre. *Outline of a Theory of Practice*. Cambridge: Cambridge Univ. Press, 1977.

Braudel, Fernand. *La Méditerranée et la Monde Méditerranéen à l'epoque de Phillip II*. Rpt. in Fernand Braudel, *On History*, trans. Sarah Matthews. Chicago: Univ. of Chicago Press, 1980.

————. *Civilization and Capitalism: 15th-18th Century.* 3 vols. New York: Harper and Row, 1979).

Braverman, Harry. *Labor and Monopoly Capital; The Degradation of Work in the Twentieth Century.* New York: Monthly Review Press, 1975.

Breene, Timothy H., and Stephen Innes. *"Myne Owne Ground," Race and Freedom on Virginia's Eastern Shore, 1640–1676.* Oxford: Oxford Univ. Press, 1980.

Breslaw, Elaine G., ed. *Records of the Tuesday Club of Annapolis: 1745–56.* Urbana: Univ. of Illinois Press, 1988.

Bridenbaugh, Carl. *Gentleman's Progress: The Itinerarium of Dr. Alexander Hamilton; 1744.* Westport, Conn.: Greenwood Press, 1973.

Carr, Lois Green, and Lorena S. Walsh. "Inventories and the Analysis of Wealth and Consumption Patterns in St. Mary's County, Maryland, 1658–1777." *The Newberry Papers in Family and Community History.* Paper 77–46. Chicago: Newberry Library, 1977.

————. "Inventories and the Analysis of Wealth and Consumption Patterns in St. Mary's County, Maryland, 1658–1777." *Historical Methods* 13, no. 2 (1980): 81–104.

Castiglione, Baldassare. *The Book of the Courtier.* Translated by Sir Thomas Hoby. 1528. Rpt. New York: AMS Press, 1967.

Chesterfield, Philip Dormer Stanhope. *Letters to His Son.* Ed. Leigh. 1776. Rpt. London: M. Walter Dunne, 1901.

————. *The Modern Chesterfield: A Selection of Chesterfield's Letters to His Son.* Ed. Robert McMundy. 1776. Rpt. Boston: R. G. Badger, 1917.

Cipolla, Carlo M. *Clocks and Culture: 1300–1700.* New York: W. W. Norton, 1978.

Deetz, James. *In Small Things Forgotten: The Archaeology of Early American Life.* New York: Doubleday, 1977.

della Casa, Giovanni. *A Treatise of the Manners and Behaviours.* 1576. Rpt. Amsterdam, N.Y.: Da Capo Press, 1969.

Doggett, Rachel, ed. *Time the Great Innovator: Timekeeping and Time Consciousness in Early Modern Europe.* Washington, D.C.: Folger Shakespeare Library, 1986.

Douglas, Mary, ed. *Food in the Social Order: Studies in Food and Festivities in Three American Communities.* New York: Russell Sage Foundation, 1984.

Douglas, Mary, and Baron Isherwood. *The World of Goods.* New York: Basic Books, 1979.

Earle, Carville V. *The Evolution of a Tidewater Settlement System: All Hallow's Parish, Maryland, 1650–1783.* Univ. of Chicago, Dept. of Geography, Research Paper no. 170.

Elias, Norbert. *The Court Society.* New York: Random House, 1983.

———. *The Civilizing Process 1. The History of Manners*. Trans. Edmund Jephcott. New York: Pantheon Books, 1978.

———. *The Civilizing Process 2. Power and Civility*. Trans. Edmund Jephcott New York: Pantheon Books, 1983.

Foucault, Michel. *Discipline and Punish*. New York: Vintage Books, 1979.

———. *The History of Sexuality 1, An Introduction*. Translated by R. Hurley. Harmondsworth: Penguin Press, 1981.

———. *Power and Knowledge*. Ed. C. Gordon. Hassock, England: Harvester, 1980.

Glassie, Henry. *Folk Housing in Middle Virginia: A Structural Analysis of Historic Artifacts*. Knoxville: Univ. of Tennessee Press, 1975.

Guazzo, Stefano. *The Civile Conversation of M. Steven Guazzo*. Rpt. New York: Knopf, 1925.

Hemphill, John M. II. *Virginia and the English Commercial System 1689–1733*. New York: Garland Publishing, 1985.

Hodder, Ian. "Postprocessual Archaeology." In *Advances in Archaeological Methods and Theory*, ed. Michael B. Schiffer, 8: 1–26. New York: Academic Press, 1985.

———. *Reading the Past*. Cambridge: Cambridge Univ. Press, 1986.

———, ed. *Archaeology as Long-Term History*. Cambridge: Cambridge Univ. Press, 1987.

———, ed. *Symbols in Action: Ethnoarchaeological Studies of Material Culture*. Cambridge: Cambridge Univ. Press, 1982.

Isaac, Rhys. *The Transformation of Virginia; 1740–1790*. Chapel Hill: Univ. of North Carolina Press, 1982.

Kasson, John. *Rudeness and Civility: Manners in Nineteenth- Century Urban America*. New York: Hill and Wang, 1990.

Kilty, William. *The Laws of Maryland 1*. Annapolis, Md.: Frederick Green Printer, 1799.

Kulikoff, Allan. "The Economic Growth of the Eighteenth-Century Chesapeake Colonies." *Journal of Economic History* 39 (1979): 277–82.

———. *Tobacco and Slaves: The Development of Southern Culture in the Chesapeake, 1680–1800*. Chapel Hill: Univ. of North Carolina Press, 1986.

Land, Aubry, ed. *Letters From America by William Eddis*. Cambridge: Harvard Univ. Press, 1969.

Landes, Davis S. *Revolution in Time: Clocks and the Making of the Modern World*. Cambridge: Harvard Univ. Press, 1983.

LeGoff, Jacques, ed. *Time, Work and Culture in the Middle Ages*. Chicago: Chicago Univ. Press, 1980.

Leone, Mark P. "The Georgian Order as the Order of Mercantile Capitalism in Annapolis, Maryland." In *The Recovery of Meaning: Historical Archaeology*

in the Eastern United States, ed. Mark P. Leone and Parker B. Potter, 235–
61. Washington, D.C.: Smithsonian Institute Press, 1988.

———. "Interpreting Ideology in Historical Archaeology: Using the Rules of
Perspective in the William Paca Garden in Annapolis, Maryland." In *Ideology, Power and Prehistory,* ed. Daniel Miller and Christopher Tilley, 25–
35. Cambridge: Cambridge Univ. Press, 1984.

Leone, Mark P., Parker B. Potter, Jr., and Paul A. Shackel. "Toward a Critical
Archaeology." *Current Anthropology* 28, no. 3 (1987): 283–302.

Leone, Mark P., and Paul A. Shackel. "Forks, Clocks and Power." In *Mirror
and Metaphor, Material and Social Construction of Reality,* ed. Daniel Ingersoll and Gordon Bronitski, 45–61. Latham, Md.: American Press, 1987.

———. "The Georgian Order in Annapolis, Maryland." *Maryland Archaeologist* 26, nos. 1 and 2 (1990): 69–84.

Little, Barbara J. *Ideology and Media: Historical Archaeology of Printing in 18th-
Century Annapolis, Maryland.* Ann Arbor, Mich.: Univ. Microfilm International, 1987.

———. "'She was . . . an Example to her Sex'; Possibilities for a Feminist Archaeology in the Historic Chesapeake." In *The Historic Chesapeake: Archaeological Contributions,* ed. Paul A. Shackel and Barbara J. Little. Washington, D.C.: Smithsonian Institution Press, 1993.

———. *Text-Aided Archaeology.* Boca Raton, Fla: CRC Press, 1992.

Lowe, Donald M. *History of Bourgeois Perception.* Chicago: Univ. of Chicago
Press, 1982.

Main, Gloria. "Inequality in Early America: Evidence from Probate Records of
Massachusetts and Maryland." *Journal of Interdisciplinary History* 7, no. 4
(1977): 559–81.

Maryland Gazette. On file at the State Law Library, Court of Appeals Building,
Annapolis.

Mason, John Edward. *Gentlefolk in the Making: Studies in the History of English
Courtesy Literature and Related Topics From 1531 to 1774.* New York: Octagon Books, 1971.

McCracken, Grant. *Culture and Consumption: New Approaches to the Symbolic
Character of Consumer Goods and Activities.* Bloomington: Indiana Univ.
Press, 1988.

McCusker, John J., and Russell R. Menard. *The Economy of British America:
1607–1789.* Chapel Hill: Univ. of North Carolina Press, 1985.

McKendrick, Neil, John Brewer, and J. H. Plumb. *The Birth of a Consumer Society.* Bloomington: Indiana Univ. Press, 1982.

Menard, Russell Robert "The Tobacco Industry in the Chesapeake Colonies,
1617–1730: An Interpretation." *Research in Economic History* 5 (1980):
157–61.

Menard, Russell Robert, Lois Green Carr, and Lorena S. Walsh. "A Small Planter's Profits: The Cole Estate and the Growth of the Early Chesapeake Economy." *William and Mary Quarterly* 40 (1983): 171–96.

Mennell, Stephen. *All Manners of Food: Eating and Taste in England and France from the Middle Ages to the Present.* Glasgow: Bell and Bain, 1985.

Miller, Daniel. *Artifacts as Categories: A Study of Ceramic Variability in Central India.* London: Cambridge Univ. Press, 1985.

———. *Material Culture as Mass Consumption.* New York: Basil Blackwell, 1987.

Miller, Daniel, Michael Rowlands, and Christopher Tilley, eds. *Domination and Resistance.* London: Unwin Hyman, 1989.

Miller, Daniel, and Christopher Tilley, eds. *Ideology, Power, and Prehistory.* Cambridge: Cambridge Univ. Press, 1984.

Nicholls, Jonathan. *The Matter of Courtesy: Medieval Courtesy Books and the Gawaioa-Poet.* Bury St. Edmunds, Suffolk: St. Edondsbury Press, 1985.

Orser, Charles E., Jr. "Toward a Theory of Power for Historical Archaeology: Plantations and Space." In *The Recovery of Meaning: Historical Archaeology in the Eastern United States,* ed. Mark P. Leone and Parker B. Potter, 313–43. Washington, D.C.: Smithsonian Institution Press, 1988.

Papenfuse, Edward C. *In Pursuit of Profit: The Annapolis Merchant in the Era of the American Revolution, 1763–1805.* Baltimore: Johns Hopkins Univ. Press, 1975.

Paynter, Robert. "The Archaeology of Equality and Inequality." *Annual Review of Anthropology* 18 (1989): 369–99.

———. "Steps to an Archaeology of Capitalism: Material Change and Class Analysis." In *The Recovery of Meaning: Historical Archaeology in the Eastern United States,* ed. Mark P. Leone and Parker B. Potter, 407–33. Washington, D.C.: Smithsonian Institution Press, 1988.

Peachman, Henry. *The Complete Gentleman.* 1622. Rpt. New York: Da Capo Press, 1968.

Pendery, Steven. *Symbolism of Community: Status Differences and the Archaeological Record in Charlestown, Massachusetts, 1630–1760.* Ann Arbor, Mich.: Univ. Microfilm International, 1987.

———. "Consumer Behavior in Colonial Charlestown, Massachusetts, 1630–1760." *Historical Archaeology* 26, no. 3 (1992).

Rainbolt, John C. "The Absence of Towns in Seventeenth-Century Virginia." *Journal of Southern History* 25 (1969): 343–60.

Rapoport, Amos. *The Meaning of the Built Environment: A Nonverbal Communication Approach.* London: Sage Publications, 1982.

Rebhorn, Wayne A. *Courtly Performance: Masking and Festivity in Castiglione's Book of the Courtier.* Detroit: Wayne State Univ. Press, 1978.

Reps, John W. *Tidewater Towns: City Planning in Colonial Virginia and Mary-land.* Williamsburg, Va.: The Colonial of Williamsburg Foundation, 1972.

Rhode, Hugh. "Book of Nurture and School of Good Manners." Rpt. in *The Babee's Book: Medieval Manners for the Young, Done into Modern English From Dr. Furnivall's Texts by Edith Rickert.* 1550. Rpt. New York: Cooper Square Publishers, 1966.

Riley, Edward M. "The Town Acts of Colonial Virginia." *Journal of Southern History* 16 (1950): 306–23.

Russell, John. "The Boke of Nurture, Folowyng Englondis Gise, by Me John Russell, Sum Time Servande with Duke Vmfrey of Glowcetur." Rpt. in *The Babes Book: Medieval Manners for the Young Done into Modern English From Dr. Furnivall's Texts by Edith Richert.* 1450. Rpt. New York: Cooper Square Publishers, 1966.

Shackel, Paul A. "Conspicuous Consumption and Class Maintenance: A Case Example from the Nicoll Site" In *The Historical Archaeology of Long Island* 1, *The Sites,* ed. Gaynell Stone and Donna Ottusch-Kianka, 156–70. St. James, N.Y.: Braun-Brumfield, 1987.

———. "Consumerism and the Structuring of Social Relations: A Historical Archaeological Perspective." In *Digging into Popular Culture: Theories and Methodologies in Archeology, Anthropology and Other Fields,* ed. Ray B. Browne and Pat Browne, 36–47. Bowling Green, Ohio: Bowling Green State Univ. Popular Press, 1991.

———. *A Historical Archaeology of Personal Discipline.* Ann Arbor, Mich.: Univ. Microfilm International, 1987.

———. "Modern Discipline: Its Historical Context in the Colonial Chesa-peake." *Historical Archaeology* 26, no. 3 (1992), 73–84.

———. "Probate Inventories in Historical Archaeology: A Review and Alter-natives." In *Text-Aided Archaeology,* ed. Barbara J. Little, 205–16. Boca Raton, Fla.: CRC Press, 1992.

———. "Town Plans and Everyday Material Culture: An Archaeology of So-cial Relations in Colonial Maryland's Capital Cities." In *The Historic Chesapeake: Archaeological Contributions,* ed. Paul A. Shackel and Barbara J. Little. Washington, D.C.: Smithsonian Institution Press, 1993.

Shamas, Carol. "The Domestic Environment in Early Modern England and America." *Journal of Social History* 14, no. 1 (1980): 1–24.

Stiverson, Gregory. *Poverty in a Land of Plenty: Tenancy in Eighteenth-Century Maryland.* Baltimore: Johns Hopkins Univ. Press, 1977.

Thompson, E. P. "Time, Work-Discipline, and Industrial Capitalism." *Past and Present* 38 (1967): 56–97.

Tilley, Christopher. "Michel Foucault: Towards an Archaeology of Archaeology." In *Reading Material Culture: Structuralism, Hermeneutics and Post-Structuralism*, ed. Christopher Tilley, 287–88. London: Basil Blackwell, 1990.

Trigger, Bruce. "Distinguished Lecture in Archaeology: Constraints and Freedom." *American Anthropologist* 93, no.3 (1991): 551–69.

Wallerstien, Immanuel. *The Modern World-System.* 3 vols. New York: Academic Press, 1974, 1980, 1989.

Walsh, Lorena S., ed. "Annapolis and Anne Arundel County, Maryland: A Study of Urban Development in a Tobacco Economy, 1649–1776." NEH Report, 1983.

Wobst, Martin. "Stylistic Behavior and Information Exchange." Univ. of Michigan, Ann Arbor, Museum of Anthropology, Anthropological Paper no. 61 (1977): 317–42.

Wolf, Eric. "Distinguished Lecture: Facing Power." *American Anthropologist* 92, no. 3 (1990): 586–96.

———. *Europe and the People Without History.* Berkeley: Univ. of California Press, 1982.

Index

Personal Discipline and Material Culture was designed by Sheila Hart, composed by the Composing Room of Michigan, Inc., and printed and bound by Braun Brumfield, Inc. The book is set in Goudy Old Style with Antique Open display, and is printed on 50-lb. Glatfelter natural.